DEAL

SAD
SMUGGLING
TOWN

Gregory Holyoake

S.B. Publications

for
Nick George
who loves Deal

By the same author
Wellington at Walmer
The Prefab Kid – A Postwar Childhood in Kent
Kent the County in Colour (with John Vigar)

First published in 2001 by S B Publications
19 Grove Road, Seaford, East Sussex BN25 1TP
telephone: 01323 893498
fax: 01323 893860
email: sales@sbpublications.swinternet.co.uk

ISBN 1 85770 246 8

Typeset by JEM Editorial, JEMedit@AOL.com
Printed and bound by Tansleys the Printers
19 Broad Street
Seaford
East Sussex BN25 1LS
telephone: 01323 891019

Cover design: Ian Fuggle
Front cover picture: Deal in a Storm by JMW Turner, courtesy Deal Town Council
Back cover picture: Junior Royal Marines Bandsmen
Title page: Victorian pot lid showing Sandown Castle
Collection: Harry Lyons

They drove to Deal, a sad smuggling town, where Lady Hales bought run goods, and wrote to ask Fanny to accept a small part of her purchase, viz, a piece of chintz.

Fanny Burney's diary

Deal foreshore and Royal Hotel

Three castles that keep the Downs © English Heritage

CONTENTS

JULIUS CAESAR

'A kind of conquest'

GAIUS JULIUS CAESAR was one of the few aggressors who have led a successful invasion of Britain. Caesar had been appointed Governor of Gaul (this region included France, parts of Belgium, western Germany, southern Holland and northern Italy) by the Roman Senate several years before he turned his attention to the English coast. The Roman general meticulously chronicled his two British expeditions in his *Commentaries* – he is the first writer to mention Britain by name – and although the precise location of his landings is not identified, historians, archaeologists and astronomers from Halley to Napoleon III have deduced that they were at Deal.

Caesar had planned his expedition long in advance. Indeed, his invasion was common knowledge among the merchant sailors who warned the islanders of their imminent peril. The information Caesar extracted from captured Gauls, who regarded it as their most important trading, religious and military centre, was deliberately contradictory and the intelligence he received from his spies, particularly regarding the Kent coastline frequently visible from France, was surprisingly cursory. He had been prevented from an earlier invasion in 56 BC by a rebellion of the Veneti, a seafaring tribe that inhabited the south coast of Brittany, who feared Roman domination would lead to cessation of a profitable trade with their allies in Britain. The Roman chronicler, Strabo, lists the exports of Belgic Britain as corn, cattle, hides, dogs, metals and slaves. Caesar's plans were further hampered by both a Germanic invasion across the Rhine and frequent uprisings among the Gauls, so his initial expedition must be regarded as little more than a reconnaissance.

Head of Gaius Julius Caesar © Musei and Gallerie Vaticani

The expressed reasons for his British campaign were threefold: he hoped for plunder, chiefly crops and minerals, and he sought to punish the Britons who actively assisted the turbulent Gauls in their conflict with Rome. The third reason was paramount because this middle-aged military commander had strong political ambitions and he astutely realised that a triumphant British campaign would greatly enhance his reputation with the Senate. Presumably, personal ambition overcame his caution in organising an ill-prepared expedition into an unknown territory so late in the season . . .

Julius Caesar was a popular military commander despite his autocratic tendencies which led eventually to his downfall. He constantly displayed brilliant leadership and he invariably led his men in the forefront of battle. He was scrupulously honest with them, particularly regarding their position before an offensive. He was a skilful swordsman, an accomplished rider and a strong swimmer. Suetonius described him as 'tall, fair and well built with rather a broad face and keen, dark brown eyes . . .' and he mischievously mentions his habit of combing thin strands of hair forward in an attempt to disguise his premature baldness. Caesar's greatest successes in warfare were achieved by his lightning strikes which were perfectly demonstrated on land and sea during his British campaigns.

Around midnight on 25 August 55 BC, the hastily-assembled Roman expeditionary force, headed by eighty transports conveying 10,000 men, set sail from Portus Itius (Boulogne) for the Kent coast. Transports had been requisitioned from the defeated Venetine navy whose country-built merchant ships, sailed by their native crews, were more suited to the heavy seas rolling in from the Atlantic. These had exceptionally high bows and sterns, flat bottoms, oak strakes and cross timbers, iron anchors and leather sails. They were accompanied by fast war galleys assigned to the quaestor, prefects, lieutenants and two generals (Caesar and his deputy). These heavy, two-level galleys known as 'labernians', were pulled by trained oarsmen who sat two to an oar. Features included an underwater ram, a low parapet and a collapsible tower for firing catapults. They had formed the squadron built the previous summer for the naval action against the Veneti which were rowed round the coast from the Mediterranean. As dawn broke this cluster of galleys and transports lay at anchor under the shadow of the soaring white cliffs.

Incredibly, Caesar took with him only two legions – the VIIth and Xth (his favourite and most reliable corps) – and the sight of such a modest army visibly cheered the waiting British chieftains.

Commius (or Comm), King of the Atrebates, had been sent ahead to act as Caesar's ambassador. Commius offered generous conditions of surrender to the British chieftains: they must pay an annual tribute, hand over prominent tribesmen as hostages and, above all, recognise the supreme authority of Rome. Caesar trusted Commius implicity although eventually he proved to be a traitor and may even have actively roused the Britons to fight against Rome. Envoys replied with a subtly-worded message which implied that they were willing to submit to Rome. All the same the chieftains realised that Caesar's terms must be treated seriously since many of their warriors were refugees from Roman oppression.

Now the Britons, after failing to forestall invasion, had decided to oppose the Roman invasion. The chieftains organised their tribes into fighting forces consisting of the major southern British tribes. Principal of these was the Cantiaci (or Cantii), who later gave their name to the county of Kent. Weapons they brandished included long swords, spears or javelins with fearsome iron tips. They wore little armour for protection but carried leather shields with bronze bindings. Elaborate helmets that have been discovered were almost certainly for votive rather than practical purposes. Warriors harangued their enemy with taunts and jeers accompanied by trumpet blasts and battle cries.

British warriors rode light wicker chariots which wreaked havoc as they careered headlong into battle. Chariots were open at both ends, carried on either two or four wheels with iron rims, and pulled by a breed of horse no bigger than a pony. Warriors threw spears indiscriminately from the chariot while scythes attached to the hubs mowed down their enemies. A rider leapt from the platform to fight on foot but when he found himself in trouble his driver raced back so that he could leap aboard to safety. Caesar admired their nimbleness. He wrote:

They could run along the chariot pole, stand on the yoke, and get back into the chariot quick as lightning . . . The terror inspired by the horses and the noise of the wheels is sufficient to throw their opponents' ranks into disorder.

The Romans, familiar with chariots for sport and transport, were alarmed to find their opponents employing them so skilfully for war.

Julius Caesar, in the prow of his galley, studied his enemy with intensity. One further reason for this expedition was to collect information about the remote island and its inhabitants. He was totally unprepared for the extraordinary apparel of the warriors who had assembled on the clifftop to confront him. He wrote:

Roman bronze of a Celtic barbarian © British Museum

All Britons stain their bodies with woad that produces a blueish colour and gives them a wild appearance in battle. They wear their hair long, shaving all parts of the body except the head and upper lip.

Southern Britain in the Late Iron Age was inhabited by Belgic and Celtic tribes which had been dominant in Europe before the Roman Conquest. They were skilled weavers and dyers and their clothes were fairly sophisticated. Although some warriors fought naked, most wore short trousers with linen tunics over which was a long woollen cloak fastened with a metal brooch. These garments

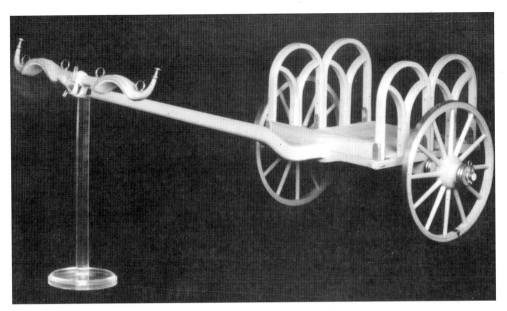

Reconstruction of British war chariot © National Museum of Wales

were striped or checkered and brightly coloured. Leather sandals were worn but helmets were often avoided since warriors were intensely vain and proud of the elaborate hairstyles that they stiffened with lime. Ornamentation was intricate – torques, armlets, buckles, brooches – wrought in bronze and coral, sometimes silver or gold.

British warriors were heroic fighters and their method of warfare was based upon individual combat rather than on organisation. Celtic battle formation was complicated since each tribe and every tribesman was allocated a traditional place in the battle line. Warriors spurned elaborate body armour but preferred to place their reliance upon magic and protection from their native gods. Warriors daubed their bodies with dye probably in intricate curvilinear patterns resembling tattoos. Chapman also says that the name Britannia derives from the root 'brith', and alludes to the Ancient Britons' practice of staining their bodies with natural dyes. The object was not only to provide protection through sacred symbols and ritual but, by their startling appearance, to strike terror into their opponents.

'I saw the armed forces of the enemy posted along the heights', Caesar reported. Presumably he had intended to make a surprise appearance in Dover Bay where he was expecting to land unopposed after his recent treaty. However, he was thwarted by the appearance of British warriors lining the peaks where he realised that it was possible for them to hurl javelins directly onto the narrow beach. Moreover, they might easily reach into his ships. 'Clearly,' he considered, 'it was no place for a landing'.

Caesar summoned his staff officers and company commanders to a council of war to consider their options.

Eighteen transport ships allotted to the cavalry which had sailed on the morning tide had been forced by prevailing winds back into the harbour at Ambleteuse.

There seemed little hope that they would arrive in time. Caesar's problem now was how to steer his ships through treacherous waters and land his depleted force on an unknown shore while enfiladed by warring tribes. Volusenus, a distinguished military tribune, had spent the week previously in his sleek war galley surveying the coastline – stealthily watched by native sentinels. He was in a position to study his charts and advise an alternative landing site further north along the coast. It is conjectured that he considered the most suitable landing place to be the sheltered beach of what became Deal and Walmer.

Accordingly, around 3pm, Caesar made a decision for action.

> Both the wind and tide were now in our favour, so I gave the signal for the anchors to be weighed. We moved on about seven miles and ran the ships aground on an open and evenly shelving shore.

He might have been wiser to venture out into the Dover Straits and await the morning tide but probably he was anxious not to allow the enemy further time to rally. From their vantage point the British chieftains watched the galleys and transports – with all sail set – turn purposely up-Channel and round the South Foreland fanned by a strong southerly breeze. Anticipating Caesar's intention, the natives rode or marched along the clifftops keeping pace with the Roman fleet.

At Walmer the ships swung shorewards. Immediately, they faced danger because Caesar had now been forced to land at low tide. There was obvious difficulty: the transports could not be manoeuvred because of the shallowness of the water neither could they be beached on account of their great size. Moreover, his soldiers were daunted by the prospect of jumping down from the high decks and wading through deep water while weighed down by full armour and heavy weapons. The Britons, sure of their ground, rode boldly into the shallows and hurled javelins ruthlessly at the hesitant troopers.

Ceasar kept to seaward in his flagship where he gave directions to his troops. First he called upon his auxiliaries, recruited from captured Barbarians, who had become an integral part of the Roman army. They were valued for their indigenous skills yet were always sent to the forefront of battles since they were more expendable than trained legionaires. He ordered them to sheer off slightly from the transports and take up a position on the enemy's exposed left flank. Then they rowed their galleys close inshore at utmost speed and opened fire with slings, arrows and catapults, hurling missiles onto the yelling tribesmen. The Britons were momentarily stunned – unnerved by the strange shape of the warships, the motion of the oars and unfamiliar machines. Yet Caesar could not pursue the advantage. His men were still two hundred yards from the shore and could not make battle formation. Caesar admits his men were 'terrified'.

At this crucial moment the aquilifier of the Xth Legion, who wore a leopard skin and bore the symbolic eagle, called upon the gods to aid the success of his venture and cried with a loud voice: 'Leap forth, soldiers, unless you want to surrender your eagle to the enemy. I, at any rate, shall have performed my duty to my country and my general'. Boldly, he sprang overboard raising the silver eagle high above the crashing waves. The rest of his company – and soldiers in nearby transports – fearing the disgrace of losing their prized emblem, followed closely and advanced towards the hostile shore.

A Roman legion presented a fighting complement of 5,000 infantry and was commanded by a Legate who was usually a senator appointed by the Emperor. Each legion was divided into ten cohorts of 480 men (eventually the first cohort was double-strength and composed of the most experienced fighters) which in turn were organised into six centuries comprising eighty men. Centuries were then split into ten small fighting units consisting of eight men, called a 'contaburnium'. Caesar's legionaires wore long, sleeveless chainmail shirts which, although heavy, allowed freedom of movement (lighter scale armour was reserved for the officers and cavalry). They had bronze domed helmets with hinged cheek guards and a horsehair crest and leather hob-nailed sandals. For colder climates, there was the comfort of a woollen cloak. Each legionary carried two iron-tipped javelins plus a short sword for thrusting, and a dagger, which hung from separate belts. An oval wooden shield held against the body gave protection along the whole of one side. According to the Roman writer Verro, their great cylindrical shields, introduced later, were copied, like the chainmail, from the Celtic Gauls.

Legionary soldiers were trained to fight in close formation so that they pressed constantly on their enemy in a tight melee. They linked shields to create a solid metal wall (the famous tactic known as a testudo, or tortoise, was reserved for storming forts). Legionaires were trained to manoeuvre in small groups to prearranged signals given by shrill blasts on bugles or trumpets. They were

Relief showing Roman galley © Musei and Gallerie Vaticani

11

assisted – although not at Deal – by cavalry, who gave pursuit with lance and slashing sword. Firm emphasis was on the foot soldier who bore the brunt of the attack. The Roman army was most skilful at fighting pitched battles and laying siege to enemy camps.

The battle at Deal was fiercely contested. The Romans, struggling to marshal their ranks, fell into great confusion. The British – unencumbered by armour and certain of their territory – attacked the soldiers from their chariots which were driven into the surf. Warriors engaged the legionaires in hand-to-hand fighting as they hesitantly disembarked, while others hurled javelins from the shore, stinging the Romans' undefended right flank. Caesar ordered his rear guard to transfer to the warship skiffs or scouting boats and race to the aid of troops in difficulty. Thus he called in all his reserves.

At this point a certain legionary, Caesius Scaeva, threw himself into a boat with four daredevil soldiers and made for an offshore rock where they hurled javelins at the enemy. The ebb tide, however, enabled the warriors to surround the rock and attack these five companions. The Britons raced at them wildly and while his friends retreated to their boat, Scaeva stood his ground and resisted the enemy. Despite sustaining horrific injuries, he slew several Barbarians before swimming to safety. Caesar instantly rewarded him for this heroic deed by making him a centurion. Local tradition identifies these rocks as the Malms which can occasionally be seen at low water during spring tides off Deal Castle. This dramatic incident (which may even be attributed to folklore) is recorded by two ancient military historians – Maximus and Suetonius.

Once his legions had landed, the battle on the beach swung in Caesar's favour. He mustered his troops into making a full scale assault which proved overwhelming. Caesar recorded:

> As soon as our men had a footing on dry land and all their comrades had formed up behind them, they charged and put the enemy to flight. But they were unable to pursue very far because our cavalry had not been able to hold their course and reach Britain. This was the one thing that prevented me from enjoying my usual good fortune.

The time was around 7pm.

British warriors revelled in fighting. In battle each man strove for his own personal glory which made for a fearsome rabble rather than an organised fighting force. All the while the Romans struggled in the water the Britons had the advantage, but once ashore the Romans' tight battle formation outmatched the natives. They charged at the warriors and put them to flight. The Britons were routed and it was only his lack of cavalry which prevented Caesar effectively pursuing his foe. The chieftains submitted to defeat, dismissed their warriors and began to sue for peace. Commius, mysteriously absent during recent events, appeared , claiming that he had been held hostage 'by the common people'. He was appointed mediator and the negotiations lasted several days. 'Peace', proclaimed Caesar, 'was thus concluded'.

The Romans made a temporary encampment while vainly awaiting the arrival of their transports. This would have covered a vast rectangular site bounded on one side by the sea and protected by a shallow ditch and embankment spiked with stakes, and a gate guarded by sentries. The large leather tents, which conveniently accommodated a contaburnium, were still stranded in France. Chapman mentions the discovery of a long V-shaped trench near Deal Cemetery in the nineteenth century, while Elvin notes the finding of a similar trench, which ran obliquely across Constitution Hill during the building of New St Mary's Church, Walmer, although their assertion that these date from the Roman Conquest must be viewed with suspicion. Camden, who published his *Britannia* in 1586, conjectured that the sandhills between Sandown and Sandwich are artificial and mark the true site of the Roman naval camp. Later discoveries of Roman pottery on Walmer foreshore and Roman coins in the sandhills dispels the theory that all the low ground between Walmer and Sandown was covered by the sea during Caesar's invasion.

On the fourth day sails borne by a gentle breeze were sighted in the Downs. The eighteen vessels bearing cavalry had finally caught up with the main invasion force. The arrival of horses would give Caesar the chance to explore the interior of his conquered territory. Yet as the transports neared the shore a sudden squall erupted. The cumbersome ships scudded before the north-easterly gale. A few limped back to France once more under cover of darkness while others perilously rode the massive waves mid-Channel. It was a credit to their masters' seamanship that not a single ship was lost. For Caesar this was a catastrophe. Not only had he lost valuable reinforcements but his own ships lay battered on the foreshore.

Caesar surveyed the carnage.

> The result was that the warships which had been beached, were waterlogged, and the transports, which were riding at anchor, were knocked about by the storm. A number of ships were shattered, and the rest, having lost their cables, anchors, and the remainder of their tackle, were unusable, which threw the whole army into consternation.

That night there was a full moon and a spring tide.

It was a disaster of the first magnitude. Caesar calmly took stock of the situation. His army was cast adrift on a foreign shore. No material was to hand for repairing the shattered vessels. There was a total lack of provisions, clothing or equipment for a protracted campaign. Unbelievably, the legionaires had cross the Channel without any baggage. It had been Caesar's intention to travel light and live off the land. Further, the approach of autumn heralded adverse weather which might make it impossible for the fleet to return to the Continent. The worst to be feared, however, was a renewed attack by the Britons.

'Troops should not be put in such a position', trumpet the authors of *The Roman Conquest of Britain*, 'and good commanders do not put them there . . .'

Caesar ordered his carpenters – part of the team of skilled craftsmen which made up his complete task force –– to repair the stricken craft. Timber and bronze was salvaged from the seriously damaged ships and used to renovate the more stable ones, while naval equipment necessary to complete the restoration was ordered from the Continent. By their industry all but twelve ships were saved

Roman coin showing Caesar's profile © British Museum

Caesar was pronounced with a hard 'C' in Latin and the 'ae' rhymed with 'eye', so that the name corresponded with the modern 'Kaiser'.

Deal's name derives from the Saxon word 'dylle' meaning 'low lying land' or 'del' referring to 'a dale or valley'.

The Druids, who formed the priesthood of the British warriors, directed their worship of spirits of nature, which sometimes involved human sacrifices, around holy oaks.

Woad, which produces an indigo pigment, grew in the sandhills near Deal.

and rendered tolerably seaworthy. The Britons, revelling in their enemy's plight, began a systematic campaign of harassment to prolong the war into winter.

Foraging parties were despatched to scour the countryside and sieze provisions from neighbouring farms and settlements. Members of the VIIth Legion, sent to reap corn, marched into a carefully baited trap. The corn had been cut everywhere except in one place so the natives guessed that this would be a tempting rendezvous. Nennius, a legendary chieftain, hatched a plot to form an ambush by concealing chariots in a wood overnight. While the soldiers laid down their arms and scattered to cut corn, they were surrounded and pelted with missiles. Sentinels on duty at the camp gates reported an exceptionally large cloud of dust rising from the standing corn and alerted Caesar who correctly interpreted this as a sign of an ambush. He commanded a detachment of the Xth Legion and raced to the scene where his prompt personal intervention rescued his men from imminent danger. Local tradition places this dramatic incident in the vicinity of Oxney, between Ringwould and Martin Mill, where traces have been identified of both a British fortified settlement served by a chariot track (Vine), and a nearby Roman encampment known as Roman Coddy, at Kingsdown (Pritchard).

British accounts of this engagement, written centuries later (and translated from ancient Welsh manuscripts in Victorian times by Reverend RW Morgan under the title *The British Kymry*) testify to a signal defeat by the Roman legions.

> The eagle itself was borne down, and Caesar in covering it with his body was assailed by Nennius. The sword of the great Roman buried itself in the shield of the British prince, and before he could extricate it, the tide of the battle separated the combatants, leaving the weapon a trophy to be long afterwards exhibited by the inhabitants.

Holinshed confirms this incident, but insists the shield belonged to a general named Belinus.

Caesar's troops made an inglorious retreat to their ship camp. They had been unable to prevent the capture of prisoners and weapons under such withering fire. Tempestuous weather called a temporary halt to hostilities since chariots could not function in miry ground. Meanwhile, the British chieftains rallied their tribes to make one final assault on the Romans and drive them inexorably back into the sea. Caesar's legions formed in serried ranks, probably protected by catapaults fired from their fort, and slowly advanced upon the painted warriors who persisted to fight in isolation. The result was inevitable. The Britons were routed, fugitives were slain and their homes razed to the ground. Commius, the Atrebatian, loaned thirty horses which he had brought from Gaul for the pursuit.

Caesar noted dryly:

> The same day the enemy sent envoys to me to ask for peace. From these I demanded twice as many hostages as before and ordered them to be sent to the Continent because it would soon be the equinox and I did not think it wise to risk sailing in wintry weather. Soon after midnight I set sail, taking advantage of a favourable wind, and my entire fleet reached the Continent safely.

As Caesar returned to France under the cover of darkness, he had time to reconsider his battle tactics. He was perfectly aware that at times his own army, although loyal to his command, had lost its morale. The islanders had the advantages of knowledge of their territory, a plentiful supply of food and the mobility provided by a powerful team of war chariots − the rapidity with which war chariots moved about the countryside indicates that there already existed an intricate network of tracks across Britain. Yet the major drawback was their outmoded form of defence. It was evident that their formidable form of guerrilla warfare was still no

Caesar's plaque on Walmer Green

match for the mighty military machine of Rome.

Caesar's conquest had been hampered by his lack of cavalry and unwieldy sailing craft. The Roman fleet was primarily employed for transporting troops, horses, artillery and supplies, while lighter galleys were used for reconnaissance and communications. The Britons, however, were skilled mariners and navigators who had been trading for centuries across the English Channel. Their sturdy craft were constructed with broad bottoms, high prows and sterns to ride the waves and glide with ease upon the foreshore.

Caesar left precise instructions with his deputy, Titus Labienus, regarding size, shape and dimensions for carpenters to construct a stouter fleet of transports suitable for local conditions. They were to have greater beam and less draught so that their decks could accommodate more troops, horses and heavy cargo. British granaries would be low in early summer – particularly after the previous year's fighting – and he was determined to travel independent of island resources. Transports were to be equipped for both rowing and sailing, which would make them comparatively independent of wind and tide. Also the addition of a low freeboard would greatly simplify loading and beaching. The shallowness of the ships, combined with their uncommon breadth, however, entailed an unforseen disadvantage: it would cause the vessels, unless the wind were right aft or on the quarter, to make a great deal of leeway. Caesar was about to experience this major flaw when crossing the English Channel.

Caesar's expections of recuperating the massive cost of boat-building by plundering Britain were questioned in a letter by the orator, Marcus Cicero:

> It is notorious that the approaches to the island are ramparted by astonishing masses of cliff; and, besides, it is now known that there isn't a pennyweight of silver in the island, nor any hope of loot except from slaves . . .

After drawing up detailed plans for invasion, Caesar dismissed his legions to their winter quarters while he returned to Rome. There he was amazed to learn that the Senate had decreed a period of public thanksgiving for his gallant endeavour to annexe a new province. His spin doctors had astutely played up the remoteness of Britain, the hazards of the English Channel and the audacity of a commander who had dared such a military adventure. Caesar determined to devote the next season's campaign to the conquest of Britain.

The second Roman invasion fleet sailed from Boulogne around 8pm on 6 July 54 BC. Caesar's intention was to travel overnight and, by carefully observing the current, make a surprise appearance on the Kent coast at dawn. An opportunity for a similar attack upon the islanders had been snatched from him the previous year. There were excellent sailing conditions – a south-westerly breeze gently ruffled the waves of the ebb tide – for this journey covering thirty Roman miles. The ships took a more direct route across the English Channel, since it is generally supposed that the treacherous Goodwin Sands did not attain their formidable dimensions until around the time of the Norman Conquest. (Curiously, Frontinus, who published a collection of successful military startegems, mentions the fact that the traitor, Commius, was pursued by Caesar, and his flotilla was stuck upon a sandbank at low tide within easy reach of land.) Caesar commanded 540 transports of the new class – sixty more remained weather-bound in port – plus a further 200 privately-owned merchant vessels which, with his twenty-eight war galleys, presented an awesome spectacle as they crossed simultaneously at sunset.

At midnight, however, the wind dropped with the result that the fleet was driven by the current along the Kent coast beyond the North Foreland. For a time the ships rode out this obstacle and drifted out towards the North Sea taking care to keep land on their port side. At first light the tide turned and the oarsmen strenuously rowed towards the familiar shore, arriving slightly north of their intended destination. The Romans had perfected a system of naval signalling which allowed Caesar to direct the operations of his fleet remotely. 'The soldiers worked splendidly, and by continuous rowing enabled the heavily-laden transports to keep up with the warships,' Caesar noted. 'The whole fleet reached Britain around midday.'

The Romans landed once more in the vicinity of Deal and Sandwich. This time, however, they were completely unopposed. The invasion force of five legions (25,000 soldiers) plus 2,000 cavalry disembarked with comparative ease and a base command was quickly established. Scouting parties were despatched and these soon returned with prisoners who supplied reliable information regarding the position of the natives. Caesar learned that a large fighting force had originally assembled on the foreshore but the natives had prudently withdrawn and concealed themselves on higher ground at the approach of his formidable fleet.

Quintus Atrias was given command of the shore camp. He was provided with ten cohorts (5,000 men, presumably drawn from all five legions) plus 300 cavalry and ordered to protect both the camp and the fleet. He was further charged with unloading heavy baggage, building defences and setting up a courier service with galleys between the two countries. Unwisely, Caesar left his warships riding at anchor – a potentially dangerous situation in view of the treacherous southerly winds then blowing – 'on an open shore of soft sand'. No trace of a Roman encampment remains although, from Caesar's description, it is assumed that it was once more in the vicinity of the gentle sandy flats beyond Sandown.

Caesar acted with the rapidity which had brought him countless victories. He headed towards the Great Stour where he knew the Britons had concentrated their forces. A midnight march covering twelve miles – lit by the light of a new moon – finally brought the Roman army into confrontation with the British forces.

The Cantii had chosen their site carefully for their initial clash with the invaders. They occupied a patch of territory across the Stour Valley two miles west of Canterbury. Here, their chariots could rush down from high ground and whip across the plain to prevent the Romans from fording the deep water. Caesar's pioneer corps, however, consisted of crack troops trained to swim with heavy equipment across the swiftest of rivers. They soon secured the crossing, enabling the infantry to proceed unhindered. A surprise cavalry attack at dawn then put the Cantii to flight.

The Cantii were repulsed and retreated to a Celtic hill fort at Bigbury Wood. This was the most important British fortress south-east of the River Thames. The Britons had blocked all the approaches by felling timber and had stocked up against a prolonged siege. Skirmishing parties made random attacks out of the woods trying to prevent the Romans from penetrating their defences. Caesar ordered his VIIth Legion to storm the hillfort which it managed with surprisingly little difficulty by late afternoon. The method was for soldiers to pile up earth against the lowest part of the fortified mound and when level with the summit breach the defences under the cover of the testudo. Caesar captured the hillfort but declined to pursue the chieftains who had escaped in the confusion. Instead, he concentrated on establishing his own fortified encampment on Barham Downs.

Next day Caesar divided his infantry and cavalry into three columns in readiness to pursue the Britons when he received devastating news from the coast. A messenger arrived from Quintus Atrias informing him that his fleet had been hammered by an easterly gale while anchored in the Downs. According to Holinshed, Caesar's 'nauie by rigour of a sore and hideous tempest was greeuously molested, and thrown upon the shore'. Walmer beach was completely littered with vessels which had been driven ashore and swamped by the thrust of the huge rollers. Caesar reported:

> The anchors and cables had not held firm and the captains and pilots could not cope with the force of the gale. As a result a great deal of damage had been caused by the ships colliding.

Caesar halted the progress of his legions and cavalry while he hurried back with a reduced force to inspect the carnage at Walmer. Forty ships were totally wrecked. Those that could be repaired were hauled to safety up the beach - a phenomenal feat. He deployed his battle-weary troops to assist the carpenters and, working in relays, they took a full ten days to repair the battered fleet. Troops were deployed to haul boats up the beach to shelter by means of capstans over greased logs. Next, they laboured to extend the fortifications of the military camp to enclose the restored vessels. Even assuming tight packing and double banking of ships, this defensive line must have stretched four or five miles along the coast. A galley was also despatched to France with orders for Labienus, who had remained behind, to construct replacement warships.

Julius Caesar spent his forty-sixth birthday at Deal (most scholars argue that he was born in 100 BC on the 12th or 13th day of the month Quintilis later renamed July in his honour). Yet it was not a time of celebration. The galley returned with news from Rome that his only child, Julia, had died in childbirth. This personal disaster now threatened opposition from his antagonistic son-in-law, Pompey, whose fine naval reputation Caesar was attempting to challenge. Time was running out for this ambitious general who was fast approaching his fiftieth year.

On 19 July Caesar once more marched his troops inland and headed towards the Great Stour. Meantime, the military position of the Britons had considerably strengthened during his brief absence. The Cantii had united with other native tribes under Cassivellaunus (Caswallon) Chief of the Catuvellauni (Cassi) whose territory beyond the Thames encompassed parts of what were to become Middlesex, Hertfordshire and Oxfordshire. Cassivellaunus, an influential warlord, was venerated by the Celts as High King of Britain.

Cassivellaunus skilfully combined the British cavalry and chariots for maximum impact. He laid ambushes to harass the Romans as they marched across Kent and he organised constant skirmishes to prevent them making camp. His ploy was to send out a detachment of warriors to entice soldiers away from their unit and then attack them with tacticly posted reserves. Caesar strictly forbade his troops to pursue the enemy in isolation realising that his soldiers were particularly vulnerable whenever they went in search of provisions. In a brisk action fought outside the Roman camp the natives impressed Caesar with their verve and dash.

Yet their success was dearly purchased in the last onset by the death of Nennius. This catastrophe was matched by the slaughter of a military tribune, Quintus Laberius Durus, whose traditional burial mound is 'Jullieberri', near Chilham. Caesar rallied his army the following day when all three legions plus the cavalry finally swept the natives from the field. Caesar noted with obvious satisfaction that this was the last time Cassivellaunus was able to meet him with full strength.

Relentlessly, the Roman army marched across North Kent until it reached the Thames. Caesar aimed to strike Cassivellaunus at the heart of his kingdom.

Immediately Caesar's army had forded the Thames - probably at Brentford - it entered the territory of the Catuvellauni. This was the most powerful tribe in southern Britain. Roman cavalry and infantry made their amphibious assault so swiftly that the Catuvellauni were overpowered. Cassivellaunus retreated to his capital at Wheathampstead, near St. Albans, where he prepared for a protracted siege. Caesar interrogated prisoners and deserters who betrayed the secret location of his impregnable stronghold which consisted of a rampart and trench screened by forests and protected by marshes. Employing identical tactics to Bigbury Wood, the Romans stormed the stronghold and put the Catuvellauni to flight.

In retaliation, Cassivellaunus ordered the four Cantii chieftains to renew their attack on the Roman ship camp at Walmer. Implicitly, they obeyed their leader even though his own defence had crumpled. Presumably, the idea was to relieve pressure on the Catuvellauni and allow them time to reform while cutting off the invaders' only means of retreat. Quintus Atrias resolutely defended his position. After tough fighting the Cantii were routed and a prominent chieftain named Cingetorix was captured. Apparently, Caesar returned briefly to Walmer to make an inspection of this latest onslaught. Confirmation of this incident is a letter written by Quintus Cicero to his older brother, Marcus.

Cassivellaunus was becoming disheartened. He had suffered too many reverses and was humiliated by the defection of his allies. Caesar's successes attracted several tribes to his allegiance. Nevertheless, Ceasar astutely realised that the British could easily hold out for the rest of the campaigning season. Summer was passing. Gaul was increasingly restless. His troops feared being stranded once more in Britain. The rival armies had reached stalemate. A negotiated peace therefore suited both Caesar and Cassivellaunus. What could not be achieved through force might be still gained by stealth. The illusive Commius appeared once more to outline the general's revised terms for the High King's surrender. Once more Commius had made himself scarce throughout the protracted campaign. Had he, in fact, been encouraging the British Atrebates (based in Hampshire) to join the combined southern tribes in opposing the Romans?

There is more intrigue. At this late point in his narrative Caesar introduces a young British prince named Mandubracius who had ingratiated himself with the Roman army. Part of Caesar's bargaining was to reinstate him as king and offer him protection.

The name 'Mandubracius' means 'black traitor'. British sources identify this scheming youth with Avarwy, son of Lugh or Lud, King of the Trinovantes (who inhabited modern Middlesex) after whose 'dun' or fortress London is supposedly named. When Lud died Mandubracius failed to inherit his father's kingdom because the law of primogeniture did not apply in Celtic society although a faction claimed he was indeed the rightful heir. Cassivellaunus was elected military dictator of the whole island instead but he treated Mandubracious fairly and compensated him with generous offers of lands under his suzerainty.

Mandubracious, however, sought to depose Cassivellaunus and seize power for himself. When he witnessed the might of the first Roman invasion, he presented himself to Caesar in Gaul and offered to hold the island a tributary of Rome upon the overthrow of Cassivellaunus. He convinced Caesar in exile that Cassivellaunus had killed his father and usurped him as chief of the Trinovantes. Mandubracius sailed with Caesar to Britain where he acted as interpreter, negotiator and guide leading him directly towards Cassivellaunus' stronghold. He escorted him on the night march to the Celtic hill fort below Barham Downs, across the ancient trackway in North Kent towards London and over the Thames at the only point where the river was fordable.

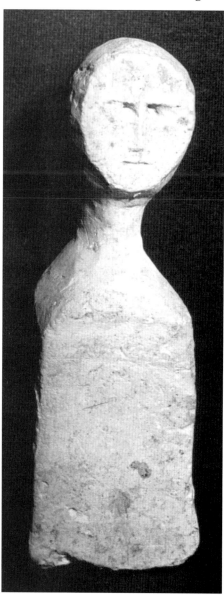

Deal Man © Dover Museum

Surprisingly, Mandubracius' accession as King of the Trinovantes was welcomed by all parties even though such connivance with the Romans inevitably destroyed the democratic structure of Celtic society. Naturally, Caesar plays down the fact that Mandubracius' treachery enabled him to travel far from base camp and swiftly conquer British territories in his *Commentaries*. Nor does he mention the lucrative wine trade which flourished between Rome and Britain immediately after his treaty. Perhaps these omissions indicate Caesar's 'secret agenda' in his second expedition to Britain, the purpose of which he keeps remarkably silent?

Caesar's forages into the country over his four months' sojourn enabled him to compare the aboriginal natives of the interior with the migrant tribes of the seashore. He noted:

The coast (was populated) by Belgic immigrants who came to plunder and make war - nearly all of them retaining the names of tribes from which they originated - and later settled to till the soil.

20

East Kent was at that time inhabited by Belgic immigrants – a mixture of Germanic and Celtic stock – who had arrived on these shores a generation before but had continued to trade with their counterparts on the Continent.

An Ancient British village possibly existed around the fortified entrenchment dating from the Early Iron Age (600-200 BC) which was once discerned on the eastern slope of the grand escarpment near the present water tower atop Mill Hill. Later Iron Age or Belgic cemeteries clustered around an earlier Bronze Age barrow were discovered when chalk quarries were developed in the nineteenth century. When these burial sites were carefully examined towards the end of the twentieth century, they were deemed to be the most significant Iron Age cemeteries in Britain.

Early excavations had revealed pottery, brooches and a puzzling pair of bronze spoons (possibly used for divination) while curious inhumations numbered a child and its lap dog and a rider with his mount. An intriguing new find in a subterranean Druid shrine was a carved chalk figurine which has become known as the Deal Man. Most spectacular discovery, however, was the skeleton of an Iron Age warrior, buried with his decorated bronze crown, an iron sword in an ornate scabbard and a ceremoniously broken shield, now exhibited in the British Museum. The wealth of Celtic art contained in this shallow grave dating from about the second century BC is said to be 'virtually unparalleled in southeast England'.

> By far the most civilised inhabitants are those living in Kent. The population is large, the ground thickly studded with homesteads . . . and the cattle numerous.

Kentish tribes clearly prospered from their double trade - maritime and agriculture. Corn was cultivated on the coast while inland sheep were reared for wool and milk, cattle for meat and leather. Timber was plentiful although minerals were sparse. Currency consisted of both bronze and gold coins or iron ingots which were imported. Lastly, Caesar commented favourably upon the climate which was more temperate than Gaul 'the cold being less severe'.

Caesar's observations, nevertheless, perpetuate several errors.

Peter Berresford Ellis, author of *Caesar's Invasion of Britain,* argues that he failed to comprehend the advanced democracy of Celtic society whose intrinsic structure was based upon humane laws and a social conscience. He champions this 'progressive' society whose members possessed highly developed artistic skills including spinning, weaving, pottery and metalwork. Their religious leaders were natural scientists with a basic knowledge of physics, medicine, astronomy, astrology and navigation. Disastrously for Rome, Caesar never truly revealed the potential wealth and natural resources of the island.

At the end of August Caesar and his legions returned to Walmer without establishing a permanent garrison in Britain. They took with them hostages to be sold abroad as slaves to finance the two campaigns. Storms continued to play havoc with Caesar's plans. He learned that although most of his ships had been repaired several of the sixty replacements had failed to reach Britain. A few were still struggling in rough weather to traverse the Channel. Patiently, Caesar waited until mid-September for the arrival of the remainder of the craft necessary to transport both his troops and hostages. The equinox was fast approaching and he feared being stranded in Britain.

Eventually Caesar decided to split his force and launched them in two shifts back to France. The second detachment packed tightly on board their transports departed in late September.

> The sea became absolutely calm so we set sail in the late evening and reached land safely with the whole fleet at dawn.

Julius Caesar was not destined to return to Britain . . .

The third and conclusive invasion of Britain took place in 43 AD. Four legions only were despatched but the number of auxiliaries deployed brought the force up to 40,000-50,000 men. Dio Cassius, a third century historian, asserts that the Roman fleet sailed in three divisions 'lest all arriving at one place (they) might be prevented from landing.' Scholars surmise that a decoy army made a landfall under the cliffs at Dover to draw the Britons westwards while another force led by Vespasian - who later became Emperor himself - made contact with British allies at Fishbourne, near Chichester Harbour. Meanwhile, the main fleet commanded by Aulus Plautius sailed up the Wantsum Channel - then a broad navigable waterway separating the Isle of Thanet from the mainland - and disembarked on the island of Rutupiae (Richborough).

Contrary winds had driven the massive fleet back when the Romans sailed overnight to make their surprise attack at dawn. A meteorite shower passing from east to west visibly cheered them since Romans had an aversion to sea voyages and this was interpreted as a harbinger of good luck. Superstitious sailors would have needed reassurance since not only did they believe they were sailing to the country at the edge of the flat Earth but they risked veering towards the Isle of Thanet, which derives from the Greek word *thanatos*, meaning death. This time the Britons failed to muster and the Roman invasion went unopposed. Further inland, a ferocious battle lasting two days took place on the banks of the Medway forcing the Britons to retreat north of the Thames. The Romans pursued their foe across the river and successfully stormed the Catuvellauni's new capital, Camuldonum (Colchester).

Emperor Claudius, Commander-in-Chief of the army, declared himself Governor of Britain. He made a triumphal entry into the new Roman province riding at the head of his troops on an elephant. Elephants struck terror into the natives in the same way as their war chariots had undermined the confidence of Caesar's troops. According to one inscription on a victory arch in Rome eleven British kings 'formally placed themselves under the sway of the Roman people'. Roman rule lasted almost four centuries and the whole of England and Wales was subdued, with Hadrian's Wall marking the northern frontier of the Roman Empire.

In the light of Claudius' spectacular annexation of Britain, Caesar's two brief forays into 'the land at the extremities of the earth' have tended to be regarded as superficial accomplishments. Fresh insurrection by the truculent Gauls prevented his hypothetical third invasion and cancelled the promised annual tribute by the defeated Britons. (Shakespeare dramatised the Britons' refusal to pay tribute to Rome in *Cymbeline*, where he refers to Caesar's invasions as 'A kind of conquest'.) Moreover, the plunder of corn and cattle was hardly worthwhile compared to the rich rewards of gold, silver, tin, iron, copper and lead which Caesar failed to discover in the island interior. One biographer Pat Southern is of the opinion that:

> The second expedition brought no profit to Rome and nothing but a reputation for daring to Caesar . . . But it is incontrovertible that he had waged war more or less for his own ends.

Julius Caesar triumphed against his adversary, Pompey, during the Civil War in Rome, while his courtship of the Egyptian queen, Cleopatra, shocked the world. Yet his dictatorship was crushed by the assassins' knives in the Senate on the Ides of March, 44 BC - ten years after he had departed from the shores of Kent. The Roman historian Tacitus belittled Caesar's British escapades and proclaimed him to be:

> The discoverer, not the conqueror, of the island . . . he did no more than show it to posterity . . . Rome could not boast a conquest.

Modern scholars tend to dispute this jaundiced view and hail Julius Caesar as Rome's greatest military commander, who not only stimulated trade with Britain but opened the way for the true conquest of a New World.

SAINT LEONARD'S

'The chirch of Dale'

SAINT LEONARD'S CHURCH has, for some 800 years, served the parish of Deal. More than any other building, it encompasses the history of the port and inevitably it is regarded as a maritime church.

The church, built over a mile distant from Lower Deal, existed in fact to serve the tiny hamlet of Addelam. The Domesday Book renders the phrase 'at Deal' as *ad Delam* which is possibly a latinised version of the Saxon *aet del ham* meaning 'at the valley settlement'. Inhabitants were concerned primarily with farming rather than fishing. Not until Stuart times, when the emergence of the Navy Yard led to the beginnings of a town built close to the shore, did St Leonard's start to accommodate the needs of a sea-faring community.

Leland, writing in the time of Henry VIII, records:

> The chirch of Dale corruptely caullid Dele was a prebbende longging of auncient tyme to S. Martines College in Dovor. Deale, half a myle fro the shore of the se, a fisscher village iii myles or more above Sandwice, is apon a flat shore and very open to the se, wher is a fosse or a great bank artificial betwixt the towne and se, and beginneth about Deal, and rennith a great way up towards S. Margaret's Clyfe, yn so much that sum suppose that this i the place where Caesar landed. Surely the fosse was made to kepe owte ennemyes there, or to defend the rage of the se; or I think rather the castinge up beche or pible.

Most of the earliest references to St Leonard's are concerned with agriculture - although not all these records present the church in a favourable light. A report of the Visitation of the Feast of the Conversion of Saint Paul in 1327 reveals that the rector, who was non-resident, offended his parishioners by causing corn to be winnowed in the churchyard; while a local farmer, Robert Byng, allowed his sheep to graze in these grounds for which offence he was 'flogged thrice'.

St Leonard's is fortunate in possessing a Frampton List of Rectors complete from 1243. The first name mentioned is the most illustrious: Richard de la Wyche (1197-1253) – known as Saint Richard of Chichester. Richard began life as a humble farm labourer but owing to his own exertions and a frugal life, he entered Oxford University and afterwards studied at Paris. His companion,

24

Edmund Rich, Archbishop of Canterbury, appointed him his Chancellor. When Edmund was exiled, Richard accompanied him and he was ordained abroad.

Returning to England after Edmund's death, he served the Vicarage of Charing and the Rectory of Deal until he was called upon by Archbishop Boniface to resume his Chancellorship. In 1245, he became Bishop of Chichester and in 1253 he died at Maison Dieu, Dover, shortly after dedicating a tiny wayside chapel in memory of his friend, now canonised. St Edmund's Chapel has been faithfully restored (it had become a smithy) and it remains the smallest chapel regularly used in England. It is the only building still standing dedicated to an English saint by an English saint.

When a modern church was built for the miners at Deal in 1934 St Richard was chosen as its patron. Richard was a gentle, loving and unworldly person and his kindly character is reflected in his prayer:

Thanks be to Thee, my Lord Jesus Christ,
For all the benefits Thou has won for me,
For all the pains and insults Thou has borne for me,
O most merciful Redeemer, Friend and Brother,
May I see Thee more clearly,
Love Thee more dearly
And follow Thee more nearly
Day by Day.

The Church of St Leonard

Deal's parish church is built on a high mound (not immediately perceptible) which was possibly a pagan moot hill. Four roads here converge, the most important being the one from Sandwich that veers sharply towards the town of Deal. Once a toll gate stood here. Until 1874, the tolls were collected by a certain Mr Parker who gave his name to Parker's Corner. This seventeenth century red brick house with double gables and tall chimneys, concealed by high walls is more commonly called Jenkin's Well. Later still, it was the Post Office.

There is an interesting run of eighteenth century buildings at the beginning of Manor Road. The Old House was formerly the Liverpool Arms, named after the Earl of Liverpool, Lord Warden of the Cinque Ports, and the Admiral Keppel (dated 1742) commemorated a naval hero. A picturesque thatched cottage was pulled down some time ago but a magnificent barn remains, converted into residential use. Opposite Holly Farm are some delightful weatherboarded cottages and Marlborough House, with its decorative shutters and shell fanlight, occupies the south-east corner of the churchyard.

St Leonard's may occupy the site of a place of worship in Saxon times but the present church is generally considered to have been built at the latter end of the twelfth century. Today, it presents a confusing mixture of architectural styles - a twelfth century nave, thirteenth century chancel, seventeenth century tower and a nineteenth century porch with annexe - yet the original building must have been a humble affair typical of the tiny Norman churches which exist still in secluded areas of East Kent.

The outline of this Norman church is best viewed from the churchyard looking to the west where the high flint walls of the early church are readily discerned. Inside, it is difficult to visualise the original structure which consists of a short chancel and a rectangular nave of three bays. During the thirteenth century the

An early postcard of St Leonard's

narrow Norman aisles were rebuilt on a grander scale with angle buttresses and north and south doorways. The south aisle was enlarged to its present width and the northern aisle extended as far as the beginning of the north gallery. The original nave wall was discovered during recent renovations.

On either side of the nave a pillar has been removed to allow for a grand elliptical arch. The north-easterly column is one of those that remain, fortunately, as it is worthy of attention. This pillar, c1180, forms the eastern respond of the north arcade of the nave and stands just above the ambo. Particularly interesting is the Corinthianesque capital of the type introduced by William of Sens and the intricately moulded foliage is clearly the work of a master craftsmen. Later masons stamped their marks on the remaining columns by carving pictorial graffiti, either mortar boards or boats - sleek galleys having tall masts with striped sails, long oars, pointed prows and high rounded sterns – evidently typical ships that passed through the Downs in the Middle Ages.

St Leonard's possessed a tower as early as the twelfth century which, according to Philip Symonson's 1596 Map of Kent was surmounted by a tall steeple. During the seventeenth century the structure crashed onto the church causing immeasurable damage. Prior to the Reformation, English churches fell into disrepair so the collapse of a steeple was not an uncommon occurrence. Funds being insufficient, St Leonard's remained towerless until 1686 when the present red brick edifice was constructed.

The tower is surmounted by an octagonal white timber lantern (which may have been intended as a gazebo) with a cupola and a weather vane. This tower, which stands 125 feet above sea level, appears on early charts of the Downs as an important landmark for shipping approaching the Goodwin Sands, and for this reason it was maintained by Trinity House. From its summit extensive views are gained over the Isle of Thanet and across the English Channel towards the coast of France.

It is not known when St Leonard's first acquired bells but the churchwardens' accounts for January 1638 contain this entry: 'Ite for a roape for the wakering bell 00-03-60', and for 5 March: 'Ite for a basericke for the third bell wheele and otherwise 00-05-06.' Presumably, then, there were three bells when the steeple fell.

Five bells cast by Christopher Hodson, a London founder, were added to the tower. There they remained for 200 years when they were recast and a sixth added in 1887 as a Jubilee gift to the town by Captain George Colman, afterwards Mayor of Deal. Since 1715 the church has owned a clock, but the existing one, manufactured by a certain Mr Farrer, dates from only 1866.

St Leonard's is entered via the tower by a handsome west door which is a splendid example of Jacobean panelling. It is made without any form of brace and has a hand-wrought latch and bolt of fine craftsmanship. A slim fifteenth century doorway leads from the north aisle to the chancel. Apart from one panel, the door itself is original, having hand-wrought hinges and studs.

Originally the pulpit (a three-decker) was sited in the south aisle and the church organ, now in the west gallery, once stood in the South Chapel. Several galleries have been added to accommodate the increase in population and the old horse-box pews were removed during the Victorian period in favour of the present seating arrangements. When the gallery over the chancel was moved to the west side some fine oak panelling was discovered at the rear. It was thought to have originated from the old chapel at Northbourne which belonged to St Augustine's Abbey. The font was presented to the church in 1851 but the fate of the old one remains a mystery. In 1979 the pulpit was replaced by a modern ambo and the carved chancel screen was repositioned along the wall of the clergy vestry. This opened up the chancel and the nave so that the twelfth century architecture can be appreciated.

The South Chapel was restored at the beginning of this present century. When the floor was lowered to conform with the level of the rest of the church an 18 inch flint wall was discovered, the foundation of the original building. Probably this chapel was entered from the south as traces of a doorway can be seen in the exterior wall. Inside, on the south wall, a fifteenth century credence remains with a stone shelf and piscina below. The Bevington organ had been the gift of Anne Oldman and the Crucifixion window - a copy of the famous painting by Guido Reni (1575-1642) was installed in memory of the Reverend Robert Patterson, Rector of Deal 1905-19.

The chancel holds several treasures including an ancient aumbry bearing traces of hinged doors, and a thirteenth century double sedilia. These ascending sedilia have columns formed from Purbeck marble and wonderfully carved arches – the eastern trefoiled, the western pointed and terminating with the head of an unidentified crowned medieval monarch.

Prize possession is undoubtedly the rare Norman piscina mounted on a shaft. It is beautifully proportioned with an octagonal shaft carved with chevron mouldings and an intricately worked capital. Evidently, early worshippers treasured their piscina for the Early English pointed arch appears to have been made later especially to contain it. The only other Norman piscina in Kent is at Ryarsh, near Maidstone.

Prior to the Reformation there were several side altars containing images of a host of saints - St Christopher, St James, St John, St John the Baptist, St Katherine, St Margaret, St Peter, St Thomas a Becket, St Loy, patron of farriers - before which lights were constantly kept burning. Thus we read that Thomas Holman, who died in 1535, was buried 'in the church before St Lowis' and he left a bequest of a bushel of barley 'to every light in the church'.

Three galleries remain - two of which have historic interest. The one over the west door was constructed by the Pilots of Deal for their exclusive use after the steeple crashed down in 1658, destroying the then existing gallery and necessitating the rebuilding of the tower. There was a great deal of controversy concerning the construction of this gallery and its legality was contested by the rector, Henry Gerard, who deeply resented it. Two small panels show pilots in the costume of the Restoration period holding sounding lines. It is a pity that other panels representing globes have not been restored as it would be fascinating to study how much of the world had been explored by that date.

A painting in the centre of the gallery features a three-masted man-o'-war, fully-rigged and flying the red ensign. It bears the date 1705. This commemorates the Great Storm of 1703 in which thirteen ships of Her Majesty's Navy were wrecked on the Goodwin Sands with the loss of 1,200 lives. Deftly, the artist has included both the bow and the stern of the vessel. An intricate ship model exhibited

Man-o'-War painting in the Pilots' Gallery

under glass was based on this painting. It was made by TW Cox to commemorate the 250th anniversary of the granting of Deal's charter.

The adjoining gallery, with its wonderfully carved panelling, carries the arms of William III (after Mary died). Originally, this was the front of the gallery, erected over the chancel facing the Pilots' Gallery, built in 1696 by Deal's second Mayor, Tobias Bowles. The arms in the clerestory of the south side of the nave are of William's successor, Queen Anne. After the Restoration in 1660, Royal Arms were ordered to be placed in all churches as a reminder to the congregation of their loyalty to the Crown in addition to God.

Three notable brasses appear in the church. On the east wall of the chapel there appears a handsome brass to the memory of Thomas Boys of Fredville, Nonington, who is shown in full armour kneeling at prayer. The knight's helmet and gauntlets lie in front of a prie-dieu on which lies an open missal. Boys was a gentleman-at-arms in attendance on Henry VIII at the Siege of Boulogne. He was rewarded for his services by being made Mayor of Calais and later appointed the second Captain of Deal Castle in the reign of Edward VI. He died aged sixty on 16 February 1562.

> Though Thomas Boys his corps in grave here ded doth lye,
> Yet Robert Boys sayth to him shall never die.

Another brass, on the left-hand side of the Sanctuary, commemorates Thomas Baker, sometimes called 'Barbor.' He is the earliest known Deputy appointed by the Mayor of Sandwich to act for him at Deal before the town was granted its charter giving it the status of a borough. Baker is depicted in a long flowing robe

The Drake hatchment, which commemorates Vice-Admiral Sir Francis Samuel Drake, a descendant of Sir Francis Drake

Hatchments are coats-of-arms painted on lozenge-shaped boards of wood or canvas and placed in churches as memorials of the deceased.

St Leonard, to whom the church is dedicated, was a sixth century French Abbot. He is regarded as the friend of outlaws and prisoners and is usually depicted girded with chains. He died about 559 AD and is commemorated on 6 November.

with wide collar and cuffs and a purse hangs about his waist. His wife wears a wimple and a full-length gown with upturned cuffs and a long girdle. Their four sons and four daughters are shown collectively on two separate brasses. When he died in February 1508, Baker thoughtfully left money for the repair of the church walls and the steeple which, even then, was evidently in decay.

The third brass is the most remarkable. It is a rare example of a chrism brass - that of a newly-baptised baby - in memory of an infant buried by broken-hearted parents under the high altar. An inscription in characters of the day reads:

Anne the daughter & onely child of Thomas Consant Pson of Deale & of Judith his wife (after 13 yeares maried) was borne ye 18th of June and died sodenly at nurse ye 20th July 1606.

The pathetic child is shown wrapped in swaddling clothes and a Latin inscription, composed by her scholarly father, at one time master at King's School, Canterbury, and afterwards headmaster of King's School, Rochester, is touchingly put into the child's mouth. It translates: 'I who so soon departed this life have soon begun to live, And I who but now was as nothing, have become one of Heaven's company'.

A further memorial in the vestry recalls Edward Bulstrode, whose body lies in a vault under the altar. He was the eldest son of Sir Richard Bulstrode who served both Charles II and James II as 'Agent, Resident and Envoy Extraordinary at the Court of Bruxelles'. He died 27 December 1718 and his armorial bearings are enclosed in a handsome monumental frame with the motto: 'Think and Thank'.

Seventeen hatchments hang on the walls. St Leonard's hatchments immortalise representatives of the Pomeroy, Serocold, Gerard, Baker, Scriven and Harvey families. The last-named resided for a time at the magnificent house known as The Oaks which later became Tormore School. A distinguished naval family, their hatchments display various nautical emblems and sailors in period costume. The most distinguished hatchment commemorates Vice-Admiral Sir Francis Samuel Drake, third son of the fourth Baronet, and a baronet in his own right. He died in 1789 and his hatchment appears above the fifteenth century door into the chancel. His tomb is located in the churchyard towards the east end of the church. He was a descendant of Sir Francis Drake, the Elizabethan seafarer, and his hatchment bears the familar Drake crest – the world surmounted by a ship and the motto 'Auxilio Divino' (by divine help). Duncomb Drake, an uncle of the above Sir Francis, lies buried before the font while another Drake hatchment - as yet unidentified - hangs in the porch. Silhouettes of sheldrakes feature on this particular hatchment.

The vestry, a parochial meeting consisting of a chosen number of ratepayers elected to carry out the government of the parish, met at first in the church or at an inn. It levied rates to pay for the care of the poor and the upkeep of the church. A room for vestry meetings was created when the west end of the south aisle was partitioned off in 1709. The seats around three sides are still in position, as is the fireplace to provide warmth. In the cupboard, high on the north wall, are the Poor House accounts dating back to 1700.

It is interesting to recall how town councils grew out of such parish meetings. At a convening of the vestry on 13 December 1698 a resolution was passed to apply to Parliament for a charter which would convert Deal into 'a Borough and Market Town'. It would ensure that the town was no longer a mere limb of Sandwich but could elect its own mayor and council to make its own by-laws. This historic charter was signed by William III in 1699 and brought triumphantly home by Joshua Coppin, elected first Mayor, to be proudly displayed in the church porch. After their inception Deal's new Mayor and Corporation attended St Leonard's with great pomp and dignity every Sunday until St George's Church was built.

Opposite the church stands the sixteenth century Court House (originally a poor house) rented temporarily by the corporation for their meetings. The first

Chrism brass at St Leonard's Church © Simon Howes

true Court Hall where the mayor, jurats and common councilmen met, was in the High Street between Market Street and King Street. It was a grand affair surmounted by a cupola with a 'fire and market bell' and a gaol at the rear. When the present Town Hall was built in 1803 Deal's impressive Charter of Incorporation was removed from St Leonard's and prominently displayed in the Mayor's Parlour.

The parish chest, which held church plate and records, appeared to be an ordinary deal box until after the last war when it was found to have the date 1661 carved on the underside of its lid. In the churchwardens' accounts for that year there appears this entry: 'Item payed Richard Beane ye joyner for makeing of a new chest, with hinges and a lock to it and for closeing up of the arch and making of benches in the church porch 01 - 06 - 10.' Later the chest was fitted with three locks of different sizes - one for the Rector, the other two for the churchwardens.

The Parish Registers are complete from 1559 when in the reign of Queen Elizabeth I every church was required to keep a record of all baptisms, marriages and burials. A nephew of Samuel Pepys was baptised at St Leonard's on 28 October 1669 and recorded as 'ye son of Beltshazzar St. Mitchell and Esther his wife.' Nieces, Elizabeth (1661) Esther (1675) and Ann (1677) are also recorded. Samuel Pepys was Secretary of the Navy and probably granted his brother-in-law the post in Deal's Navy Yard.

Ravages of the Plague are also recorded in the register and bear testimony to the virulence of the disease probably introduced by sailors into the port:

1663: 45 burials
1664: 78 burials
1665: 210 burials
1666: 333 burials
1667: 29 burials

The first outbreak occurred among the seamen of the fleet of Deal so that from 1665 to 1666 the records of burials of sailors are frequent (ie 'Seaman from the Swann'). From the latter end of 1666 the names of townsfolk are in the majority until the subsidence of the contagion the following year.

A plan of the seating survives, dating from about 1618, which was drawn up to settle matters of controversy. This torn and damaged document mentions all the principal householders in the parish and where they sat. Curiously, the men sat separately from the women. The Porter of Sandown Castle occupied a reserved pew, but where the garrisons of Deal and Sandown Castles, who were required to attend divine service at St Leonard's were accommodated is not specified. Poor families, we know, sat humbly upon forms against the west wall. This rough plan is endorsed by the churchwardens, one of whom, John Marlton, could sign only by making his mark.

George Whitefield, one of the earliest Methodist ministers, visited Deal at the beginning of 1738 when embarking on his first missionary expedition to America. After rounding the North Foreland his ship *Whitaker* was becalmed in the Downs for several weeks and so Whitefield, already acknowledged as the

The Manor House, where Deal's first mayor, Joshua Coppin, lived

greatest preacher of his age, took the opportunity to attend the three Anglican churches - St Leonard's, St George's and St Nicholas', Sholden.

Whitefield - like the Wesley brothers - sought to please the Almighty by his methodical approach to worship, which involved fasting, prayer, studying the scriptures, regular attendance at church and partaking of Holy Communion. The young cleric presented a startling appearance – tall, handsome, with piercing blue eyes, a squint and a fluffy white wig. Undoubtedly, he was a remarkable preacher - powerful, eloquent, melodious - who elicited a strong emotional response from his congregation. Thousands flocked to hear him and his presence set Deal in 'a holy flame'.

Spurned by the intolerant Dr Nicholas Carter, perpetual curate of St George's, George Whitefield was welcomed by the Reverend Herbert Randolph, rector of St Leonard's. The church was packed to capacity and resourceful folk even climbed upon the leads to peer in through the topmost windows. After visiting the sick and bereaved of the parish, Whitefield turned his attention to the blaspheming boatmen. At St Leonard's he had taken the opportunity to denounce smuggling, which he recognised as 'a sin that does most easily beset the Deal people'.

Finally, Whitefield set sail down the English Channel upon 'a pleasant fare gale' on the first stage of his voyage to Georgia. Strangely, the south-west wind which had prevented him from sailing earlier blew home another fervent methodist, John Wesley, who arrived in the Downs, depressed and disillusioned, after his own disastrous tour of America.

St Leonard's churchyard has an unusual number of seventeenth century headstones (before 1668 people who could afford it were buried inside the church). The earliest surviving stone is dated 1675 but there are at least ten headstones earlier than 1700 - the oldest normally small and lacking sculpture. In 1690 the outline of a skull and crossbones appears for the first time and later embellishments include hour glasses, scythes, picks and shovels, all symbols of mortality. Fashion changes . . . and the cherub head appears as the eighteenth century progresses, accompanied by the Grecian urn. Other ornamentations to be found are the Tudor rose, an anchor and a snake swallowing its tail - a striking representation of eternity.

Occasionally, the lettering on the stones is exceptional. A particularly fine example is on the tomb of 'Presillow ye wife of William Garner of Deal, blacksmith who departed the 24th day of January, 1695, aged 40 yeares who had 7 children and now alive William, Presillow, Elizabeth, Mary, Joanah and Thomas'. The stone of Esther, wife of John Baker, has carved at its base (now concealed) the trademark of a stonemason, John Peach - a peach with a single leaf on its stem.

Against the north wall of the tower lies the table tomb of the fiery Thomas Powell who died in 1703. Early in the reign of Queen Anne 'a Society for the Reformation of Manners' was formed, and this gained national support. Mayor Powell rose to the challenge of suppressing vice and immorality in Deal. Zealously, he closed all shops, inns and coffee houses which opened on Sundays, rebuked those who used vile language and drove undesirables out of town. His diary details his religious fervour. He placed a seaman in the stocks for swearing, he publicly whipped a prostitute and he prevented a stage coach from leaving for Canterbury on the Lord's Day. He betrayed his immense pride when marching through the town at the head of the procession of jurats and common councilmen attending afternoon devotions at St Leonard's. His account of the occasion was:

> After prayers, when we came to sing Psalms, being part of the 75th Psalm, and at particular verses which were very appropriate to certain persons present, I stood up, spreading my hands, pointing round the church to some whose ill lives I knew, as well as their conversations, which this Psalm most peculiarly hinted at.

For these achievements Powell earned a mention in Trevelyan's *Social History of England*.

Joshua Coppin, 'First Mayor of ye Corporation of Deal', who died in 1721, lies buried in the nave. He lived at the Manor House whose interior boasted a magnificent carved oak staircase and a remarkable bedroom which, according to Roget, was 'fitted up like the cabin of a ship by a retired admiral'. From the rooftops smugglers used to signal to ships arriving in the Downs. The Gaunt family lived there from the mid-eighteenth century until 1916 and they took pride in the extensive gardens. Manor House was shamefully demolished (apart from the coach house) last century.

The walled burial ground in Church Path (once called Stone Lane) was purchased at the end of the eighteenth century and served the parish until Deal Cemetery was opened. The grand mausoleum in the centre contains the earthly

Deal Parochial School

remains of the Harvey and Cannon families. An earlier 'Strangers' Burial Ground', where the bodies of drowned sailors thrown up on the foreshore were laid to rest, had been in use since 1668. Inexplicably, this site was considered suitable for the building of modern homes at the far end of St Patrick's Road.

The rectory was built by the Reverend William Backhouse during the latter part of the eighteenth century. This is a symmetrical red brick building having an elegant porch with fanlight and a series of shuttered windows. It replaced a former parsonage and, like the church, reflects a confusing mixture of architectural styles. A medieval cellar, rubble-walled, retains a lancet-headed recess for a lantern, and traces of a Tudor doorway. The kitchen is Jacobean, the living rooms are Georgian and the extension is Victorian. The house has now been converted into flats and replaced by a modern rectory in Addelam Road.

A charity school was opened in the village for thirty-five children in 1786. The Rector, William Backhouse, encouraged his parishioners to sponsor each child's education for one year. Among the subscribers was Deal's celebrated blue-stocking, Elizabeth Carter, who volunteered fifteen shillings a year. Children attended for five years and were taught reading and writing plus the catechism. Afterwards, they received a presentation copy of *The Whole Duty of Man*. The minute book from 1790 to 1812 survives.

In 1853 Deal Parochial School was built by public subscription on a site described as being on 'ye Turnpike Road which leadeth to Sandwich', in London Road. The architect was a Mr Poynter from Westminster. The cost was £2,300 and the school was featured in *The Illustrated London News*. There were two long halls, one for boys, another for girls, with an infants' room adjoining. Each classroom had a gallery, high windows and access to a playground. Houses were provided for the master and mistress (Mr and Mrs CJ Hopping) and for the infants' teacher (Miss SA Cooper). The school was the combined responsibility of the three parishes – St Leonard's, St George's and St Andrew's. In 2001 a modern school was opened in the grounds of the abandoned Royal Marines' South Barracks.

TUDOR FORTRESSES

' Three Castles that keep the Downs'

'THE THREE CASTLES that keep the Downs' - Walmer, Deal and Sandown - were built by Henry VIII to defend our vulnerable coast from imminent invasion from the Continent. Curiously, none of these Tudor fortresses experienced hot fighting until the English Civil War because of the superiority of the English fleet.

Henry VIII had not expected to become king. His older brother, Arthur, had been groomed for kingship and married a young Catholic princess, Catherine of Aragon, to secure a Spanish alliance. Shortly afterwards, Arthur died and Henry inherited the throne in his teens to become the youngest king in Christendom. When he was crowned in 1509, he continued the lucrative alliance by marrying his brother's widow. Catherine was demurely pretty - she had grey eyes and golden brown hair - and their union produced one daughter, Mary. Henry was

Deal Castle by George Shepherd, showing the toll gate

in love with Catherine and he wrote poems expressing his constancy and devotion.

At first, King Henry was content to leave affairs of state to able ministers such as Cardinal Wolsey while he pursued a life of pleasure. As the years galloped by, however, he increasingly took over the reigns of government, and he became particularly concerned about the line of succession. After two decades of marriage his wife had failed to provide a male heir to ensure the Tudor lineage. Henry had grown tired of Catherine, who had turned into a portly matron. When riding at Hever Castle in Kent he fell under the bewitching spell of the owner's daughter, Anne Boleyn, whom he made pregnant, and secretly married. Henry now had two wives . . .

The King ordered Cardinal Wolsey to petition the Pope for an annulment of his first marriage. Campeggio, the Papal Legate, arrived at Deal, travelled to London with great pomp, but transferred the case to Rome. The Pope declined Henry's divorce, so he dismissed Catherine, abolished the monasteries and proclaimed himself Head of the Church in England. In 1538 Pope Paul III formed an alliance between Francis I of France and Charles V of Spain and proposed a religious crusade against the tyrannical king of England. Ironically, by now, both queens were dead. Hastily, Henry set about fortifying the southern coastline.

William Lambarde, who wrote his *Perambulation of Kent* just thirty years after the castles were built, gave this account of their construction:

> King Henrie the Eight . . . with all speede, and without sparing any cost . . . builded Castles, platfourmes and blockhouses, in all needefull places of the Realme. And amongst other, fearing least the ease and advauntage of descending on lande at this part, shoulde give occasion and hardinesse to the enemies to invade him, he erected (neare togither) three fortifications, which might at all times keepe and beate the landing place, that is to say, Sandowne, Deal and Walmere. Al which (togither with some others newly built upon the coast of Sussex) and their captaines he recommended to the surveigh, controlment, and correction of the Wardein of the Cinque Portes.

Henry took a personal interest in the progress of his castles since it represented a mammoth investment. There is a strong tradition that the king inspected the sites prior to their construction although there is no mention of a visit in the State Papers. Hall, who chronicled Henry's reign, records that His Majesty 'took very laborious and painful journeys towards the sea coast' to inspect his defences and that during one excursion into Kent, on Easter Day, 1539, he was attended by 'three score unknown ships lying in the Downs'.

The immediate coastline was further defended by a sequence of bulwarks which were heavily manned by gunners. There were at least four of these 'eminences of earth' but the most important were the Great (or Black) Bulwark and the Little (or White) Bulwark. These primitive turf mounds were connected by trenches to form a chain of fortifications about three miles long. Hasted, who asserts the bulwarks existed prior to the construction of the castles, adds further details: 'They had embrasures for guns and together formed a defensive line of batteries along that part of the coast where was deep water, and where ships of war could approach the shore to cover the disembarkation of an enemy's army'.

Architect of this unique trio of castles was a German, Stephan von Haschenperg. He had been responsible for a similar project at Calais (English territory until 1559) and was the 'deviser' of nearby Sandgate Castle. Promptly, he

fell out of favour with Henry VIII through avish overspending and he was dismissed from service in 1543. One contemporary account ridicules him by saying he 'behaved lewdly and spent great treasure to no great purpose'. The Royal Works played a significant role in preparing the final plans, which consisted of a domestic drum surrounded by semi-circular platforms mounted with a vast number of heavy guns. These remarkable fortresses demonstrate the advance in technological warfare - from crossbow to gunfire - and represent the last stage in castle design, which began 500 years earlier with a simple motte and bailey.

Accidentally, the design of the Henrican castles reflected the shape of the Tudor rose. From the air the plan is shown to consist of an immense round tower

Henry VIII © National Portrait Gallery

surrounded by a double circle of bastions or 'lunettes' (forming the petals). Deal - the 'Greate Castle' - is *sex-foil* while Walmer and Sandown are both *quatre-foil* in style. The castles were purposely positioned more than a mile apart to minimise accidents from striking each other by their own powerful cannon. At the same time Lower Deal was slow to develop as inhabitants, naturally, did not wish to risk their homes being caught by friendly fire.

The Tudor fortresses contrasted with the outmoded Norman castles, fine examples of which can be studied at Dover, Canterbury and Rochester. These each boasted a tall, square keep, from which arrows rained down upon the enemy, built on a hilltop and protected by a curtain wall. Haschenperg's curious design provided levels of circular platforms allowing cannon to be positioned a full 360 degrees for maximum coverage. Moreover, the thick walls of the semi-circular bastions were intended to deflect enemy cannon balls, and the low, squat profile made the castles difficult to target, particularly from the sea.

A central keep in each contained the living quarters, kitchen, bakery with huge ovens, a deep well and basement stores for ammunition. The winding walls at the base of the bastions were pierced with 53 gunports from which the dry moat could be raked with gunfire. Vents above these gunports were intended to carry away noxious smoke and fumes while a postern gate leading into the moat presumably provided a sally-port.

This novel design also incorporated a number of traditional features. The gatehouse of Deal Castle, constructed in the bastion on the landward side, was reached by a draw-

Anne of Cleves, by Holbein © Louvre Museum

bridge over the moat and was protected by a portcullis and five *meurtrieres* or 'murder holes' through which boiling oil could be poured onto invaders' heads. The stout oak arched door - it contains a wicket - weighs three tons and is studded with 1100 iron bolts. Spiralling around the keep at Deal are remnants of a double staircase which led to the captain's private apartments, and also took the gunners to the roof. Deal Castle was furnished with a trumpet and drum for communication.

Sir Edward Ryngley was appointed overseer of the works and his staff included two paymasters, a comptroller, a master carpenter, a master bricklayer and the master mason from Hampton Court. Thomas Wingfield, who represented Sandwich in Parliament, was promoted from paymaster to Captain once building was completed. His arms comprised three pairs of angel wings. He and his Deputy were charged with victualling royal ships stationed in the Downs.

Iron-studded door of Deal Castle, showing the 'murder holes'

Workforce at the castles fell from 1400 to less than 500 in winter. Oddly, the first recorded strike took place at Deal Castle, where workmen downed tools and demanded a rise of one penny, from 5d to 6d per day. Sir Edward dealt with the matter swiftly, thus winning the certain approval of his sovereign. Five of the ringleaders were sent to Canterbury, four to Sandwich Gaol. Reluctantly, the labourers returned to work . . .

Materials for the castles came from various sources. Limestone, known as Kentish rag, was mixed with Caen stone plundered from the recently dissolved monasteries - the Carmelite Friary at Sandwich is one suggested source - while bricks were manufactured locally. Chalk and flint were quarried at Mongeham where the disgruntled workmen, breaking their backs to provide materials for the defence against Catholic invasion, joked that they were digging the 'Pope's Hole'.

All three castles were built in eighteen months - a phenomenal feat. The total cost, including earthen gun platforms, was £27,000. Work probably began in March 1539 (although the scheme for coastal defence was projected six years earlier) and progressed at an astonishing rate so that they were completed at the beginning of October, 1540. Sixty hostile ships which had anchored in the Downs on Easter Day earlier that year found the virgin castles so much of a deterrent that they retreated without firing a shot. Meanwhile, Thomas Cromwell, the King's chief minister, made frantic preparations for a 'garrison for the king's new castles and blockhouses in the Downs' which he meticulously recorded in his *Book of Remembrances*. In accordance with Henry's policy of making any defence the responsibilty of the immediate district, garrisons were all drawn from this area while the officers were selected from local gentry. One drawback was that the soldiers were required to provide suitable weapons - dagger, sword, halberd, bill - at their own expense.

Even before it was finished Deal Castle received a royal visitor. Cromwell had arranged the marriage between Henry VIII and Anne of Cleves. The purpose of this alliance with an obscure provincial court was because the Duke of Cleves exerted enormous influence over Protestant Germany, which could counterbalance the powers of France, Spain and the Pope. Henry's fourth bride-to-be travelled across land from the district of the Lower Rhine to Calais, then English territory, where she was delayed over Christmas 'for want of a prosperous wind'. A fortnight later this demure Catholic princess was escorted with great pomp and ceremony across the English Channel by a fleet of fifty ships decorated with silk and gold banners, under the command of the Earl of Southampton. Anne arrived at Deal in the late afternoon of 27 December 1539 and, according to Holinshed, 'taried there but a certeine space in a castell newlie built'.

Lady Anne rested and dined at Deal Castle - 'bleak, grey stone in cold December' - in a sumptuously furnished apartment. Afterwards she was escorted by Thomas Cheyney, Lord Warden of the Cinque Ports, the Duke and Duchess of Suffolk, the Bishop of Chichester and a large retinue of knights and esquires to Dover Castle. From thence, despite driving rain, she travelled in splendour across Kent from Canterbury to Greenwich. Henry was so excited at meeting his unseen bride - spurred on by Holbein's flattering portrait - that he hurried to Rochester in disguise. When he met Anne secretly at the Bishop's Palace on New Year's Day he was dismayed to find her plain, foolish and ill-mannered. 'I like her not,' was his ominous comment. Thus the king's sexual appetite once more placed the country in jeopardy. Cromwell paid with his life for this disastrous marriage between 'England's lion' and a 'Flanders mare'.

Elizabeth I inspected the castles during her royal progress through Kent in 1573. After leaving Dover, the Queen journeyed through Walmer and Deal before being carried on a litter along the Ancient Highway to Sandwich. She arrived

Walmer Castle by George Shepherd

41

Deal Castle © British Museum

there on 31 August and lodged at Manwood House where her father, Henry VIII, had stayed twice before.

John Leland, the antiquarian, extolled the virtues of the castles shortly after their completion in a couplet contained in his *Cygnaea Cantio*:

Renowned Deal doth vaunt itself
With Turrets newly raised.

Ordnance for the castles remains a mystery since the number and type of cannon varied constantly. Small arms, including bows and arrows, were retained at first but the arquebus fired on the matchlock principle soon became common, particularly in the gunports covering the moats and the courtyards. During the mid-sixteenth century great guns at Deal Castle comprised one cannon, three culverins, four demi-culverins, five sacres, two minions and one falcon. The brass cannon's bore was seven inches and its extreme range was over three miles, while the lesser guns such as the falcon carried smaller shot further but did less destruction. Towards the end of the sixteenth century a rare long culverin (the name derives from the French word '*couleuvre*' meaning grass snake) was introduced at Deal; this had a bore of almost five inches and an extreme range of seven miles. A combination of firearms ensured that the occupation of the Downs by an enemy fleet would prove an impossibility unless the guns were first silenced.

Deal Castle sounded its guns more in protest than in anger when the admiral of a fleet of Hollanders failed to strike his flag as he approached Walmer Castle in June 1628. He was fired on as he passed into the Downs and forced to haul down his colours. Englishmen obliged ships of all nations to acknowledge their supremacy of the seas by lowering topsails and striking their flags when sailing in territorial waters. Further, there was a custom that the culprit was billed for the warning shot. Earlier, when Henry IV of France despatched his statesman, later Duc de Sully, in a ship commanded by a vice-admiral, to congratulate James I on his accession, his mission was interpreted as arrogance and he was fired on by Admiral Mansell for daring to hoist the flag of France in the presence of that of England. Saluting, clearly, was regarded as a serious matter in the seventeenth century.

Whenever the threat of invasion passed the castles were put into 'care and maintenance' with a reduced number of veteran gunners. Captains constantly petitioned the Treasury for urgent repairs but with little success and the castles fell into ruinous states. John Heyden, Captain of Sandown, reported in 1615 that the sea wall of his castle was perished, the stone work and lead decayed, the bridge and stairs rotten and the glass broken. Sir John Hippisley, Lieutenant of Dover Castle, warned Charles I that 'the castles in the Downs must be repaired or the country cannot be in safety in the event of a war with France'. Despite this alarm nothing was achieved even though, by now, there was not a single barrel of gunpowder left in any of the castles.

William Byng, Captain of Deal Castle, catalogued the decay:

> The ruines dayly increase in soe mutch that if sume course bee not taken before winter the sea will swallow them up . . . the gate of Wallmer Castle is so decaied, that it is not to bee opened and shut, but with very great danger of our lives to knock us on the heade with the loose stones hanging over, and the court of guard, the cheifest roome of use, is only held up by propes the which also give waye; the bridges are so unfitt to be drawen up at nights . . . . the powdar houses so leaky that wee are fayne to stor the powder in the vaultes . . . and the lanthorne of Deal castle, a sea marke, utterly decayed, of which the sea men mutch complaine . . .

Byng, a Royalist expelled from Deal Castle during the Civil War, was perhaps the most strenuous opponent of the expansion of Lower Deal. He complained bitterly about the daily encroachment of cottages built upon the foreshore, obstructing the field of fire. His successor appointed by Parliament was equally zealous. A warrant was issued by the Earl of Warwick, Admiral of the Fleet and Governor of 'the three forts which command the Downs', in 1643 against John Hollman, Robert Smythe and William Matthews: 'We are ordered by Parliament to prevent the erection of buildings on the waste of the said castles which would

A direct hit by a bomb in 1941 demolished the 1802 Governor's Lodging at Walmer Castle. Local opinion was that Hitler had done the town a favour.

Caen stone from the demolished Sandown Castle was spirited away for private or public use and turned up in the most unlikely places - a Wesleyan chapel, boatmen's rooms and the abutment to Deal Pier.

Persistent rumours that the walled garden at Deal Castle was a burial ground for horses killed in the Napoleonic Wars are unconfirmed.

The Duke of Wellington, when Lord Warden of the Cinque Ports, was a frequent worshipper at Old St Mary's Church. Each Sunday he rode over from Walmer Castle, a great Bible tucked under his arm, and tied up his horse to the ancient yew tree near the porch. He would curl up in one corner of his private pew directly beneath the pulpit and fall asleep, snoring loudly.

shelter a foreign enemy by hindering the plying of the ordnance.' The three culprits were ordered to demolish their new dwellings forthwith.

At the commencement of the Civil War Parliament held all three castles, but in 1648 there was a Royalist uprising in Kent followed by a mutiny among the Downs Fleet. The initial cause of the rebellion was the declaration by Parliament that Christmas Day should in future be observed as a fast. Sandown Castle declared for King Charles, who was at that time imprisoned in Carisbrooke Castle on the Isle of Wight, and Deal and Walmer Castles accordingly changed their allegiance to the deposed monarch. Lord General Fairfax mercilessly subdued the rebels at Maidstone with his New Model Army which he despatched from London. Afterwards, he directed his trusted friend, Colonel Nathaniel Rich, assisted by 2,000 infantry and modest cavalry, to recover Dover Castle for the Roundheads before turning his attention to the three castles protected by Royalist ships now commanded by James, Duke of York, who was Lord High Admiral.

Deal, Walmer and Sandown were the last three fortified posts to hold out for the King in East Kent. That June, Colonel Rich took steps to reduce them, deliberately concentrating on one at a time. First, he laid siege to Walmer Castle. Conditions for his troops were appalling - their trenches were waterlogged, the weather was bitterly cold and there was a distinct lack of artillery. After waiting one whole week for the delivery of a mortar there was a further delay until an 'Ingenier' arrived to demonstrate how to fire this devilish new device.

Royalist sympathisers sent ships from France to attempt to relieve the beleaguered garrisons and there were minor skirmishes involving troops from Deal Castle. The Governor of Walmer Castle taunted his oppressors by hoisting a flag painted with a coffin to remind them of their inevitable fate. Another time desperate soldiers faked an explosion, threw a dummy of the Governor over the ramparts and pretended to surrender in order to tempt the Roundheads into the gatehouse where they could open fire. After three weeks, however, Walmer Castle capitulated and Colonel Rich - now armed with a pair of cannons - turned his attention to the remaining two castles. Anticipating trouble, timid Deal folk abandoned their houses and made for the country . . .

In mid-August, the gallant young Prince of Wales ventured over from Holland to make a dramatic attempt to relieve his castles. Under cover of darkness he landed a force of 500 soldiers and 250 seamen, plus a handful of London apprentices, but no horses, under the direction of Major-General Gibson. They were joined by reinforcements from Sandown Castle for a secret rendezvous in the sandhills. The plan of campaign for the Royalists was to make a wide detour by marching to firmer ground at Upper Deal. From thence they intended swooping down upon the Roundheads locked in their landward trenches at Deal Castle, surprising them from the rear.

A seaman deserter alerted Colonel Rich to the ambush and he sent 300 musketeers and 100 of his redoubted horse to repel the invaders. Wisely, they retired to marshland where they knew heavy horses could not follow, but the cavalry pretended to retreat and so lured the Royalists into the path of the musketeers. The intruders broke and fled but were pursued by the cavalry right up to the drawbridge of Sandown Castle. Prince Charles' troops suffered terrible

Sandown Castle

injuries in the melee and less than 100 of his men escaped unharmed to their attendant ships.

Both besieged garrisons were further discouraged by Cromwell's victories in the North, news of which was conveyed to them by notes attached to arrows fired into both castles. Inevitably, Deal and Sandown Castles succumbed, despite the fact that there were sufficient stores and ammunition to withstand a prolonged siege. Colonel Rich surveyed the damage at Deal: 'The castle is much torn and spoiled with grenadoes, as Walmer was, or rather more.' Parliament ordered the immediate renovation of all three castles and the transference of wounded soldiers to Greenwich Hospital. Thus terminated the Kentish Rising of 1648.

During the Dutch Wars of the 1650s and 1660s the three castles proved invaluable in protecting shipping in the Downs but by the end of the seventeenth century they became practically obsolete. Celia Fiennes, daughter of a Cromwellian colonel, journeying through Kent in 1697, dismissed them as 'three little forts or castles . . . which hold a few guns but I should think they would be of little effect and give the enemy no great trouble'. Daniel Defoe also belittled the castles in 1722 as 'two small works of no strength by land and not much use by sea'.

Deal Castle is strangely positioned nineteen-twentieths in the parish of Walmer. At one time there was a single storey residence reserved for the Governor's Lodging. This was rebuilt on the sea-ward side in 1802 by Lord Carrington in anticipation of his residency as Captain. When he presented the exorbitant bill to the Treasury he found Prime Minister William Pitt's response uncompromising: 'Those who made the alterations had best pay for them'.

The Captain's sizeable walled garden opposite the castle is shielded by a cottage, coachhouse and stables. It appears to date from the 1720s when the castle was converted into comfortable accommodation for its Captain, Admiral Sir John Norris. A map of 1753 shows the garden laid out with a broad, central path and planted with numerous strips but later it was divided into four quarters by tree lined paths. Originally, the purpose of the garden was to provide vegetables for the garrison and it retained this horticultural function until the mid-twentieth century.

One mile northwards are the few remaining traces of Sandown Castle, first styled 'Castle at Sandhyll next to Sandwyche'. Only a small portion of the west bastion survives with the spandrels of a ceiling to a lower room visible from the beach. Traditionally, Queen Elizabeth I momentarily lodged at the castle in 1573 during her royal progress through Kent, and Charles II, when Prince of Wales, landed there from a ship in the Downs. The most famous resident, however, was the regicide, Colonel John Hutchinson, who was incarcerated in a squalid chamber at the base of the central tower. Apparently, his portrait, chair and conveyance were on exhibition long after his demise.

Sandown Castle fell victim to the sea as early as 1785 when the moat was flooded. It was repaired and garrisoned during the Napoleonic Wars but the waves continued to erode the foundations. The drawbridge, portcullis, inner courtyard, four circular bastions, ramparts and keep with its immense thick walls - even the meadow on the sea-ward side - all succumbed to the sea. After its occupation by the Coast Guard, Sandown Castle became dangerous and the War Office ordered its demolition in Victorian times.

Walmer Castle has been the official residence of the Lords Warden of the Cinque Ports since the early eighteenth century. After the Norman Conquest five south-east coastal towns were formed into the Cinque Ports in order to protect the country from invasion. They comprised Sandwich, Dover, Hythe, New Romney and - across the border into Sussex - Hastings. Rye and Winchelsea were later incorporated into this confederation by King Richard I as 'Ancient Towns'. Deal, although never a Cinque Port, was affiliated with Sandwich as a 'limb'.

Prior to the Norman Conquest the Cinque Ports were responsible for forming a primitive royal fleet. Eventually they were required by law to provide jointly at their own expense up to fifty-seven fully-crewed ships for the monarch's use for a total of fifteen days each year. Further, they were charged with defence of the realm and the protection of cross-Channel trade. The considerable power of the Cinque Ports declined only when Henry VIII established the Royal Navy.

Edward I granted a Charter to the Cinque Ports in 1278 whereby they were awarded special privileges in return for loyal ship service. These included exemption from national taxes, the right to raise tolls on passing merchant ships, a claim on all wreckage washed on their shores and the authority to hold their own courts of justice. The Court of Shepway - where dignitaries of the Cinque Ports gathered - is marked by a modern stone cross near Lympne. Most jealously guarded was the right to hold the ornamental canopy over the sovereign at every coronation - a custom which continues to this day.

The office of Lord Warden was instituted in the thirteenth century to oversee and regulate affairs of the Cinque Ports. Edward I combined this with that of the Constable of Dover Castle and Admiral of the Cinque Ports. It was the most powerful appointment in the realm and provided a direct link between local government and the monarch, who tended to regard it as a personal patronage. It was endowed with special privileges and at first carried a generous salary.

First resident Lord Warden was Lionel Sackville of Knole, who succeeded Queen Anne's dull husband, Prince George of Denmark, when he died in 1708. Lionel Sackville, first Duke of Dorset, was only twenty years of age when this tremendous honour was bestowed upon him. He frequently fell from favour yet he managed to be appointed to the office on three separate occasions and he officiated in this role in 1727 at the coronation of King George III. Thereafter, this office has remained a lifetime appointment.

An impressive painting by Wootton on the grand staircase at Knole depicts the procession of the Duke of Dorset to Dover Castle after he had taken the oath of office for the third time at the Court of Shepway in 1727. The occasion was marked by a sumptuous banquet prepared by 'Mr. Russel, the Dover cook'. Lionel Sackville proceeded to convert the southern fortress into a comfortable residence befitting a high ranking nobleman and the plans for his renovations completed in the late 1730s are extant. The principal alteration was a red brick projection on the north-east bastion facing sea-wards which has remained (though sometimes rebuilt) the living rooms of successive Lords Warden. It features prominently in the famous Buck engraving dated 1735. Despite the tremendous cost the Duke of Dorset appears to have occupied these lavish new apartments for a few weeks only each summer. During his tenure a small plot of land called the Governor's Garden began to be cultivated and this formed the basis of the celebrated gardens of Walmer Castle.

When the Duke took up residence at Walmer Castle, the Lord Warden had already begun to lose the greater part of his civil jurisdiction owing to the decay of the Court of Chancery over which he had presided. He still retained his authority over the Court of Admiralty, which dealt with maritime affairs, and the Court of Lodemanage responsible for appointing and regulating Channel pilots. He held supreme command of all the military forces within his jurisdiction and he appointed a number of posts, including Justices of the Peace, Members of Parliament for Dover, the Lieutenant of Dover Castle

Lionel Sackville, Duke of Dorset
© private collection

and the Captains of the three castles in the Downs. Further, he presided over the Assemblies of Brotherhood and Guestling.

The list of Lords Warden includes the most illustrious people in history since the foundation of the Cinque Ports in the reign of Edward the Confessor. The successor to the Duke of Dorset, however, is generally considered to have been the dullest – Robert d'Arcy, Earl of Holderness. This Gentleman of the Bedchamber accompanied George II to Hanover and was present at the Battle of Dettingen in 1743 which was the last occasion when a reigning monarch led his soldiers into battle. Lord Curzon, in his history of Walmer Castle, reports that he was 'solid and steady in character and mediocre in talents' and he ascribes to him only one contribution in his role of Lord Warden - the introduction to Walmer Castle of sash windows.

A succession of four Prime Ministers were appointed next as Lords Warden. King George III insisted on regarding the Cinque Ports as an example of personal patronage and in July 1778 he duly appointed Lord North. Frederick, Lord North, was an amiable, witty and dignified man but he proved a blinkered statesman. He has the unenviable reputation of forfeiting the American colonies during his Premiership. Naturally, his appointment was unpopular and questions were asked - perhaps unfairly - regarding his salary in Parliament. Late in life he inherited the title of Earl of Guilford, and the family home at Waldershare, near Dover. When he finally visited Walmer Castle he was too infirm and blind – it was said he was unable to distinguish the colour of his wine – to appreciate it.

William Pitt was appointed Lord Warden in 1792 at the age of thirty-three, having already been Prime Minister for nine years. Apparently, George III refused recommendations since he had resolved to confer this office on his favourite politician as a mark of high esteem. Pitt - permanently in debt - gratefully accepted both the salary and the residence. There he received famous statesmen at a period when England was under constant threat of invasion from Napoleon during the years following the French Revolution. He leased extensive lands surrounding the castle and with the aid of his eccentric niece, Lady Hester Stanhope, began to create the beautiful gardens which are still enjoyed by visitors today.

King George's choice for Lord Warden after Pitt's untimely demise was Robert Banks Jenkinson, Lord Hawkesbury and Second Lord Liverpool. Previously he had been elected by Pitt as Colonel of the Cinque Ports Fencibles, an army of regular troops - infantry and cavalry - enlisted for home service at the commencement of the French Wars. 'Jenks', 'Jinks' or 'Jawkes', as he was derisively called, appears a colourless character who kept his private life separate from his public career. An astute politician and an able minister, his appointment as Lord Warden was nevertheless met with dismay. Historians, unkindly, forget that he was Prime Minister when the decisive Battle of Waterloo terminated the Napoleonic Wars.

Lord Liverpool stayed frequently - spring and autumn - at Walmer Castle particularly during the last decade of his life. When he first arrived he was impressed by the garden which, he says, 'abounds in flowers', thus indicating that Pitt and Hester's creations continued to flourish. He installed mauve tinted panes in the sash windows on the seaward side of the castle to spare his wife's eyesight and he acquired the sizeable cottage (where Pitt had lodged his distinguished guests) now known as Liverpool House which stands at the entrance to Castle Meadow.

In the summer of 1820 Lord Liverpool lent the castle to the newlywed Duke and Duchess of Clarence (later William IV and Queen Adelaide). Prior to her betrothal, the German Princess Adelaide had landed at Deal where she was so delighted by the warmth of her reception that she afterwards remained a generous benefactor. She contributed funds towards the building of St Andrew's Church and the Royal Adelaide Baths which stood on the beach opposite the present Adelaide House.

William Cobbett, that indefatigable rambler, penned a portrait of the castle as he rode on horseback from Dover to Sandwich in midsummer 1823:

> After coming through the village of Walmer, you see the entrance to the Castle away to the right. It is situated pretty nearly on the water's edge, and at the bottom of a little dell, about a furlong or so from the turnpike road.

This picturesque scene owed no little part to Lord Liverpool who permanently secured the vast estate surrounding the castle from a wealthy landowner, George Leith, thus ensuring successive Lords Warden enjoyed greater privacy.

A letter from his sister-in-law, Mary, Countess of Erne, a welcome guest in the autumn of 1820, enthused about his recent alterations.

> I arrived first yesterday, and as it was so fine, insisted upon Lord Liverpool shewing me all his improvements. They really are very great. The plantation has grown and flourish'd so as to afford a great deal of shady and sheltere'd walking – and there is besides a sea-walk (as he calls it) which for the purpose of taking sea-views into one's eyes, and the sea air into one's lungs . . . is perfect.

This 'sea-walk', which ran along the top of the beach before the castle, was originally laid out by Pitt but extended towards Kingsdown. At first it was known as Liverpool Walk, then The Marina.

Lord Liverpool was further a benefactor to the village of Walmer. He donated funds for the enlargement of Old St Mary's Church and also purchased the communion plate, while his wife presented a handsomely-bound Bible and prayer book.

Perhaps the most illustrious Lord Warden was the Duke of Wellington who had finally defeated Napoleon at the Battle of Waterloo. When the Duke was installed in January 1829 he was so delighted by his 'charming marine residence' that he returned his salary into public funds. He altered the castle hardly at all, strictly declining to do anything which might 'weaken the defences'. For almost a quarter of a century the Iron Duke resided for a third of every year - generally in the autumn - at Walmer where he endeared himself to the inhabitants.

His neighbourliness was legendary. He attended balls at the Assembly Rooms, went on shopping sprees to Dover, bathed from the beach at Walmer and rode over uninvited to chat to the miller at Ripple Mill. He was often to be seen

During the Duke's temporary sojourn at Walmer Castle he invariable reposes on the Camp bedstead which formed his Graces couch, through the Peninsular Campaigns. the highly prized articles of furniture being regularly conveyd from Downing Street to Walmer Castle when ever the Duke visits the later place. vide Morning Herald.

Cartoon of Wellington carrying his famous camp bed © Victoria and Albert Museum

hurtling down country lanes driving a succession of carriages pausing only to offer a military salute rather than the fashionable gesture of raising his top hat.

The Duke was not always recognised, however, for Captain Gronow relates the story of the time Wellington visited the parish church (Gronow unhelpfully identifies this as 'Trinity') where he ensconced himself in a spacious pew in front of the pulpit. After a short time the owner of the pew, a lady 'of portly and pompous appearance', entered. She cast a scowl at the intruder whom she did not recognise and curtly requested him to leave. Obediently, Wellington did as he was commanded and, while searching for another pew, pointedly informed the sextant: 'Tell that lady she has turned the Duke of Wellington out of her pew'.

At Walmer the Duke displayed his inordinate fondness for children. He was often to be seen playing football with his grandchildren on the ramparts or fighting a mock Battle of Waterloo with cushions in the drawing room. Once he dressed up as a Christmas tree with toys pinned about his person to entertain his young guests. When a timid woman inadvertently strolled into the paddock with her two children she was invited to return the following day when the Duke personally conducted them on a tour of his estate. On that occasion - as was his custom - he enquired of each child: 'Are you for the army or the navy?' According to their reply he presented a gold sovereign attached to either a red ribbon (for the army) or a blue one (for the navy).

Highlight of the Duke's residency was a visit by the young Queen Victoria and Prince Albert. The Queen decided to take a seaside holiday at Walmer Castle in the autumn of 1842. The royal couple enjoyed informal strolls along the beach with their dogs towards Kingsdown. On one occasion they took shelter from a sudden squall in the hovel of a retired boatman, Thomas Erridge, who was later rewarded with a handsome pension. Prince Albert revelled in a tour of the South Foreland Lighthouse, then under construction, and a trip to the Goodwins to inspect Captain Bullock's Beacon of Refuge for shipwrecked mariners. The Queen enjoyed a ride in an open carriage around Walmer village and an excursion to Ramsgate Harbour. The holiday - extended by a week when the Queen caught cold - coincided with the Princess Royal's birthday and an impromptu regatta was organised in celebration by the Deal boatmen. Lady Lyttleton, royal governess, remarked in her diary upon the castle's 'outward rudeness mixing very oddly with the numbers of smart servants and courtly whispers'.

The Duke of Wellington died in the castle after a brief illness in November 1852. His body lay at Walmer for a full two months before being transported by train at night for a state funeral in London. His study bedroom remains almost exactly as he knew it with the mahogany desk in the window recess where he stood to write letters, the wing armchair in which he died and the narrow camp bed that accompanied him on several campaigns. When Lady Salisbury enquired how he could sleep in a bed in which there was little room to turn, his classic reply was: 'When it's time to turn over, it's time to turn out.'

A modest museum displays several relics of the Iron Duke including his gruesome death mask, his uniform as Lord Warden and, naturally, a pair of the famous Wellington boots.

Later Lords Warden numbered Lord Dalhousie, Governor-General of India, who was an absentee Warden, and Lord Palmerston who, apart from attending an impressive Grand Court of Shepway, distanced himself from official functions. Lady Palmerston, however, enthused about the house and gardens to her husband: 'I am sure you will be delighted with the place, and the sea is covered with shipping and a beautiful sun to light them up,' she wrote. About

The Duke's study bedroom © Victoria and Albert Museum

51

this time it was discovered that the magazine of gunpowder used for firing the guns on ceremonial occasions was situated directly under the kitchen!

George Leveson-Gower, Second Earl Granville, however, enjoyed a period of cosy domesticity at Walmer Castle during his tenure and involved himself in local affairs. He succeeded Lord Palmerston as Prime Minister in 1851 and followed him as Lord Warden in 1865. He played a major part in the Great Exhibition of 1851. Walmer Castle was his only country residence and he turned it into a cosy family home for his young bride and their children. Highlight of his residency seems to have been a visit to Walmer funfair where he toured every attraction from an Amazon to an animal freak show. He was dissuaded from riding the merry-go-round because of the risk of inviting ridicule from the press.

Earl Granville made several alterations to the structure of the castle, notably increasing the accommodation above the gatehouse, adding a cupola, new stables and kennels. He took a lively interest in the gardens and restored the original plantings by William Pitt and Hester Stanhope. His designer was William Masters from the renowned Exotic Nursery, Canterbury. In particular he created the double row of undulating yews and herbaceous borders which comprise the famous Broad Walk; he developed the wide grass stepped terraces and he lavishly stocked the walled garden with standard roses and bedding plants. Further he improved the moat with a serpentine path; he established an avenue of oaks at the castle approach and planted the ramparts with creepers.

Lady Leveson-Gower named the Walmer lifeboat *Centurion* on 15 November 1874. The RNLI presented her with a painting of this vessel rescuing the crew of a schooner, *Hero*, from the Goodwin Sands, which she hung in her apartments. Earl Granville was instrumental in erecting the stone cross which marks St Augustine's landing at Ebbsfleet.

WH Smith was the only commoner (apart from Pitt) until then to hold the office. He was first Lord of the Treasury and afterwards Leader of the House of Commons. More famously, he is remembered as the founder of the stationery firm whose bookstalls flourished on railway stations. He was in such poor health when he arrived at Walmer that he was driven around the castle grounds in a bath chair although he did enjoy several carriage rides and cruises in his beloved yacht *Pandora*, from which fluttered the Lord Warden's flag.

At sea the Lord Warden is entitled to a salute of nineteen guns within the limits of his own Admiralty. At one time Prime Minister William Gladstone visited Mr Smith at Walmer Castle, and he was escorted out to a man-o'-war stationed in the Downs. As the Lord Warden approached the vessel a salute was duly fired but it was mistakenly acknowledged by the Prime Minister who took the compliment to himself. In the same circumstances the Lord Warden may also hoist the standard of the Cinque Ports and the Lord Warden's flag. This gorgeous confection of blue, red and yellow in which are quartered monsters – half lions, half ships – castles, anchors and a vessel in full sail once caused consternation at Dover where it was mistaken for a distress signal and a pilot was forthwith despatched, much to Mr Smith's bewilderment. Traditionally, Walmer Castle hoists the Union Jack since it is a royal castle and until Victorian times a salute was fired on the sovereign's birthday.

Mr Smith's great contribution was to collect and display relics relating to previous Lords Warden, especially the Duke of Wellington. He died in office at Walmer and was succeeded by the Marquis of Dufferin and Ava who was, at that time, British Ambassador in Paris.

Another Prime Minister, Robert Cecil, Lord Salisbury, who briefly held this post, inexplicably shunned Walmer Castle in favour of the South of France. This is strange since, as a youngster, Cecil had enjoyed romping in the grounds when the Duke of Wellington was Lord Warden. Lady Salisbury, who was not enamoured by the Duke, dreaded living in the shadow of the famous soldier-statesman.

> I think I shall hate it, tinsel picturesqueness and false sentiment . . . I have no sympathy with either. I shall lock up the relics and use the room . . . Queen (Victoria) says it is the most uncomfortable house she ever was in.

Local inhabitants loudly expressed their disapproval when she desecrated the Iron Duke's shrine.

However, Lady Salisbury appreciated the walled garden with its rose-strewn trellised arbours and pallisaded fruit trees. The sheltered moat produced early strawberries and ripe figs while the kitchen garden incorporated a tomato house, a vinery and fernery. The Salisburys were followed by Lord Curzon, Viceroy of India, a wealthy aristocrat who expressed delight at being appointed to such an honorific office. His pride soon turned to bitterness when his wife became fatally ill within weeks through a deficiency in the drains. He protested angrily that it was a 'charnel-house . . . unfit for human habitation' and 'an ancestral doghole'. Lord Curzon of Kedlestone, not surprisingly, resigned the post after four months and returned to India. Gallantly, he continued to compile notes for a history of the Castle and its Lords Warden, which were published posthumously.

King Edward VII took the incident most seriously. He personally inspected Walmer and declared the castle unfit for habitation. When he conferred the post on the the Prince of Wales it was on the strict understanding that he did not take up residence. Adamantly, the Prince refused to nominate the magistrates of the Cinque Ports, to attend to business of Dover Harbour Board or to convene the Court of Shepway. After two years the exasperated Brotherhood and Guestlings of the Cinque Ports publicly declared that the Prince's refusal to be installed as Lord Warden or to fulfil the duties of his office was 'detrimental to the interests of the Ports and would imperil one of the most ancient Institutions of the Kingdom'. 'No nonsense this time,' he retaliated, 'I shall stick to my guns and resign.'

The opportunity was taken during the absence of this royal Lord Warden to open the castle to the public for the first time. The next Lord Warden was Earl Brassey. He was the son of a railway contractor who first entered the legal profession, turned to politics and was elected to Parliament in 1868. He inherited a fortune from his father which enabled him to make substantial alterations to improve the living accommodation at the castle. It also allowed him to indulge his passion for yachts by sailing round the world. A jovial fellow, he endeared himself to the local population by arriving at Deal Pier in his private steam yacht, *Sunbeam*.

Earl Beauchamp was installed as Lord Warden in the summer of 1914. Countess Beauchamp took a particular delight in the castle gardens and was often photographed admiring the flowers. Croquet was played on the lawn and the walled garden contained a tennis court. A gentle slope led down to the moat since at that time the lawn mower was pulled by a pony. Earl Beauchamp resigned as Lord Warden in 1933 and emigrated to America.

He was followed by the Marquess of Reading. Lady Reading was the person who recreated the Duke of Wellington's study according to details depicted in a contemporary watercolour by Thomas Shotter Boys. She fitted a replica carpet and hung identical trellis-patterned wallpaper before positioning original furniture and ornaments.

Next Lord Warden was the Marquess of Willingdon, who played brilliant cricket for Cambridge and was a favourite tennis partner of George V. Lady Willingdon had steps built into the curtain wall of the moat so that she could not be observed crossing to her beach hut for her regular swim.

Winston Churchill added lustre to the post when he was appointed in 1941. Britain was then at war with Germany and the enemy forces were within sight as they assembled along the coast of France. Like Pitt and Wellington before him he organised a voluntary militia to defend the vulnerable south-east coastline. Churchill revelled in the duties, the ceremonies and the uniform of Lord Warden yet, although clearly honoured by his appointment, he showed little interest in his maritime residence.

There was a break with tradition with an overseas appointment for the succeeding Lord Warden – Sir Robert Menzies, the former Prime Minister of Australia. His terms of residency coincided conveniently, it was noticed, with Canterbury Cricket Week.

Present Lord Warden – another break from tradition was made by the choice of a woman, Queen Elizabeth, the Queen Mother, as the present Lord Warden. Queen Elizabeth was installed on 1 August 1977 and afterwards she set a welcome tradition of staying at Walmer during midsummer, ariving by helicopter and residing at the castle. The Lord Warden currently occupies an apartment built over the north-east bastion by Lord Granville.

Queen Elizabeth has involved herself with the community during her informal visits over more than twenty years. She named the Dover Lifeboat *Faithful Forester*; championed the Downs Sailing Club and regularly attended services at New St Mary's, Walmer. Further afield, she has unveiled the Battle of Britain Memorial on the White Cliffs; been made a member of the exclusive Winkle Club at Hastings and taken a ride on a steam train at Tenterden. Unwittingly, she became embroiled in a dispute over the introduction of wildfowl on to the pond at the neighbouring Lord Warden Avenue estate.

As a tribute to the Queen Mother, English Heritage commissioned Penelope Hobhouse to convert the walled kitchen garden on the south side of Walmer Castle into a landscaped garden. Features number a central canal, topiary pyramids, a folly formed from yews and a box parterre-shaped in the letter 'E'. The garden is planted with Californian poppies, salvias, lilies and clematis interwoven with Her Majesty's favourite roses and is designed to be at its best when the Queen Mother is in residence in July.

Queen Elizabeth the Queen Mother
© East Kent Mercury

SAMUEL TAVENOR

'A man of war, a man for peace'

CAPTAIN SAMUEL TAVENOR, Governor of Deal Castle, became a Baptist and itinerant preacher and was imprisoned for his faith in Dover Castle.

Samuel Tavenor (or Taverner) was born at Romford, Essex, in July, 1621. He entered young into the army and by his reliable and spirited conduct soon earned favour and promotion. At the age of twenty-two he was made Captain of a Troop of Horse, and an early posting brought him into Kent.

During the Civil War the three castles of the Downs were first held by the Royalists. In July 1648 Parliament recognised that '. . . the enemy increases in numbers about Deal and Walmer so our forces there are like to have a hard service'. Later that same month, despite reinforcements sent by the Prince of Wales, Walmer Castle surrendered to the Roundheads. Colonel Rich was entrusted with its command and from there he successfully masterminded the capture of the remaining two castles – Deal and Sandown. When Colonel Rich was rewarded by being made Captain of Deal Castle, he appointed Tavenor as his Lieutenant.

War broke out between England and Holland in the summer of 1652. The Admiralty had repeatedly pressed for increased armament to protect 'ships which ride under (the) castles', while intensive recruitment 'by beat of drum' among the seamen along the coast proved surprisingly successful. Preparations for possible invasion included the hire of a house for service as a hospital fully equipped 'with a surgeon and other necessaries' to deal with the wounded.

The following year Samuel Tavenor received a commission from the Lord Protector, Oliver Cromwell, in recognition of his loyal service, by which he was made Governor of Deal Castle.

> A man of war, and yet a man for peace,
> Who fought on purpose that the wars might cease.
> His parts and courage so conspicuous were
> That of Deal Castle he was Governor . . .

The document concerning Tavenor's appointment reads:

> Oliver Cromwell Lord Protector of the Commonwealth of England, Scotland and Ireland. To all whome there present may concern.

Know ye that I reposeing spetiall trust and confidence in the fidelity and integrity of you Samuell Tavernour, Doe here by constitute and appointe you to be Governor of Deal Castle, and of all the forces of and within the same. Which said Castle, together with all the ordnance and ammunition stores and habiliments of war and those unto belonging you and by virtue hereof to receive and take unto your charge and ye said buildings and fortifications thereof you are to uphold and maintaine in good repair, which ye shall defend and keepe for ye use and service of the Comon Wealth and shall not render or suffer the same to be rendered delivered up to any person or persons whatsoever, unless he or they be thereunto authorised by myselfe. And you shall duely exercise the officers and souldiers within the said castle in armed and doe your best endeavour to keep them in good order and discipline, commanding them to obey you as their Governor. And you are to observe such orders and directions as you shall from time to time receive from myselfe.

Captain Tavenor was expected as part of his normal duties to liaise between Parliament and the Navy stationed in the Downs and to submit daily reports to the Admiralty. Promptly, he reported on 3 January 1653 the sighting of the Dutch fleet in the English Channel. He received the thanks of Parliament on several occasions for forwarding such valuable intelligence.

At the same time Captain Tavenor showed his compassion by involving himself in local charities. In 1653 he recommended a widow with seven children for poor relief on the grounds that her husband, a Deal pilot who had supported Parliament in the Civil War, had 'lost much in the Kentish rebellion' and in 1656 he spoke on behalf of a gunner's mate from the castle convicted of stealing. The man was acquitted but Tavenor's trust in him was misplaced for he was soon afterwards charged once more with receiving goods from prize ships.

He was incensed when Deal folk set up maypoles to celebrate the pagan festival of Maying. Openly, they decked the poles with the Royalist flag and toasted the return of the exiled Prince Charles. Captain Tavenor resisted sending his troops to fire warning shots into the drunken crowd although he firmly opposed the restoration of the Stuarts.

In 1649 Tavenor had married Ann Gibbs of Word (Worth) by whom he had thirteen children. One daughter, Priscilla, was born on 24 December 1654 in Deal Castle. Ann Tavenor died, aged forty-two, in 1665 and she was buried at St Leonard's churchyard. A second marriage the following year to Susanna Harrison of Dover, proved childless. This marriage took place at Canterbury 'in ye presence of Edward Prescott and Thomas Partridge and others, ye 14th day of June, 1666'.

Edward Prescott, a local farmer from Guston Court, was leader of the General Baptist sect at Dover. As Governor, Samuel Tavenor often conversed with him and Court attempted to convert him to Baptist principles. One story relates how Tavenor was pursuaded to attend an open-air meeting of believers in fields next to Deal Castle. He went along through curiosity but was ashamed to be seen in their presence because of his rank. He hid behind a hedge but was so impressed by their preaching that he, too, became convinced of their doctrine. Tavenor was baptised - by immersion - in the Delf Stream at Sandwich on 13 April 1663 and he joined the Arminian Baptists meeting at Dover.

At that time Baptist dissenters were widely scattered along the coast from Sandwich to Hythe. They numbered well over 200 and were grouped loosely in one fellowship at Dover. Since 1654, Richard Hobbs, 'a worthy, pious good man', served as Elder. Believers met in private houses and in the open-air since they were legally denied official meeting houses. Tradition asserts that clandestine meetings took place at dead of night in the sandhills between Deal and Sandwich.

The landing of Charles II at Dover Harbour in 1660 plunged the believers into deep despair. The Baptists feared that the Restoration would lead to further persecution since the Merry Monarch was no friend of Puritans. The Five Mile Act in 1665 harassed dissenters by forbidding them to inhabit certain areas. Deal, then not yet a corporate borough, was outside the limits of the Act and therefore attracted many dissenting groups who settled here. An eminent group of Baptist officers and sailors - who received their teaching initially from the Continent - gathered regularly at the house of Joan Culmer at Lower Deal where they were ministered to by Pastor Hobbs.

Tavenor's token

Inevitably, Captain Tavenor's period of office terminated after the Restoration. Although he was expelled from the castle he continued to live in the area. He had, in any case, found a military life incompatible with the Christian calling. Shamefully, his name was blackened by the authorities. He was not only branded as a 'schismatic' by Richard Watts, Magistrate of Deal, but later a damning report was also sent to the Archbishop of Canterbury by Benjamin Harrison, vicar of Saint Clements, Sandwich. Harrison, who had been repeatedly persecuted by Cromwell's soldiers, now preposterously accused Tavenor of concocting a plot hatched at Partridge's meeting house in Guston for a Dutch invasion of England.

Tavenor moved to Dover in 1655. There he rented a house and set up business as a grocer in Market Lane. This shop became sufficiently large to be entrusted with the supply of necessaries for the Guard of James, Duke of York, in 1674. Apparently, his business spread into other areas because there is a record that Tavenor supplied a barrel of gunpowder to the Corporation, probably for the defence of the harbour.

At least one tradesmen's token of his survives, listed in George Williamson's *Trade Tokens Issued in the 17th Century*. This token, a halfpenny, dated 1669, bears the Tavenor arms, granted 1575. Such tokens, usually brass farthings, were issued by the Corporation and local tradesmen to ease the chronic shortage of small change and also to advertise the public house or shop.

Tavenor beame a zealous preacher promoting the cause of religion in the district. Through his efforts many folk were added to the General Baptist community in south-east Kent. His shop became the focus of religious activity in

Dover. For this, he was greatly persecuted and often arrested while preaching, and hauled before the magistrates. There he testified boldly to the truths he professed.

On 21 January 1670 the King's brother, James, Duke of York, wrote to his Deputy, the Lieutenant of Dover Castle, stating that Charles II had been informed that there were several conventicles and unlawful meetings in the district and that the magistrates had proved lax in enforcing the laws against them. The Privy Council, in response, swiftly summoned before them Samuel Tavenor, Edward Dell, Nathaniel Berry, Symon Yorke, Anthony Street and Richard Matson, Mayor of Dover.

Tavenor refused to curtail his preaching and he was clapped into the dungeon at Dover Castle. His confinement was terminated by certain friends who had influence at court. It is thought that William Kiffin, the wealthy and prominent Baptist to whom Charles II was under some obligation, might have had a hand in this. At the same time the Dover Corporation had been instructed to seal up all Nonconformist meeting houses in Dover.

Tavenor's evangelism continued, nonetheless, and in October 1681 he became joint Elder with Richard Cannon, under the direction of Thomas Partridge who was ruling Elder, of the Dover Baptists. The community had by now become so large that Tavenor sub-divided it into three congregations – Dover, Deal with Sandwich, Folkestone with Hythe. These three churches, amicably organised, promised to meet collectively each May, an event which continued for the following fifty years.

The General Baptist Chapel at Deal dates from this period. It was built c1681 under Tavenor's direction on land probably owned by Joan Culmer. It stands on the east side of the High Street (once called Lower Street) and marks the original level of the old Sea Valley. Hasted mentions:

A handsome meeting-house between which and the street is a piece of ground on each side of the wall of the house which is used as a Burial ground having many graves and headstones.

Little remains of the original interior but in the floor of the vestry there is a tombstone which covers Anthony Atkinson and three other people who were interred there between 1770 and 1775. Atkinson died on 14 October 1775, aged sixty-four, and he left a small endowment. Graves were to be found along the approach to the chapel until they were destroyed in the First World War.

On the Ordnance Survey map of 1871 the building is marked 'unused' and this, sadly, has been its fate throughout most of its long history. Extensive repairs were carried out in 1922, when the facade was considerably altered as a consequence. A shell which demolished part of neighbouring Comarques also battered the chapel, then known as Central Hall, during the Second World War. Now a private residence, its bizarre exterior disguises the true age of this historic building.

General Baptists (as opposed to the present Particular Baptists who follow Calvinist teaching) believed that all men are saved ultimately. They later merged with Unitarians who preach the One-ness of God. Above the doorway of the

The General Baptist Chapel

General Baptist Chapel at Deal there was once conspicuously placed the legend: 'God Is One'.

Meeting-houses were eventually allowed to open under licence but persecution for these early Baptists remained a reality during the Stuart period. In 1682, Tavenor's enemies came with a false warrant and seized his shop goods and furniture to the value of £91 6s 11d. Discovering the illegality of the proceedings, he was able to demand the return of all his possessions from the magistrates. This incident led Tavenor and nine other like-minded men to sign a document promising to refund any believer whose goods were confiscated because of meetings held on their premises.

Persecution became so great that Tavenor was obliged to remove to London. While there he continued to preach as often and as publicly as he could, composing hymns and writing epistles to encourage and console his friends. Sixteen hymns attributed to him were long preserved by the Tavenor family.

Samuel Tavenor had been falsely accused at one time of helping to bring about the Dutch invasion. Ironically, he did survive to witness the accession of the tolerant William of Orange and his English wife, Mary II. Tavenor immediately returned to Dover and secured permission to use the south-end of his dwelling in Market Lane for public worship. The license was granted by Thomas Bedingfield, town clerk, on 20 April 1692:

> These are to Certifie whome it may concerne that att an adiournment of the Genrall Sessions of the peace held for the Towne and Port of Dovor in the County of Kent on Tuesday the nynetenth day of Aprill Anno dno 1692 in the fourth yeare of their Maties Reigne. It is Registred according to the directiuons of an Act of Parliament made in the first yeare of their said

maties reigne - Intituled an Act for exempting their maties protestant Subjects dissenting from the Church of England from the penalties of certon Lawes: That the dissenting protestants who scruple the Baptizing of Infants have appointed their meeting place for exercise of religious worshipp to bee att the South end of the dwelling house of a Mr Samuel Tavenor neere the market place in Dovor aforesaid dated att Dovor aforesaid the twentieth day of Aprill Ann Dno 1692.

Tavenor was elected pastor, and was again assisted by Richard Cannon, a descendant of Captain Cannon, Deputy Governor of Dover Castle during the Commonwealth. Baptisms were performed at this time in the stream at nearby River. A winding path which connected Tavenor's dwelling with the Market Square became known as Tavenor's Lane. This exists as a small cul-de-sac above the Prince Regent public house behind the Market Square.

In addition, Tavenor gave a portion of his land for burials. Tavenor's garden thus became The Old Baptists' Burial Ground and it was here that the Captain was buried when he died aged seventy-six on 4 August 1696. An entry in the minute book of the Baptist congregation records:

> Bror. Sam. Tavenor by his Last will and Testament gave to the poor of this congrigation three pounds and the same was distributed amongs them accordingly by his executors in the year 1696.

The burial ground, which was later merged with St Martin's cemetery, lay between Princes Street and Market Street. Also buried there were Samuel, his eldest son, who died aged thirty in 1682, described as being a 'chyrurgion' (surgeon) and Susanna, his second wife, who died in May, 1701. In her will she left £8 to be distributed among the poor. A wall tablet marked the site of the original meeting-house and described Tavenor as 'Elder of ye congregation of Baptist believers at Dover, 14 years and nine months.' Recent road construction has demolished this ancient burial ground and shattered the inscription on the tomb of this remarkable man:

> Enclosed within a valient Captain lies,
> Holy and humble, pious, grave and wise,
> A Gospel pastor, faithful to his trust,
> Courageous for his God, here lies in dust,
> Expecting to be raised with the just.

Richard Cannon succeeded as minister of the Dover Baptist Congregation and in about 1712 John and David Simpson became joint pastors. Baptist services continued in Tavenor's private house with adult baptisms in the Dour Stream at River, near Dover, until 1745, when the first chapel was built in Market Lane.

A Unitarian Baptist, Benjamin Martin, was ordained pastor in 1800 and under his leadership a new meeting house was built nearby in 1820. Dover's Unitarian Chapel still stands on a prominence overlooking Snargate Street. It is an imposing yellow brick building comprising an irregular octagon with a crypt and vaults

Tavenor's tomb and burial ground © Dover Museum

below, vestries on two floors at the east end and a grand, central Venetian window. A recent fire devastated this perfectly preserved Georgian preaching house although many of the original features survived, including horsebox pews, semi-circular gallery, a Holdich organ (1855) replacing the central pulpit and a concealed baptistry (full immersion font). This body of worshippers, which soon became exclusively Unitarian, has the distinction of establishing Dover's first Sunday School in 1803 by Priscilla Pierce, granddaughter of Captain Samuel Tavenor.

JOHN HUTCHINSON

'Imprisonment of a regicide'

ON A WINTRY January morning in 1649, Charles, King of England, was executed before a vast crowd gathered outside the Banqueting House at London's Whitehall. A great groan went up as the King's head was severed and spectators rushed forward to soak their handkerchiefs in the royal blood. For Royalist sympathisers who witnessed this gruesome spectacle on this bleak, bitter day, this was the death of 'King Charles the Martyr'.

The King's 'unreasonable stubborness' in refusing to accede to the demands of Parliament, his unyielding belief in the Divine Right of Kings and his unpopular Catholic marriage to Henrietta Maria of France had embroiled the nation in bitter turmoil. The culmination of four years' Civil War between Crown and Parliament was this unique act of English regicide.

'Men wondered that so good a man should be so bad a king,' wrote Lucy Hutchinson, wife of a Puritan colonel who was one of the judges to condemn Charles I. (The death sentence had been cast by a single vote: sixty-eight against sixty-seven). While admiring the King's undoubted talents and patronage of the arts Lucy objected to Charles' absolutism and commented that he was 'the most obstinate person in his selfwill that ever was, and so bent upon being an absolute uncontrollable sovereign, that he was resolved either to be such a king or none'. In her biography of her husband, *Memoirs of The Life of Colonel John Hutchinson*, she traces his brief military career and inevitable arrest and imprisonment as a regicide after Cromwell's demise.

Lucy Hutchinson was the daughter of Sir Allen Apsley, Governor of the Tower of London, a fervent royalist who had served during the reigns of Elizabeth I and James I. Lady Apsley, her mother, had learned chemistry and physics from such distinguished Tower prisoners as Sir Walter Raleigh. Lucy, born in the Tower *c*1620, acquired these skills from her mother and she put them into practice when she became a country gentleman's wife. During the Civil War she treated the wounded of both sides. Presumably these acts of compassion earned her subsequent favours when her husband was imprisoned at the Restoration of the Monarchy.

Lucy married John Hutchinson in 1638 at a time when her face was disfigured by smallpox. The priest was 'affrighted' to look upon the bride. She bore John four sons and four daughters - her firstborn children were twins, Edward and

Thomas. Inevitably, the network of intermarriages between upper class families led to relatives finding themselves on opposite sides during the Grand Quarrel which flared up in 1642. This would explain, in part, the absence of atrocities, reprisals and recriminations against certain leaders during the Commonwealth.

It might be remembered, too, that this was not merely a political war but a religious one where men fought according to their conscience - the 'Arminian' or High Church supporters of the Monarchy whose beliefs centred upon sacramental and ritualistic worship, against the Calvinists or Puritans whose lifestyle was influenced by a personal response to the life of Christ.

John Hutchinson took the Parliamentary side during the Civil War, receiving in 1643 a commission from Lord Fairfax to raise a regiment-of-foot. Appointed Governor of Nottingham Castle, he distinguished himself by defending the town from repeated Royalist attacks. According to his wife, he was nominated much against his will to act as one of the King's judges and he signed the death warrant only after great deliberation and prayer. This warrant – perhaps one of the most important single documents in English history – was greatly amended before signatures were appended. King Charles, it read, was:

Colonel John Hutchinson
© National Portrait Gallery

. . . to be putt to death by the severinge of his head from his body . . . in the open streete before Whitehall uppon the morrowe . . . between the houres of Tenn in the morning and Five in the afternoon.

Lord Protector, Oliver Cromwell, attempted to persuade Colonel Hutchinson to take office under his leadership as a reward for his loyal service. Surprisingly, Mrs Hutchinson expressed extreme dissatisfaction with Cromwell during his brief regime. She approved her husband's decision, therefore, to retire into private life and take little active part in public affairs during Cromwell's Commonwealth.

Hutchinson retreated to Owthorpe, his family home in Nottinghamshire, where he remodelled the handsome stone mansion.

After the Restoration in 1660 Charles II was swift to bring retribution upon those he considered to be 'the immediate murderers' of his father. Oliver Cromwell's corpse was exhumed and his head disported on London Bridge as a warning of the price of rebellion. Direst penalties were inflicted upon the remaining regicides and during a series of trials at the close of that year many were condemned to be hanged, drawn and quartered. More fortunate regicides were merely imprisoned, forfeited their properties and then paraded annually through the London streets to suffer abject humiliation from the scornful crowds.

Ironically, Hutchinson had been elected to the Parliament which invited Charles II to return, while realising all too well that he would be a victim of the new king's vengeance.

Lucy Hutchinson and one of her sons
© National Portrait Gallery

He confessed openly his 'penitent sorrow' and, although he escaped the ultimate penalty, he was soon arrested on suspicion of being connected with a plot to restore 'the old Parliament, gospel ministry and English liberty'. He was confined without trial in the Tower of London where the new Governor treated him with severity. Eventually, in May 1664, he was transferred to Sandown Castle, making the journey under armed escort by boat to Gravesend and then on horseback to Deal.

When Colonel Hutchinson arrived at Sandown Castle, according to his wife, he found it:

> . . . a lamentable old ruin'd place, allmost a mile distant from the towne, the roomes all out of repair, not weather-free, no kind of accommodation either for lodging or diet, or any conveniency of life. Before he came, there were not above halfe a douzen souldiers in it, and a poore Lieftenant with his wife and children and two or three Cannoneers, and a few Guns allmost dismounted, upon rotten carriages.

Once Hutchinson reached the castle a company of foot was despatched from Dover to help guard the place . . . 'pittifull weake fellows, halfe sterv'd and eaten up with vermine, whom the Governor of Dover cheated of halfe their pay and the other halfe they spent in drinke'. Obviously, the Colonel's captors expected the unhealthy condition of the castle would soon do its ghastly work and they were not to be disappointed.

The Colonel's victuals were dearly bought in the town and were horribly dressed by a sutler who lived on the premises. For beds he was forced to send to a nearby inn and at an exorbitant rate hire three - for himself, his servant and a fellow prisoner named Gregory. He had to glaze his own chamber which was a thoroughfare room having five doors to it, one of which 'open'd upon a platform that had nothing but the bleake ayre of the sea, which every tide washt the foote of the Castle walls.'

The salt air made the room so damp that the Colonel's leather hat case and trunks would be daily covered in mildew even in summer. The distraught Mrs Hutchinson complained:

> Wipe them as cleane as you could one morning, by the next they would be mouldie againe . . . though the walls were foure yards thick, yet it rain'd in through cracks in them, and then one might sweepe off a peck of salt peter off them every day, which stood in a perpetuall sweate upon them.

Despite these discomforts the Colonel remained remarkably cheerful, making the most of his unenviable situation. Eventually, the wife of the Lieutenant of Sandown Castle, realising that the Colonel could not stomach his revolting food, offered to feed him. They came to an arrangement whereby the Colonel and his servant boarded with her for twenty shillings each week although he had to provide his own wine and linen.

By far the worst of his sufferings was that he had to endure the presence of Captain John Gregory, an uncouth character, loud-mouthed and ill-mannered. Although Gregory, 'alias Thompson, Smyth, and Harte', had been imprisoned with Hutchinson in the Tower, many of the Colonel's friends suspected him of being a 'trapaner' (agent provocateur) planted to ensnare him in unguarded moments.

All this time Captain William Freeman of Sandown Castle had access to a warm room with a bed which he craftily reserved for rental to his distinguished prisoner. The alternative room, apparently, would have offered little comfort for 'this too was so darke one could not have read by the fire or the bedside without a candle at noone day'.

Shortly afterwards, Lucy Hutchinson followed her husband to Sandown. Denied accommodation at the castle, she took lodgings with her son and daughter in the 'cut-throat towne of Deal'. From there they walked daily to dinner and back again at night until the Lieutenant's wife agreed to cater in addition for Mrs Hutchinson and her children. But the meal, although plentiful, was poorly dressed and served only to bring home to the family their painfully reduced circumstances.

Yet all these privations the Colonel bore with commendable dignity. He appeared, according to his wife, 'never more pleasant and contended in his life'.

Alternative recreation being unavailable, he found diversion in 'sorting and shaddowing' cockleshells which his family gathered on the foreshore. So accomplished did he become at sketching seashells that he gained numerous admirers. Yet these were trifling treasures: his constant study was the Holy Scriptures. He would read no other book.

Once, when his wife was weeping, the Colonel tried to raise her spirits by assuring her that the Parliamentary cause would one day be revived. Should he die a prisoner, he declared, 'my blood will be so innocent I shall advance the Cause more by my death hasting the vengeance of God upon my unjust enemies, than I could do by all the actions of my life'. Another time, Mrs Hutchinson heard rumours that her husband was to be transported to Tangiers or to some equally remote destination. To this the Colonel confidently replied: 'Prithee, trust God once with me: if he carrie me away, he will bring me back againe.' Lucy Hutchinson wrote:

> Sometimes he would say that if ever he should live to see the Parliament power up againe, that he would never meddle any more either in Councells or Armies: and then sometimes againe, when he saw or heard of any of the debosheries of the times, he would say he would act only as a Justice of the peace in the Country, and would be severe against drunkards, and suffer none in his neighbourhood.

After Hutchinson had been a prisoner for some time, the Governor of Sandown Castle, Captain William Freeman, offered him his own room for twenty

Sandown Castle

shillings a week, to which the Colonel readily consented, providing his wife were allowed to lodge with him. This Freeman refused without an express order which was endeavoured but not obtained.

Next, Freeman demanded of the Colonel a mark a week for fees but the Colonel told him that unless he could show how it was due by any known law, he would not pay. Exasperated, Freeman consulted his superior, the Governor of Dover Castle, how he might obtain money from his prisoner and he was advised to lock the Colonel in a dungeon. But this action the unscrupulous fellow dared not attempt.

On a subsequent visit to the castle, Freeman repeated his insolence by calling out to the Colonel without the courtesy of his title. Turning to his Lieutenant, the Governor ordered:

> Captaine Moyle, I ordeine you to quarter Hutchinson and Gregorie together in the next roome, and if Hutchinson will make a partition at his owne charge, he may have that part of the chamber which has the chimney, and for this I expect a mark a week of Hutchinson, and a noble of Gregory; and if they will have any enlargement besides, they must pay for it.

Colonel Hutchinson spurned the Governor and directed his wife to report his deplorable treatment to Henry Bennet, Secretary of State – later First Earl of Arlington. This she did, making a passionate plea desiring him either to procure an order for removal or else for better accommodation. She showed the letter to Captain Gregory before it was sent for it represented his condition equally with that of her husband.

Shortly afterwards, a certain woman of ill-repute, who styled herself 'Mrs Montague' came from London to visit Captain Gregory, posing as his sister. 'They had bene continually in private with doores lock'd upon them,' confided Mrs Hutchinson, 'which the Garrison, believing her to have bene his sister, did not suspect; but her carriage was so light that all thought her scarce a modest woman.' At first Colonel Hutchinson alone suspected the deceit but he kept the matter quiet, thinking that the woman would soon return to London. When the Captain informed the Colonel that a second woman would be joining her, Hutchinson admonished his fellow prisoner for blatant immorality. Captain Gregory flew into a rage and threatened Mrs Hutchinson with violence so that the Colonel physically restrained him and threw him out of the prison door.

The following morning, Gregory challenged Colonel Hutchinson to 'fistycuffes'. When Captain Moyle heard of the affray he jokingly offered to lend Hutchinson his sword to run the Captain through. The outcome was that Captain Gregory was confined to his cell under close guard until Colonel Hutchinson intervened on his behalf and once more secured the rascal's liberty. Yet this 'pittiful, carnall, spiteful, passionate, wretched man' was by no means reformed and took to excessive drinking with the guards and spreading lies and rumours about the Colonel.

Not long afterwards, the Colonel's brother, George Hutchinson, arrived from London with an order signed by Secretary Bennett to allow the Colonel leave to walk by the seaside with a keeper. Permission for this concession had been

The 'cut-throat town' of Deal

obtained with difficulty by Sir Allen and Lady Apsley. Colonel Hutchinson was naturally overjoyed at this news.

Lucy Hutchinson realised by now that she would never gain admission into the castle so she rented a house in the town to which she intended bringing the remainder of her young family that winter. As it drew near to the close of the year, Mrs Hutchinson, having completed preparations for the house, decided it was necessary to return to Owthorpe in Nottinghamshire.

When the time came for her departure she left with a sad and heavy heart fearing that while her husband lay so near the shore he might be secretly 'shipt away to some barbarous coast'. But the Colonel was so confident of seeing Owthorpe again that he gave his wife directions for planting trees and renovating their mansion. His brother and daughter stayed behind at Deal, visiting him each day, and he walked with them under armed supervision along the seashore.

On Saturday 3 September Colonel Hutchinson went for his usual stroll. When he returned he found himself in excruciating pain and shivering violently. The next day he felt slightly better but on the Monday he was confined to bed. For several days he lay in this feverish state. He rose only to refresh himself for short periods and to read his Bible.

Each day the Colonel grew visibly weaker until it was at last thought advisable to consult a doctor. Lucy Hutchinson recorded:

> There was a country phisitian at Deale, who had formerly belong'd to the Armie, and had some guifts, and used to exercise them among godly people in their meetings. But having bene taken there once by the persecutors, and being married to a wicked and unquiet woman, she and the love of the world had perverted him to forsake all religious meetings; yet the man continued civill and faire-condition'd, and was much employ'd there-abouts.

After a thorough examination this doctor advised consulting Dr Jachin, an eminent physician from Canterbury. Dr Jachin was immediately summoned and he arrived at Sandown on the following Saturday. As he rode across Kent he enquired of the messenger concerning the conditions of Colonel Hutchinson's confinement and, when told, declared that his journey would be to little purpose for that 'the place had kill'd him'.

Although both doctors were attentive in applying remedies and administering cordials (for a time they even employed a night nurse) there was nothing they could do to allay the pitiful conclusion. They advised George Hutchinson that his brother would soon become delirious and that if the Colonel had anything to say he should speak while possessing his full senses. Dutifully, George relayed the doctors' alarming news and asked his brother if he had yet made his peace with God. 'I hope you do not thinke me so ill a Christian,' Colonel Hutchinson retorted, 'to have bene thus long in prison and have that to doe now!'

All day the Colonel remained quite sensible and cheerful. As his daughter, Barbara, sat weeping at his bedside he sought to comfort her with kind words. Yet even as he spoke his pulse grew low and he weakened rapidly. His family and friends realised that he lay dying and prepared to write down his last words. When they mentioned Lucy's name he whispered: 'Alas, how will she be surprized.'

The Colonel died in 'a vile chamber, untrim'd and unhung, in a poor wretched bed,' bewailed Lucy Hutchinson. And she added practically: 'It being the Lord's day, about 7 o'clock at night.' Hutchinson had charged his wife upon his demise 'to shew her selfe in this occasion a good Christian, and above the pitch of ordinary women'. She was now a lonely middle-aged Puritan widow living with her young family in reduced circumstances in a country for which she could have little moral, religious or political sympathy.

The moment the Colonel died his brother despatched a messenger to convey the tragic news to Owthorpe. None of the Colonel's possessions could be removed from the castle until a warrant came from Secretary Bennet to deliver to Mrs Hutchinson the body of her husband and all his belongings. These meagre possessions - furniture, bedding, fire irons, a trunk packed with clothes, all valued at £22 18s - were distributed among the poor. His 'vest, sute and cote and 3 pair of stockings and the velvett capp' went to his keeper, Captain Moyle; Lucy had 'the velvett goune' and to her servant went 'the ould Black sute and hatt and shoes'.

Assoone as newes came to Owthorpe, the Collonell's two eldest sonnes and all his household servants went up to London with his horses, and made ready a herse trickt with scutcheons, and six horses in mourning, with a mourning coach and six horses to waite on it, and came downe to Deale with an Order from the Secretary for the body; but when they came thither the Captaine Freeman, in spite, would not deliver it, because Mrs Hutchinson herselfe was not come to fetch it. So they were forc'd, att an intolerable charge, to keepe all this equipage att Deale while they sent to the Secretary for another order, which they got directed to the Lieftenant in the absence of the Captaine, and assoone as it came deliver'd it to him, who immediately suffer'd them to take away the body, which they did at that however, though it was night, fearing a further dispute with Freeman, who, after the body had bene ten dayes embalm'd, say'd he would have a Jury empanell'd and a Coroner to sitt on it, to see whether he died a naturall death.

All this delay was calculated to cause the Colonel's family great expense and deep distress. During the long wait in the town his daughter, Barbara, became ill with grief. At last the body was conveyed with its handsome equipage to Canterbury and on through Kent towards London. As the cortege approached a country fair one foolish priest accosted the mourners and insisted the body be buried in his parish. 'But they broke several of their heads, and made their way cleare, having beaten off all the Towne,' reported Lucy. Fortunately, this was the only harrowing incident on the journey to Owthorpe. As the sad procession passed through Southwark, over the bridge and through the heart of the City to lodgings in Holborn, not one reviling word or indignation was spoken. Many people were deeply moved at that 'sad witnesse of the murderous cruelty of the men then in power'.

Finally, the Colonel's body was 'brought lamented home, and lay'd in his owne vault' in the church at Owthorpe. The tomb bore a lengthy epitaph composed by Lucy Hutchinson:

> He died at Sandowne Castle, in Kent after
> 11 months harsh and strict imprisonment
> - without crime or accusation -
> upon the 11th day of Sept. 1664,
> in the 49th yeare of his age,
> full of joy, in assured hope
> of a glorious resurrection.

At the close of her biography Lucy Hutchinson added some strange details concerning her husband's demise. First, she related how Captain Samuel Tavenor, Governor of Deal Castle during the Civil War, a man 'that had some little skill in Astrologie', foretold the Colonel's death. He studied the Colonel's sign, consulted the stars and drew his horoscope, which artfulness Mrs Hutchinson dismissed as 'vaine and foolish.' It is tempting to speculate that the Colonel's fortitude in the face of certain death contributed towards Tavenor's conversion to Christianity. The Captain had been present when the Colonel expired and also at his embalming and he tried to convince Mrs Hutchinson that her husband had died from poisoning.

Secondly, Lucy Hutchinson narrated a ghost story concerning a mysterious cloaked figure which haunted Sandown Castle:

> 'The Castle had bene sayd to be often disturb'd with evill spiritts before the Collonel came: but in all the 4 months that he was there, there was (not) aniething seene or heard till about a fortnight before his death, when allmost every night the souldiers that were on the guard and the people in the Castle, all but the Collonell, heard att midnight in the kitchin greate noyses

and preparations for getting meate, pumping water, and winding up the jack, and washing the kitchin when the maid was in bed and no body there. But the Collonell never heard any of this: only one Lord's day at evening, his chamber being over the kitchin, and his wife and children and his brother with him, wee did certeinely all thinke we heard the jack wound up when we were after assur'd there was no such thing being done, no bodie being then in the kitchin. And this was the Lord's day before Mrs Hutchinson went. But after he was dead those noyses ceast, and nothing more was heard. But the spring after, there came an apparition of a gentlewoman in mourning, in such habitt as Mrs Hutchinson us'd to weare there, and affrighted the guards mightily at the first, but after a while grew familliar to them, and was often seene walking in the Collonell's chamber and on the platforme, and came sometimes into the guard among them. Which is certeinely true, but we know not how to interpret it . . .'

Lucy Hutchinson's account of her husband's brief imprisonment, written directly after the Colonel's death, was eventually published by a descendant, the Reverend Julius Hutchinson, in 1806. Lucy had no thought of publication in her own lifetime and therefore she felt no constraints on what she might say about those people - whether Royalist or Roundhead - of whose actions she disapproved, which gives her narrative a certain astringency. Her account of the war years was based upon entries she made in her notebook soon after the events described, which gives her story the immediacy of a diary. Intended primarily for the preservation of the memory of the Colonel and the instruction of their children, the manuscript is of small significance as a general history of the Civil War. Lucy over-rates the Colonel's political importance and is partial and prejudiced in her notices of her enemies. Yet the biography retains a peculiar value among seventeenth century literature - for as a picture of a Puritan gentleman and his family, Lucy Hutchinson's memoir is truly unique.

Death warrant of Charles I – Hutchinson's signature is third in the third column © House of Lords Record Office

WILLIAM PITT

'A d——d bitter pill'

WILLIAM PITT, the greatest of the Lords Warden, was resident at Walmer Castle for a period of fourteen years during which time he actively involved himself in affairs of war and peace. Pitt was instrumental in landscaping the estate around the castle, turning it into a place of beauty rather than a mere fortress, and he laboured ceaselessly to secure the Kent coastline against the anticipated invasion of Napoleon Bonaparte which earned him the title: 'The Pilot that Weathered the Storm.'

When Lord Guilford died in the summer of 1792 King George III did not hesitate to appoint Pitt to succeed him as Lord Warden of the Cinque Ports. The King's letter arrived post-haste the following day. Pitt at that time was thirty-three years old and he had already been Prime Minister for almost nine years.

Having this morning received the account of the death of the Earl of Guilford,' penned the King, 'I take the first opportunity of acquainting Mr Pitt that Wardenship of the Cinque Ports is an office for which I will not receive any recommendations: having positively resolved to confer it on him as a mark of that regard which his eminent services have deserved from me. I am so bent on this that I shall seriously be offended at any attempt to decline.

William Pitt, from a painting by John Hoppner © National Portrait Gallery

The King's choice of Lord Warden was a popular one and there was not one single voice of dissent.

To William Pitt the royal command was exceedingly welcome. He could never manage his personal funds and was chronically in debt , which is ironic since he was formerly in charge of the nation's finances as Chancellor of the Exchequer. This prestigious new appointment, however, not only confirmed the King's confidence in his abilities but relieved him temporarily of his pecuniary embarrassment. The post had become a lucrative political sinecure and carried with it an annual salary in excess of £3,000.

Britain's youngest Prime Minister took up immediate occupation of Walmer Castle. He arrived early that September and continued the tradition of spending the autumn at his seaside residence until his premature death in 1806. King George, nervous that his favourite statesman was to inhabit a castle close to the hostile French coast, secretly charged Lord Amhurst, Commander-in-Chief, to organise a round-the-clock armed surveillance.

As an additional precaution the drawbridge was raised every night at Walmer Castle. On one occasion this caused acute distress to a messenger from an alderman of Canterbury who arrived with a gift of a turbot just as the drawbridge was being drawn up. The unlucky servant was forced to parade all night cradling the fish before the bridge was lowered early the next morning.

Invariably, William Pitt travelled from Downing Street to Walmer in a post-chaise and four - an extravagant mode of transport - breaking his journey perhaps to visit friends in North Kent. When the carriage arrived the horses were detached and stabled inside the castle gateway. This practice continued during the residency of a later Lord Warden - the Duke of Wellington - which custom elicited the jest from George IV: 'Pray is the entry to the castle still through the coach-house?'

Pitt planned a scheme of improvements, converting the interior from military to domestic use which was first begun by Lionel Sackville, First Duke of Dorset. At first the Lord Warden inhabited a modest panelled room in the central part of the castle although 'Pitt's Room' is no longer open to the public. He deliberately chose a room facing the stark wall of a bastion surmounted by a cannon in order not to be distracted from his studies. Lord Stanhope commented on his odd choice of workroom in a letter to Lord Granville in 1842:

> Mr Pitt's own room seemed rather strangely chosen. It looked neither to the south nor yet to the sea, and had, on the whole, a gloomy aspect. For many years it continued exactly as Mr Pitt left it, with the same paper on the walls. But when the castle was lent to the Queen and Prince after they married, the wall of Mr Pitt's room was pulled down so as to join it to another apartment, and make a new dining room. On Her Majesty's departure, however, the wall was rebuilt . . .

An alternative room on the first floor is furnished in his preferred style to show to modern visitors. Pitt's Museum displays a woven-patterned carpet and plain dimity curtains, engravings and furniture, some of which came from Holwood, his country villa near Bromley, which he was forced to abandon through financial difficulties. Furniture which has survived includes a set of thirteen mahogany chairs which were originally cane-seated with squab cushions; a set of eight satinwood armchairs and a scarlet leather-covered

74

gaming or library chair. The occupant sat astride the chair in a reverse position, with his arms on the padded rests to read a book propped on a rest fixed to the back of the chair.

Later Pitt expanded the Lord Warden's living quarters by turning a separate Gunner's Lodgings adjoining the south-west bastion into two main apartments for himself and his niece, Lady Hester Stanhope. Lady Hester slept on the ground floor and Pitt above, probably in the room which became the Duke of Wellington's study. Pitt's new winter quarters were certainly an improvement. They were warmer not only on account of the thickness of the walls but because their aspect is due west. He added a wide staircase linking these two apartments plus the long corridor which runs the entire length of the castle on the first floor. It seems likely that the doorway opening onto the wooden bridge over the moat leading to the garden was constructed at this time.

Pitt made further alterations to the dining room by adding an alcove, panelling and fireplaces while the spacious drawing room was created from two small rooms on the eastern extension overlooking the sea. 'The Castle is greatly improved since you were here,' wrote Lord Carrington to Lord Camden from Walmer Castle in 1785. 'It is thoroughly cleaned and repaired, and out of two old Drawing Rooms opposite the Dining Room is made one large handsome room.' Unfortunately, food still came via a circuitous route from the kitchen below and was invariably cold.

Pitt's embellishments to the sea-ward wing inspired Lord Carrington, Captain of Deal Castle, to make improvements on an even grander scale to his own living quarters. When both repairs were completed Lord Carrington jovially approached Pitt. 'I suppose the time is now come when we may apply to the

Walmer Castle

*William Pitt's
reading chair*

*When Lord Warden,
Pitt equipped a room
above the stables at
Walmer as a study and
employed a woman to
cook him meals –
although his favourite
was said to be a
ploughman's lunch.*

*Pitt's predilection for
alcohol led one wit to
remark that if there were
one thing Pitt liked
better than a glass of
port, it was a bottle!*

*'Military and naval
characters are constantly
welcome here,' Lady
Hester Stanhope wrote
from Walmer. 'Women
are not, I suppose,
because they do not
form any part of our
society. You may guess
then, what a pretty fuss
they make of me.'*

Treasury to defray the cost of our alterations?' he enquired. Pitt's response was unequivocal: 'Whatever alterations we have made must be paid for out of our own pockets.' Lord Carrington was dismayed that he had now to fork out himself to the tune of £7,000.

Also at Walmer a partition was built dividing up the guest bedroom into a dressing room with a recess for the four-poster which was later used by Queen Victoria. The erroneously-named Prince Consort's Room was actually Pitt's library (Prince Albert slept in the same bed as Victoria when they were on holiday at Walmer). Pitt was highly satisfied with his skilful modernisation. 'I should be very glad to show you all the improvements of this place both in beauty and comfort,' he wrote to Addington (later Lord Sidmouth) on 5 September 1802.

The 'Great Commoner' continued to conduct parliamentary affairs with zest from the comfort of his castle. Politicians, statesmen and reformers flocked to Walmer for over a decade to discuss affairs of national importance in an informal atmosphere. Distinguished visitors included Grenville, Dundas, Hawkesbury and Castlereagh. Lord Chatham, Pitt's incompetent elder brother, mulled over tactics for warfare; William Wilberforce, the social reformer, expressed surprise at the warmth of his reception while Lord Mornington (later Lord Wellesley) remarked upon the spectacle of 100 sailing ships passing through the English Channel. At one time Pitt offered the castle to George III to convalesce when he was suffering one of his periodic bouts of madness.

Certainly, Pitt was a generous and welcoming host. He revelled in the opportunities for recreation which this unique site offered, perfectly blending the sea with the countryside. He joined his guests partridge shooting, riding with the hounds and hunting basketted hares. He often went sailing in the Downs and is said to have benefited from the invigorating salt air. He took immense pride in pointing out to visitors the coastal views from the ramparts before conducting them around his expanding estate. On Sundays Pitt's guests at Walmer Castle accompanied him to Old St Mary's Church, where he disciplined himself by committing to memory the dullest sermons.

Accommodation at the castle was admittedly scanty. To solve the problem of lodging his numerous guests Pitt rented a cottage which stood at the entrance to the grounds from the village. Pitt's cottage was later enlarged and subsequently used for a similar purpose by both Lord Liverpool and the Duke of Wellington. It took from the former the name which it bears today, Liverpool House. The property was acquired from the Leith family, whose ancestor, George, was a naval surgeon who amassed a fortune by contracts with the Admiralty to render medical assistance to the sick and wounded landed at Deal during the French Wars.

Pitt made it a strict rule that the younger guests, irrespective of rank, were required to lodge at Liverpool House. 'Better that these young lords should walk home on a rainy night than old men,' he would say. 'They can bear it more easily.' In 1804 he lent it to his nephew, Philip, Lord Mahon, and his pretty and talented bride, Catherine, daughter of Lord Carrington. Their marriage had been solemnised in the dining room of Deal Castle with Pitt in attendance. Their eldest son, Philip, afterwards the fifth Earl Stanhope, was born in Liverpool House in 1805. He became the biographer of both Pitt and Wellington.

Gradually the Lord Warden extended his territory. He created a path along the beach in front of the castle for the Preventive Men although at that time the sea almost reached the moat. He leased further land, including the present kitchen garden, the pleasure gardens and castle meadows which extended northwards beyond the Governor's Garden. This was the site of Walmer Lodge, which became the home of Countess Stanhope, who was an intimate friend of the Duke of Wellington. Walmer Lodge became derelict last century and the land which formerly doubled the castle estate was sold for redevelopment.

Another worthwhile acquisition was a farm adjacent to the castle. Surprisingly, Pitt soon won the regard of his neighbours as an accomplished gentleman farmer. He kept fine horses and fat hogs. He grew hay and corn. His foray into farming was no mere whim, however, since he was convinced that by growing corn he would be benefiting the country should there be an invasion.

Almost for the entire duration of Pitt's occupancy of Walmer Castle Britain was at war with France. Heroically, he saw it as his principal duty as Lord Warden to protect the Kent coast from impending invasion. From the declaration of war by France on 1 February 1793 to the Battle of Trafalgar on 21 October 1805, Pitt, both as Prime Minister and, when he was briefly out of office, as a private citizen, consistently thwarted the repeated attempts of Napoleon Bonaparte, who rose swiftly from First Consul to Emperor of France, in his attempts to dominate the English Channel.

Bonaparte shrewdly realised that without control of this sea he could never lead a successful campaign against Great Britain. 'If we can be masters of the passage for twelve hours,' he once crowed, 'England will cease to be . . .'

A vast camp sprang up overlooking the heights of Boulogne. Inland, thousands of troops stood to arms while fleets of warships were mustered along the French coast ready to attempt the hazardous crossing. Britain was in mortal danger.

William Pitt immersed himself in the security of the nation. He raised the Militia, the Regular Army and the Sea Fencibles (local mariners enlisted for home service) so that at the height of his defensive campaign total manpower of the British and Irish Forces approached half a million. Beacons, watch-houses and telegraph stations sprang up across Kent and the activities of the troops - marching and drilling - was on a scale never before seen in our county.

The Lord Warden called a special deputation of the Cinque Ports and their Members in order to project a local fighting force in April 1794. Pitt was warmly received at Dover Castle with an artillery salute and he was attended by a captain's guard and a military band. He proposed a voluntary force whose expense was to be borne entirely by public subscription. Pitt headed the subscription list himself with a donation of one thousand pounds from his limited funds. The force raised was to be expressly voluntary except when called out to repel invasion or - ominously - to suppress riots when it immediately came under Military Law. It consisted of both infantry and cavalry and was commanded by Robert Banks Jenkinson (afterwards Lord Hawkesbury and Second Earl Liverpool). It was termed The Cinque Ports Fencibles.

Deal was the likely point of invasion and Pitt ensured that it was effectively ringed by an intense concentration of defences. Two batteries (the solid base of one still stands), each manned by 200 soldiers and ten officers, were constructed on the foreshore north of Sandown Castle. Walmer Barracks, consisting of 1100 infantry, a squadron of cavalry and a naval hospital, were established in 1795 and a shutter telegraph system linking the Admiralty with the Downs was constructed in 1796. Dragoons galloped along the foreshore watching for the enemy's ships while Sandown Castle, despite its dilapidated condition, was garrisoned with a company of artillery.

Further afield, Pitt ordered the construction of Martello towers along the south coast, and the Royal Military Canal to defend Romney Marsh. The Lord Warden was indefatigable in leading the war effort and was observed cantering over the cliffs to inspect the army camp at Shorncliffe; riding out to review raw recruits on Barham Downs, near Canterbury, and sailing out to investigate French vessels captured in the Downs. Tragically, he was examining the fortifications of Dover Castle in the company of the Duke of York when an artilleryman was blown over the wall during the firing of a royal salute.

Despite his industry he was repeatedly criticised by certain members of the government. At the very moment that Napoleon was patrolling the sands at Boulogne, peering at the White Cliffs of Dover through his telescope, the blinkered aristocrat, Lord Grenville, was busy watering his rhododendrons. Nonetheless, the general public appreciated his concern. William Wordsworth composed a noble sonnet extolling the virtues of the Men of Kent. Even the caustic satirist, Peter Pindar, not normally a favourable critic, was inspired to voice his approval in doggerel:

> Come the Consul whenever he will -
> And he means it when Neptune is calmer -
> Pitt will send him a d——d bitter pill
> From his fortress, the Castle at Walmer.

This stirring rhyme echoed the sentiments of even the humblest boatmen, for one local wit extemporised with this verse found pinned to the gates of the Navy Yard:

Let Envy rail and Disappointment rage,
Still Pitt shall prove the wonder of his age;
Let peace and virtue all his steps attend,
The King's best subject and his Country's friend.

Occasionally, Pitt received welcome news at Walmer. When the French invaded Holland they commandeered the Dutch fleet which immediately became an additional threat to the safety of Britain. Admiral Duncan successfully blockaded the Dutch harbours after a decisive battle at Camperdown in October 1797. The Lord Warden was entertaining guests when a smuggler burst into the room - interrupting their indulgence in a bumper - with the news of this important victory. The following year news of an even greater event was relayed to the castle. Nelson had vanquished Napoleon at sea in the Battle of the Nile thus ensuring that danger of an invasion was temporarily suspended.

In July 1801 Vice Admiral Lord Nelson was himself sent to Deal 'on a particular service' to watch the harbours of Calais and Boulogne. Napoleon had been observed assembling a flotilla of gunboats with which to invade England and Nelson was commanded to organise a midnight raid using special flat-bottomed boats built in the Navy Yard to tow the enemy's ships into the Channel and there either sink them or set them alight. 'This Boat warfare is not exactly congenial to my feelings,' complained Nelson. In the event the attack on the French coast proved disastrous and many of his trusted men and commanders were killed or horribly injured, including his close companion Captain Edward Thornborough Parker who lies buried in St George's churchyard. Nelson, posted to Deal to deal with the French threat, hated the town. He moaned that it was 'the coldest place in England, most assuredly'.

Constantly seasick, permanently cold and racked with toothache, Nelson avoided company until his mistress, Emma Hamilton, arrived to stay at The Three Kings (Royal Hotel). Emma was accompanied by her complaisant husband, Sir William, who spent most of his time fishing with a reformed smuggler, Yawkins.

Nelson did, however, make a grudging social call on William Pitt (who was not at that time Prime Minister) at Walmer Castle. His diary records:

October 11 – I see Billy Pitt has arrived, as the colours are hoisted. I will see him before I leave the station: he may perhaps be useful to me one day or other.
October 12 – This being a very fine morning and smooth beach, I went with Sutton and Bedford and landed at Walmer, but found Billy fast asleep so left my card.

The fact that William Pitt lay so long in bed does not indicate his laziness. On the contrary he often slept no more than three or four hours a night and was normally an early riser. There is a disputed tradition that Pitt slept on a truckle bed at the castle although, given his erratic sleeping habits, this seems perfectly feasible. All his endeavours on behalf of his country, however, took a marked toll on his health. Sir Walter Farquhar, an ex-army surgeon, arrived from Ramsgate to advise on his stomach disorder while the local apothecary, Dr Benjamin Hulke, attended to his gout. His treatment involved fitting 'rather a larger shoe than common on one of his feet'.

The Lord Warden made a return courtesy call on board *Amazon* and invited Nelson to dine. This the Admiral declined. He was conscious of his deformities and avoided society when in Deal. Nelson planned a further call at the castle later that same month although whether the visit was actually paid is not known. A myth that the two great leaders did meet at Walmer persisted into the last century. Indeed, a bedroom at the castle erroneously labelled 'Nelson's Room' displayed several relics, including a fine tallboy with a black band and an inscription – Sacred to Nelson. (Furniture, too, went into mourning when Nelson died). A rascally housekeeper, Mrs Allen, used to point out a dark stain on a table where Pitt and Nelson allegedly spilled wine when they caroused at the castle.

After Pitt had resigned as Prime Minister in 1799, owing to his dispute with the king over Catholic emancipation, he lived almost exclusively at Walmer until his return to power four years later. He forfeited Downing Street and was forced to sell his country seat, Holwood, although his creditors threatened to pursue him to Walmer and seize his horses, his carriages and his furniture. He remained for a time in poor spirits and became almost a recluse. Certainly his activities were innocuous - reading the classics, playing chess and indulging in a mild game of cards.

At the depth of his despair William Pitt received an unexpected visitor who gave this ailing, middle-aged, confirmed bachelor a new lease of life . . .

Pitt's lonely life at Walmer was transformed with the arrival of his eccentric niece, Lady Hester Stanhope, in August 1803. Lady Hester had endured a bizarre childhood in her Kentish home at Chevening. She had contrived an escape from her tyrannical father when she went to stay with her grandmother, the Dowager Countess of Chatham (Pitt's mother) at Burton Pynsent in Somerset. For a time she toured the Continent but her travels were curtailed by the renewal of the French Wars. Upon the demise of the kindly Lady Chatham, Pitt welcomed his talented, spirited, vivacious niece into his home. Their union surprised everyone. Yet it soon became apparent that Hester was devoted to Uncle William and their brief time spent together proved to be the happiest of both their lives.

Immediately, Hester found herself reunited with members of her family. Pitt had previously arranged for her sister, Griselda, to lodge in a cottage near Walmer Castle. Her younger brother, James, had transferred from the Navy to the Army and joined the Guards stationed at Dover; her favourite middle brother, Charles, was quartered at Ashford with the 57th Regiment while her eldest brother, Philip (Lord Mahon) had been appointed by Pitt Lieutenant-Governor of Dover Castle. Hester wrote:

> To express the kindness with which Mr Pitt welcomed my return and proposed my living with him would be impossible. Here, then, am I happy to a degree, exactly in the sort of society I most like. There are generally three or four men staying in the house, and we dine eight or ten every other day.

Hester was not at all daunted by the prospect of taking up residence along this vulnerable part of the coast. 'I should not be the least surprised any night to hear of the French attempting to land,' she wrote conspiratorially to a friend. 'Indeed, I expect it.' And she boldly predicted: 'Those who do succeed (in landing) will neither proceed nor return.'

Hester took a keen interest in Kent's new military defences and accompanied her uncle on reviews, expressing her admiration on how expertly his troops were drilled. She did not baulk at the hard riding involved in visiting the stations situated between fifteen or twenty miles apart, nor at remaining mounted perfectly still for hours at a time watching parades during appalling weather. 'I have been so drenched that as I stood, my boots made two spouting fountains above my knees,' she comically reported.

Lady Hester Stanhope
© National Portrait Gallery

After the collapse of the Peace of Amiens in 1803 Britain entered the final stage of the war with France. Immediately, Bonaparte renewed his frenzied measures for the invasion of England. He ordered new docks to be built, roads repaired and the ports enlarged. Boulogne was to be the main point of embarkation but flotillas were also asembled at Dunkirk and Cherbourg. At the height of hostilities the combined French fleet consisted of 3,500 vessels - gunboats, sloops, pinnaces, armed fishing smacks and flat-bottomed boats to be employed (rather precariously) as transports. Intelligence indicated that Napoleon planned to make his assault in the third week of October. Deal, clearly, was once more at the forefront of battle.

Britain had unwisely fallen into incredible somnolence during the period of illusory peace. The Fencibles, horse and foot, had been disbanded; the Militia were allowed to drift away and the Volunteers had gradually dwindled. The Regular Army comprised 90,000 infantry, 15,000 cavalry and 70,000 artillery

*William Pitt as Colonel Commandant of the
Cinque Ports Volunteers © English Heritage*

which was no match for Bonaparte's forces assembled on the Continent. The Admiralty had also reduced naval personnel from 130,000 to 70,000 and ships-of-the-line in commission from more than 100 to forty. When Addington, the new Prime Minister, introduced a Military Service Bill providing for the enrolling and training of volunteers, the tremendous response proved an embarrassment to his policy of prevarication. Not only did this prove his incompetence as a war leader but testified to the general public's determination to resist the evil Corsican.

Pitt resolutely refused to abandon his post at Walmer while wind and tide favoured invasion. He organised armed resistance along this accessible coast from Ramsgate to Rye. Hastily, the Lord Warden raised a new volunteer force at Walmer in July 1803. As Constable of Dover Castle he summoned a meeting of delegates from the Cinque Ports to discuss the urgent situation and once again he contributed £1000 from his depleted funds towards their expenses. He also took steps to secure enlistment to the new Army of Reserve. By the end of the year more than 10,000 Kentish men had enrolled as volunteers and a further 1,000 in the less popular Army of Reserve.

Pitt's Volunteers at Walmer, who assembled on a makeshift parade ground in a field at Sandown, consisted of two (later three) battalions which included a chaplain, Richard Harvey, and a surgeon, William Hulke. The Lieutenant Colonels commanding the two battalions were Pitt's nephew, Lord Mahon, and Lord Carrington, Captain of Deal Castle. Curiously, the Cinque Ports Volunteers appear to have been commanded by two colonels, for one of them was certainly Lord Hawkesbury. It was with great pride that William Pitt as Colonel Commandant rode ahead of his 3,500 irregular troops at drills, parades and reviews along the coast. A painting by Hubert depicts the Lord Warden on horseback, sabre drawn, sporting his scarlet uniform with white collar and facings and cocked hat with plume on the beach before Walmer Castle.

The Lord Warden's industry was not confined to land. He organised a fleet of Deal luggers and armed them according to their size with either 12 lb or 18 lb carronades. On 15 September thirty-five local fishing boats converted for warfare were reviewed by Pitt and his party, which inevitably included Lady Hester, from the ramparts of Walmer Castle. At noon the Lord Warden's flag was saluted by the boats anchored in a line opposite the castle and afterwards the Lord Warden embarked on a tour of inspection on board a lugger steered by Thomas Canney, Warden of the Pilots. This was Canney's last moment of glory for shortly afterwards he was drowned in a yachting accident. As Pitt deftly sailed in and out of the line of luggers he was greeted with hearty cheers by the crews. The fleet then performed some clever manoeuvres which satisfied Pitt that this country was ably prepared to repel Boney, 'both afloat and ashore'.

Lady Hester, naturally, was a member of the party rowed out to view a captured French gunboat anchored in the Downs and she frequently inspected troops stationed at Walmer. She reported, confidently:

> We are in almost daily expectation of the coming of the French and Mr Pitt's regiment is now nearly perfect enough to receive them. We have the famous 15th Light Dragoons in our barracks; also the Northampton and Berkshire

Militia. The first and last of these I command, and have an orderly dragoon whenever I please from the former, and the band of the latter . . .

All these military tours of inspections turned her head for she brazenly stated that she had been left in charge of the country's defences, acting as the official substitute for the Lord Warden whenever he was indisposed. 'I have my orders how to act in case of real alarm in Pitt's absence,' was her absurd claim.

Lady Hester's domestic talents, however, were indisputable and greatly valued by the Lord Warden. Whenever he suffered a renewed bout of illness - painful vomiting and stomache cramps - she proved an attentive nurse. Pitt stubbornly drank alarming quantities of port, madeira, claret and burgundy - all the most toxic wines - and in consequence his gout became exceedingly painful. Meticulously, he applied for a sick note from Mr Hulke each time he was absent from Parliament.

Deftly, Hester warded off society women determined upon matchmaking their unmarried daughters with England's most eligible bachelor statesman. She endeavoured to tidy up his papers carelessly strewn about the living rooms, cluttering up the sofa. Once Pitt panicked and commanded his gardener, Burfield, to search his library for missing documents contained in an elusive green bag, to be forwarded speedily to Downing Street. At night, Hester lay quietly awake listening for her uncle's footfall in the room where she slept directly beneath his bedroom . . .

Now there were lighter moments at the castle. On one occasion members of the Stanhope family were engaged in a cushion fight and were attempting to blacken their uncle's face with burnt cork. At that moment Lords Castelreagh and Liverpool were announced. These dour gentlemen were forced to wait until the mock battle had been fought and won.

Most importantly, Lady Hester assumed the role of hostess at Walmer Castle. Tall, stately, aristocratic with dazzling complexion and expressive features, she was a decided ornament to the bleak, desolate castle. Swiftly, she transformed Pitt's masculine domain into a warm, friendly, inviting home. Her uncle's hospitality still demonstrated his sadly reduced circumstances. All the same she nobly managed to entertain his guests - 'vulgar sea captains and ignorant militia colonels' - with two or three servants in attendance whereas before they had both been accustomed to a servant standing behind every chair waiting to serve each guest personally at table. Invariably, at these social gatherings Pitt was attired in his official Lord Warden's uniform of blue jacket with red collar and facings.

Often Hester was the only woman present at these intimate supper parties held at the castle on alternate nights. Pitt's visitors were mainly political luminaries - Addington, Castlereagh, Canning and Liverpool - all of whom appreciated her inspired wit, dry humour and gift of mimicry. She revelled in the attention she received upon these occasions and was flattered when her opinion was taken seriously. Pitt was often horrified at her indiscretions although he indulged her exuberance with a fond patience and forgave her boldest escapades.

King George, recognising that the country was facing a time of national crisis, recalled Pitt and asked him to form a government in the spring of 1804. Although

Pitt was enfeebled through ill health he was determined to pursue his aggressive war policy. The coalition government which included four future Prime Ministers (Portland, Perceval, Liverpool and Canning) was in effect a one-man administration. His exertions on behalf of his country contributed to his premature demise. Ironically, Pitt resumed his seat in the House of Commons on the day that Napoleon crowned himself Emperor in Paris (18 May 1804).

Lady Hester naturally accompanied her uncle to London. She was instantly recognised as the confidante of the Prime Minister and lionised among the high society of London. Once the King himself expressed admiration for her political talents. At the same time she was secretly nursing a broken heart. Hester was suffering from the unrequited love of the stylish Lord Granville Leveson-Gower (later First Earl Granville) who had been in constant attendance at Downing Street. She retreated to Walmer to heal her wounds but there her name was soon linked with another of Pitt's acquaintances, General Sir John Moore, recently returned from Egypt and placed in command of Shorncliffe Camp.

General Moore was handsome and graceful. He had perfect manners and a winning address. The Lord Warden frequently rode over to Sandgate to consult his young friend although Moore privately doubted that the nation was in such imminent peril. On one occasion Pitt introduced Moore to his niece and the pair began to enjoy a close intimacy. The gallant officer, who later took command of the British forces in Spain, remembered Hester when he lay dying at Corunna.

Ramparts, Walmer Castle

The Glen, created from a quarry by Lady Hester Stanhope

Lady Hester threw herself into a challenging project to keep her mind free from affairs of the heart - creating a woodland garden at Walmer Castle.

William Pitt was an accomplished landscape gardener and he must surely have begun to cultivate the land which surrounded the castle as sufficient funds became available. Curzon makes it clear that originally the ground owned by the Crown extended no further than the moat, but that successive Lords Warden privately purchased land from their neighbours. Pitt, too, gradually increased his boundaries. First he acquired the castle meadows extending northwards towards Walmer Lodge; then the kitchen and flower gardens, and lastly the paddock which reaches westwards from the castle towards the quarry from which stone for the castle was obtained. Probably, he began to 'beautify' these acquisitions, creating a kitchen garden, a walled garden and an oval lawn in the centre of which he planted clumps of limes.

Hester, realising her uncle's passion for gardening, began to improve upon his schemes during the late autumn and winter of 1804-1805. Artfully, she enlisted soldiers from the militia quartered at Dover Castle and set them to 'level, turf and plant' under her personal supervision. Burfield, the gardener, was despatched to Maidstone to collect hardy 'creepers, furze and broom' that would soften the wilderness swept by the harsh sea breezes. Hester even charmed the new Lord Guilford of Waldershare Park near Dover into donating prize trees and shrubs which she planted to tremendous effect in the deep quarry beyond the paddock. The picturesque effect of these fern-clad hollows at the western extremity of the castle grounds was judged to be a scene of 'great rustic beauty'. And it may have been this pretty dell referred to by William Cobbett when he passed through Walmer on horseback in 1823.

Hester's planting strayed beyond the quarry because she wrote to Mr Adams, Pitt's private secretary, telling him that the opportunity to acquire free trees and shrubs from Waldershare Park was too good to miss.

> I have been employing myself to cultivate a frightful barren bit of ground behind the castle . . . It may be years and years before such an offer of plants might again be made; and buy them you cannot, of a considerable size at least. Little things make no show.

Later, Hester recalled her uncle's pleasure at being shown her surprise garden when he returned from London during the Easter recess of 1805.

> When Mr Pitt came down, he dismounted from his horse, and ascending the staircase, saw through a window which commanded a view of the grounds the improvements that had been made . . . And, though it was just dinner-time, he would go out, and examine it all over, and then was so profuse in his praises.

Sadly, the chalk pit which Lady Hester converted into a 'pleasaunce' has fallen into neglect so that it is difficult to imagine The Glen in its former glory. Once more, Pitt took immense pride in his improvements. 'The picture from my windows this morning is as delightful as in the middle of summer,' he wrote to a friend on a mild day in February, 1803.

The enfeebled Prime Minister was determined to continue with his scheme to strengthen coastal defences against French invasion and he summoned a Council of War at Walmer Castle. Present were Lord Melville, First Lord of the Admiralty, General Hope and Sir Home Popham who was in charge of the Sea Fencibles. They masterminded a plan to destroy the French flotilla still anchored at Boulogne. Three smacks, loaded with barrels of gunpowder and covered with flint stones, were silently manoeuvred a short distance within the coast of France. These were then ignited by five sloops equipped as fireships and towed within the French harbour. Rumour persisted that forty French ships had been destroyed although *The Times* belied this claim. In reality not a single enemy ship had been affected by this cunning ploy.

Later these war leaders were joined by General Sir John Moore, commander of Shorncliffe Camp; Sir Sidney Smith, commander of the naval fleet stationed off the coast of Holland; Lord Keith, commander of the squadron in the Downs and General Don, commander of an imminent diversionary expedition to Germany. Their itinerary included a debate concerning a scheme for the attack upon the French flotilla at Boulogne. Experiments were conducted in their presence - Congreve's combustible rocket and Francis' combustible bomb - which were seriously considered for further attacks upon the enemy fleet.

During his last week at Walmer Pitt was experimenting with a secret weapon - a torpedo. An American, Robert Fulton, arrived on 14 October to demonstrate his deadly double torpedo, which he called a catamarin, in the Small Downs. Inquisitive crowds watched his careful preparations although the real test was held on the following day in the presence of high ranking officers of the Army and Navy. Pitt had been recalled to London on urgent business but Lady Hester remained behind to report on the success of this novel demonstration.

Late that autumn afternoon Fulton's experiment took place in earnest. An area of calm water had been cordoned off where a captured Danish brig, *Dorothea,* lay anchored about one mile offshore. At a signal from Fulton - he waved a handkerchief tied to his cane - two fast ten-oared galleys rowed out commanded by Lieutenant Robinson. In the stern of each vessel was a torpedo – quaintly described as a 'globe or coffer' – loaded with 180 lb of gunpowder, attached to the same stout cable. As the galleys approached the *Dorothea* they separated - one kept to the larboard, the other the starboard - but remained parallel so that the long rope became taut and the two torpedoes were released simultaneously. These were carried by the tide under the hull of the brig where they wrapped themselves round the anchor chain. Their clockwork detonators were timed for fifteen minutes.

Suddenly, there was a tremendous explosion. *Dorothea* was thrown into the air, she split in two and disappeared without trace in a seething cauldron. The spectators watched in stunned silence as wreckage floated to the surface. Fulton and his party retired to the castle to toast their success and found that several windows had been shattered by the blast. A later attempt was made to set the French ships alight by 'sky-rockets', but this proved a complete fiasco since only a couple of houses near the harbour caught fire.

Pitt's government approved Fulton's underwater bombs and recognised their effectiveness in destroying enemy ships riding at anchor. A lucrative contract was signed and a quantity of torpedoes was ordered to be manufactured at Chatham Dockyard. Fulton's further invention of a miniature submarine, *Nautilus,* was unwisely ignored by the Admiralty. He returned to New Jersey where he received recognition as the pioneer of the first commercially-successful paddle steamer. Meanwhile, Admiral Lord St Vincent, who had become the new First Lord of the Admiralty, dismissed both torpedoes and submarines as an unneccessary mode of warfare.

In late autumn 1805 Lady Hester left Walmer to join her uncle at Putney where they rented Bowling Green House in the heart of the London countryside. The Prime Minister's health continued to deteriorate so he reluctantly accepted his doctors' advice to take the healing waters at Bath. Pitt left town huddled in the corner of his carriage, wrapped in Hester's eiderdown against the cold early that December. News of Napoleon's defeat at Trafalgar - tempered by Nelson's death - lifted his spirits temporarily and upon his return to the City he received a fleeting visit from his friend, Lord Wellesley, recently retired as Governor-General of India. His indomitable spirit eventually succumbed to his painful illness, hastened by overwork and excess of alcohol, on 23 January 1806 - twenty-five years to the day when he had first taken his seat in the House of Commons.

During his lifetime Pitt had been constantly criticised by certain members of the cabinet for making expensive preparations against an invasion which never materialised. He was lampooned by the press and ridiculed in cartoons. One caricature depicts Pitt and Napoleon as fighting cocks threatening each other from rival clifftops across the Channel, while another pictures Napoleon being rowed over to Walmer Castle where he is challenged by Pitt, wearing Volunteer uniform, leaning over the battlements and presenting a musket: 'Who goes there?' Nevertheless, the exiled Emperor, who had even struck a medal to sport for his triumphal entry into London, subsequently revealed to one of his captors that his planned invasion had, indeed, focused on the coast between Margate and Deal.

Long after she had left Walmer, Hester Stanhope retained an interest in local affairs. Pitt's elderly housekeeper was married to a respected Deal boatman, Peter Atkins, whose lugger, *Noble*, assisted in the daring rescue of the *Endeavour*, a West India ship, homeward-bound, wrecked on the Goodwin Sands in 1807. Disgracefully, the boatman was arrested for having appropriated a missing cask of rum from the wreck and charged with 'piracy upon the high seas'. Tried in London, he was sentenced to death. Convinced of his innocence, Hester campaigned for his release. The boatman received a pardon conditional upon his quitting the country. He emigrated to Rio de Janeiro where Sir Sidney Smith, who had been a frequent visitor to Walmer Castle, placed him in charge of the Navy Stores belonging to the British Admiralty.

After her uncle's death Hester was again homeless and her life thrown into turmoil. Realising that she had no future in Britain she began a self-imposed exile and turned tragedy into triumph as she toured extensively throughout the Near East. She was the first of the celebrated nineteenth century women explorers and also the first European to venture deep into the Sahara.

She faced danger from shipwreck, war and plague and befriended kings and beggars alike when she visited Egypt, Syria and Lebanon before she finally became a recluse, walled up by her own command, in a crumbling monastery in Djoun. Her exceptional horsemanship, her charitable acts and her absolute courage earned her the regard of even the the most hostile Bedouin tribesman who dubbed Lady Hester Stanhope 'The Queen of the Desert'.

ROYAL MARINES

'Soldiers that serve at sea'

ROYAL MARINES - 'soldiers that serve at sea' - have until the last decade always had a strong presence in the town since their formation in the reign of Charles II. Deal witnessed the evolution of the Corps from humble beginnings to one of the best disciplined and most effective fighting forces in the world.

During the turmoil of the Civil War, when England was a nation divided against itself, the proportion of seamen to soldiers had fallen drastically. At the

Junior Band of the Royal Marines trooping after church parade at South Barracks in 1976 © Crown copyright

Restoration of the Monarchy in 1660 an attempt was made to redress the balance by James, Duke of York (later King James II) who held the post of Lord High Admiral. At that time a second war with Holland seemed imminent.

During a meeting of the Privy Council in the Palace of Whitehall on 25 October 1664 King Charles directed that:

> Twelve hundred land souljers be forthwith raysed to be in readiness to be distributed into his Majesty's Fleets prepared for sea service.

This new regiment of sea-soldiers was to be known as the Duke of York and Albany's Maritime Regiment of Foote or the Lord High Admiral's Regiment. It was the first of several Regiments of Marines, as they were styled, which were formed between this time and 1755 when the present Corps was established in continuity. Initially, The Admiral's Regiment was part of the Army under General Monck, Duke of Albemarle, later created Admiral, who led his men into their first battle against the Dutch at the North Foreland.

Colonel Sir William Killigrew, nephew of the Duke of Albemarle, was commanded to beat up drums and raise 200 soldiers in the City by the Lord Mayor of London. Further licences were issued in 1666, 1667 and 1672 and from these precedents it became the custom for colonels of the Regiments of Marines to recruit in the capital. Today, Royal Marines retain their right to march through the City of London, where the original regiment was raised from the trained bands, 'bayonets fixed, drums beating and colours flying'.

From their early days detachments of marines have been stationed at Deal and Walmer. At the commencement of the Second Dutch War, Charles toured the district and his brother, the Duke of York, was placed in command of the Channel fleet. In 1665 a Yellow Company was quartered at Deal Castle under the command of Captain Silius Titus. The platoon had been entrusted with the defence of the Navy Yard and thus the first links between town and Corps were formed.

Colonel Titus (1622-1704) was a turncoat who allegedly wrote an inflammatory pamphlet, *Killing No Murder*, that incited people to assassinate Oliver Cromwell although Titus had himself at one time championed the Parliamentary cause. He was denounced by Cromwell as a Royalist agent when it was known that he had devised a plan for King Charles's escape from Carisbrooke Castle. Charles implored him:

> I pray you, thinke which way I shall remove the Bar out of my Window, without noise & unpercaeved; & what tyme it will take me to doe it.

When he became a Gentleman of the Bedchamber to Charles II, Titus used his position to persuade the king to build a Royal Observatory at Greenwich to study the position of fixed stars in order to determine longitude.

Resolutely, Titus defended the Kent coast against Dutch invasion even though his troops were hampered by the plague. In 1670 he sold his commission to Francis Digby, also a marine, who subsequently perished in a battle against the Dutch at Sole Bay. Intriguingly, this was the first occasion when the Lord

Admiral's Regiment was referred to as marines. 'Those Marines of whom I so oft have wrote you,' reported one ship's captain, 'behaved themselves stoutly.'

Laker rehearses a comical story about 'a fiddling boy' who was pressed by seamen into service around this time. Quick-witted, he pretended that he belonged to the Yellow Company at Deal Castle. In timely fashion, the infantry did indeed come to his rescue and there was a tremendous fracas between the soldiers and the sailors on the beach. Law enforcement officers eventually arrived to break up the affray and the lad escaped with just a few bruises . . . and a broken fiddle!

During the late seventeenth and eighteenth centuries marines were constantly deployed to defend the Navy Yard, often referred to as the King's Buildings. They were quartered in the Old Barracks, situated behind Admiralty House in Five Bell Lane (now Queen Street) which were demolished in the nineteenth century. One responsiblity was to guard gold bullion, accumulated from privateering and prize capture during wars, which was stored in a strongroom in Admiralty House before transference under military escort to London. Wisely, gold was landed when ships were anchored in the Downs to prevent possible recapture by enemy warships or privateers.

First permanent home of Royal Marines in Kent was established at Chatham in 1755 and the barracks occupied in 1779. Divisions were also at Portsmouth, Plymouth and Woolwich. The Woolwich Division was short-lived and closed in

East Barracks, originally a naval hospital, which became
the home of the Royal Marines Band

South Barracks

1869. Deal, because of its proximity to the Continent, has been closely associated with the corps since its formation. Records from the old Navy Yard reveal that Royal Marines from Chatham and Woolwich were on duty in Deal, being quartered in the town until the Deal Depot was established in 1861. Deal Depot was the last Royal Marines establishment to survive in Kent.

Originally, the uniforms for marines were surprisingly colourful. A private serving when the Corps was founded wore a long yellow jacket with silver buttons and turned-up red sleeves, plain brown hat, a jabot, silver-buckled shoes and a satchel in which he carried musket shot. Officers of that period, who had the distinction of wearing a feather in their caps, each carried a sword and pistols. Yellow, incidentally, was the favourite colour of the Lord High Admiral.

In 1685 the Duke of York succeeded his brother to the throne as King James II and the style of the Regiment was altered to the Prince of Denmark's Regiment after James's indolent son-in-law. The colour of the uniform was subsequently changed to red. A sergeant in 1780 wore a crimson cutaway coat and grey trousers with black cocked hat, boots and spats. Bright uniforms rendered the Marines an easy target for snipers. It was not until after the Indian campaigns of the Victorian era, however, that their fighting uniforms evolved into a sensible dull khaki, providing maximum camouflage. The Admiralty insisted that each division had its own tailors and bootmakers and all ranks were measured personally for their ceremonial uniforms, a practice which continues to this present day.

After the French Revolution the new Republican regime announced that all governments were their enemies, and inevitably declared war on Britain. At the commencement of hostilities expeditionary forces were despatched simultaneously to the Low Countries and Toulon where the marines first encountered a young French artillery captain named Napoleon Bonaparte. During the three French Wars, which stretched from 1793 to 1815, these brightly-uniformed sea soldiers occupied the vulnerable position of manning the riggings of England's Royal Navy fleet. Afloat they served with equal distinction in the battles of Glorious First of June (1794), at St Vincent and Camperdown (1797), also in Nelson's victories at the Nile (1798) and Copenhagen (1801). When war with France halted temporarily in 1802, George III conferred a lasting mark of his approbation upon the corps by commanding that in future the men be styled 'Royal Marines'.

At Trafalgar, 2,600 Royal Marines were present and, owing to their exposed position on deck and aloft, their casualties were high. It was a chance shot from an enemy sniper that felled Nelson. Mortally wounded, he was carried below deck by Sergeant Secker of the Royal Marines. At the close of that fateful day, 21 October 1805, the French Commander, Villeneuve, proffered his sword in submission to Captain Atcherly of the Royal Marines who had boarded *Bucentaure* with a corporal and two privates. Nelson's body - pickled in rum - was brought back to England aboard HMS *Victory* for burial at St Paul's Cathedral. His flagship rode at anchor under a north-east gale in the Downs for three days in December. All the Deal, Walmer and Kingsdown boats flew their flags and pennants at half-mast in respect for the dead hero.

When George IV decided to present new Colours to the Royal Marines in 1827, he was advised of more than 100 notable actions in which they had excelled.

North Barracks

The Commandant's galley

The King commanded that a globe encircled with laurels should be their distinguishing badge as the most appropriate emblem for the corps 'whose duties carried them to all parts of the globe in every quarter of which they had earned laurels by their valour and good conduct'. He also directed that his own cypher, GR IV, should be carried in perpetuity in addition to the motto *Per Mare, Per Terram* (By sea, by land).

Peculiarly, the Royal Marines with the Royal Navy are accorded the privilege of remaining seated during the Loyal Toast. This tradition arose from those days spent serving aboard the old wooden battleships when there was little headroom between decks to stand and toast the sovereign's health.

The exploits of the Royal Marines through the ages are legion. From the close of the Napoleonic Wars until the First World War they were rarely absent from active service, being engaged in the numerous small wars that accompanied the expansion and consolidation of the British Empire. During the Victorian age of Imperialism the Royal Marines saw action in Burma, Mexico, Japan, Canada and New Zealand. They participated in the Indian Mutiny, the three Chinese Wars, the Crimean War, the Zulu Wars and the Boer War. More recently, they took part in the amphibious landings to recapture the Falklands Islands in 1982, and in Sierra Leone in 2000.

Walmer Barracks, the home locally of the Royal Marines, appears to have been constructed for the Army shortly after the French Revolution. They were built in anticipation of Napoleon's invasion on the orders of Prime Minister William Pitt, then Lord Warden of the Cinque Ports. Troops were immediately drafted to this exposed coastline and billeted in the three castles or at neighbouring farms and inns. Additionally, there were small army barracks in Queen Street and West Street to accommodate French prisoners-of-war who were employed in the construction of the new army barracks.

The actual date of the foundation of Walmer Barracks is not certain but in the accounts of the Barracks Master General for December 1795 items are mentioned indicating that these buildings were already under construction for infantry and cavalry. Originally, they were intended for accommodation of 1100 foot and a squadron of cavalry with stabling for sixty-three horses. The combined North, South and East Barracks have extensive parade grounds and occupy an area of about twenty-eight acres. Almost immediately after war was declared with France, the barracks were occupied by the Army. The first occupants were the 15th Light Dragoons but following the second Peace of Paris in 1815 many troops were withdrawn from Lower Walmer.

South Barracks was then used partly as headquarters for the Coastal Blockade employed in combating smuggling. When the Blockade Men were disbanded South Barracks continued to serve as a Coast Guard station until 1840 when, together with North Barracks, it was occupied by a detachment of Royal Artillery. For almost thirty years the barracks were occupied by line regiments until in 1869 the buildings were transferred to the Admiralty in exchange for barracks and other property in Woolwich. Henceforth, they formed a full scale Depot Royal Marines, Deal.

The first reference to the foundation of the Deal Depot was on 7 May 1861. This deals with the authorisation of stores which included 'coals, candles and straw' for the use of the ranks about to occupy Deal Barracks. Four days later detachments arrived from Chatham and Woolwich to form the nucleus of the new establishment and the following Saturday 100 recruits from these divisions arrived to start training. Among those despatched were a captain, a lieutenant, nine sergeants, seven corporals, thirty-five privates and 'three undisciplined second lieutenants'. These ranks were accommodated in part of the Royal Naval Hospital (later known as East Barracks) which had housed small detachments of Royal Marines ever since the Crimean War.

Shortly after occupation of the Walmer Barracks a Beating Order was issued by the Officers' Mess Committee to muster recruits in the town. 'These are to authorise you by beat of drum or otherwise to raise volunteers at Deal, for Her Majesty's Corps of Royal Marines, for the purpose of completing the said Corps to its establishment; and all Her Majesty's Justices of the Peace, Constables, and other Civil Officers whom it may concern, are hereby required to be assisting you in providing quarters, impressing carriages and otherwise as there shall be occasion.' Eligible recruits were to be forwarded for approval to Chatham.

The main administration block was in part of South (or Cavalry) Barracks which still retained tethering rings from the time it had stabled horses for the Army. The classic facade of the Infantry Barracks and Officers' Mess still faces Dover Road. Formerly, there was a garden at the rear but the stables and coach house remain intact. The Gymnasium, Armoury, Sergeants' Mess, Recreation and Reading Rooms - and even a miniature rifle range - were all added once the Royal Marines were in full occupation. The corps recruited separately for two divisions - the Royal Marines Light Infantry (RMLI) and the Royal Marines Artillery (RMA) - until these fighting forces were amalgamated into the Royal Marines in 1923.

Originally, North Barracks was also built as a military hospital. It is marked as such on 'A Map of the Hundreds of Cornilo and Bewsborough with the Liberty of the Town of Deal' c1800. Line regiments occupied the barracks until

1840 when these were replaced by a detachment of Royal Artillery. The building consisted of three main blocks, joined by an imposing colonnade, facing the parade. Old stables and tack rooms remain backing onto the strip of land bordering the boundary wall known as the Soldiers' Burial Ground. There is further burial ground behind East Barracks. It is estimated that 2500 souls are interred in the combined graveyards, and parish registers meticulously record the names of British soldiers, Russian prisoners-of-war, convicts from prison hulks and seamen aboard the Coastal Blockade guard ships. The most frequent entry reads 'body washed ashore', and these anonymous victims of the French Wars were buried in open pits. One of those laid to rest was Algernon Stephens (died 1865) Lieutenant of the 1st Royals, who carried the colours at Waterloo.

The Globe Theatre was built around the turn of the nineteenth and twentieth centuries. It boasted a raked stage and a high tower for flying in scenery. From the late 1940s until the early 1960s it was regularly used as a cinema and for performances of variety and light opera, including Gibert and Sullivan. During summer, a professional theatre company presented weekly repertory and there were frequent performances with famous actors prior to long runs in London's West End. The celebrated Sergeants' Mess pantomimes commenced here in 1947 to raise funds for charities. The first panto, *Cinderella*, was written by Captain Wilberforce and Dennis Chinery, the latter being a dentist in the Infirmary. The last, *Aladdin*, was performed in 1995. Invariably, the orchestra was from the School of Music who had to wait for the 'top brass' to be seated in the front row of the tiny balcony before they could strike up their opening chords.

The foundation stone of the Depot church, dedicated to Saint Michael and All Angels, was laid by Lord George Hamilton, Captain of Deal Castle and a former

Babes in the Wood at the Globe Theatre

First Lord of the Admiralty, in 1905, and two years later it was consecrated by the Archbishop of Canterbury. Stained glass windows commemorate the lives of distinguished Royal Marines while memorial boards recall bandsmen lost in two world wars. The colours of Woolwich Division proudly fluttered from the ceiling of this mammoth building which could accommodate 1000 worshippers. St Michael's replaced the Victorian Garrison Chapel and School in Canada Road. This school was intended for the children of Royal Marines instructors and staff and it was staffed by Naval Warrant Officers assisted by Royal Marines SNCOs. There was both a junior and an infant department joined by a playground where Royal Marine cadets paraded the Union flag on Empire days. The school closed in the 1920s when the chapel was converted into a concert hall.

An infirmary, now demolished, was built at the turn of the century to replace the ancient Royal Naval Hospital. This was situated in Blenheim Road on the site of an old drill field where Elvin once observed the gyrations of the unique bicycle platoon. The Bicycle Corps, a separate army unit, was formed around 1850. Members were all volunteers and they were required to provide their own bicycles (a few troops rode tricycles). Alas, they never saw action although they provided valuable experience to the Army Cyclist Corps in World War One. Royal Marines Commandos employed bicycles in the Second World War.

Additionally, a swimming pool filled by tidal sea water was built on the seaward side of the Strand in 1892. Its construction was a result of sixty-eight Royal Marines drowning through their inability to swim during the collision of HMS *Victoria* and HMS *Camperdown* off Tripoli in 1893. The first Superintendent of Swimming was Lieutenant HD Farquarson, RMLI, who had saved the life of Midshipman (later Admiral) Jellicoe during the disaster, for which bravery he was awarded a bronze medal from the Royal Humane Society. The intricate

Young Royal Marine recruits at the time of World War One

Church parade at Deal in June, 1913

ornamental brickwork depicting the globe surrounded by laurels was rescued when this prime site was turned into a doctor's surgery, and is now displayed at Deal's Maritime Museum.

East Barracks, which dates from 1812, is located along the Strand and faces Walmer foreshore. It is a long, elegant, brick building surmounted by a fine cupola and at one time all the windows were shuttered in Continental fashion. There was once a large boat shed and at the rear an old parade ground. Grim and bleak on a winter's morning, hemmed in by stables, stores and an ominously named Dead House, it is easy to imagine the harsh discipline of the Army which went unchecked in former times.

The history of East Barracks is peculiar. Formerly there stood on this exposed site an old hospital which is described as having belonged to 'a gentleman of the name of Leith' and it may originally have been a French prison. Care of the sick and wounded soldiers and sailors landed at Deal assumed great importance in the late eighteenth century since many major battles were fought in the Downs. It proved impossible to find accommodation for these unfortunate victims of war until two naval surgeons, Leith and Packe, bargained with the Admiralty to 'victual and render medical assistance to the sick and wounded' around 1776. As 'contractor' to Deal Hospital, Leith received seven shillings per week for every patient entrusted to his care and soon the welfare of these men was secure.

In 1809, during a violent storm, the hospital was struck by lightning and rent from roof to foundation. The authorities decided upon the demolition of the old building and the erection of a more commodious hospital upon the same site. Accordingly, the foundation stone of the Royal Naval Hospital was laid 'in the presence of all the officers' by Commander Perser Dowers on 4 June 1812. By the end of that year the building was sufficiently advanced to receive its first 100

Royal Marines; Depot Band, Deal

patients. After the cessation of the French Wars the Admiralty took over possession of the Naval Hospital which it continued to operate until 1900.

A description of the hospital in 1890 appeared in Charles Elvin's *Records of Walmer*: 'The hospital is a fine building, situated on the Strand close to Deal, and occupying, with its various accessories, an area of about four and a half acres. Its pedimented front, 365 feet in length, which faces towards the sea, has a plain portico in the centre; and the roof is surmounted by a cupola containing a clock with four dials.' Weights and chains for this clock were encased and passed through the barrack rooms below. During the Second World War the cupola was used as a spotters' post to watch for enemy aircraft approaching Deal. Inside there is still wartime graffiti scratched on the wall.

Later additions included 'a house for the dead and the insane' which was eventually put to a more congenial use as a musical instrument repair shop. The old operating theatre and autopsy room, an oval shaped extension beneath the clock tower, still remains with its gruesome slate slabs. There is also evidence of an underground mortuary reputedly haunted by ghosts of past casualties. Royal Buildings, southwards, originally accommodated the Superintendent and surgeons and, afterwards, the Commandant and Senior Officers of the depot. The Commandant boasted not only a private open carriage but a sleek, white-painted galley.

The Depot Band was formed in 1890. It was run on the same lines as the three other divisional bands (Chatham, Plymouth and Portsmouth) but was regarded as an independent unit and virtually did its own recruiting. Musicians joined this band from other service bands, frequently the Army, or even from civilian life, and there they remained for the rest of their careers. Bandsmen wore small round caps with peaks edged with gold lace, and scarlet tunics with gold-laced edging and black trimmings. A Victorian bandmaster would have marched with a variety of instruments including french horns, piccolo, flute, oboe, clarinet, bassoon, cornets, trombones, baritone, euphonium, bombardons and drums. The Depot Band was abolished in 1930 and replaced by the Royal Naval School of Music which had been formed to produce continuous service musicians for the Royal Navy in 1903 at Portsmouth. At that time a Major Royal Marines (called the Superintendent) was in charge of the School of Music which was self-contained in East Barracks.

When the Royal Naval School of Music returned to Deal in 1950 after evacuation to the Isle of Man during the Second World War it was restyled The Royal Marines School of Music. East Barracks became its home and parts were conveniently converted into a music library, practice rooms and instrumental workshops. The Commandant, Royal Marines School of Music, was also appointed Commanding Officer of the Depot. Henceforth, the band service administration on a worldwide basis was carried out alongside the organisation of the rest of the Depot in South Barracks.

Universally, the Royal Marines School of Music is regarded as one of the finest musical companies in the world. It is required to form and train bands for service in the Royal Navy and Royal Marines, providing military, orchestral and dance bands on every conceivable occasion. Their repertoire covers every category of music including jazz, pop, classical, light concert music and big band sound. A high degree of versatility is required because only small bands can embark on ships. Also their prime duty is with the Royal Navy which means that a large percentage of their service remains at sea.

The purpose of the band is still to provide music for ceremonial occasions but in addition musicians are also trained soldiers and they provide a key military role as part of a fighting force. They were involved in manning the gunnery fire control system, an important and dangerous duty, during the Second World War. The casualty rate was phenomenal with more than 200 bandsmen killed in action on battleships. From the 1960s they were also trained in musketry at the ancient Kingsdown Range. Their usual role in wartime, however, is to act as stretcher-bearers and first-aiders, which skills they were required to exercise during recent conflicts in the Gulf and Falkland Islands. More peaceably, Junior Musicians, Junior Marines and RM Cadets combined at one time to present their own military and musical tattoo at Deal.

The origins of the Royal Marines Band Service stretches back to the days of Drake and Hawkins when drummers signalled the changing watches or beat the men to quarters. In the six companies of the Duke of York and Albany's Maritime Regiment of Foot - the forerunners of the Royal Marines - the Colour and Drum provided a rallying point in close battle. For this reason even today it is the drums and bugles of the Royal Marines Buglers Branch which lead the band on ceremonial parades. The regimental march of the Royal Marines is *A Life On The Ocean Wave*. Ironically, this music, which is essentially British, was inspired by the New York waterfront where composer, Henry Russell, was walking with poet, Epps Sergeant. It was transposed from a ballad to a march by Jacob Kappey, Bandmaster of the Chatham Division, who was German. It was adopted as the regimental march in 1882. The tune revered by the Victorians continues to electrify modern audiences.

During the 1950s, Lieutenant Colonel Sir Vivian Dunn was appointed to the newly-created post of Principal Director of Music for the amalgamated Royal Marines Band Service. Wherever he served, Sir Vivian endeavoured to raise the standard of civilian music and he popularised military music among residents by introducing regular band concerts. Soon after his retirement he was awarded an EMI gold disc to mark the sale of more than one million records by bands of the Royal Marines. For his service to four sovereigns aboard the royal yachts and on their tours of the Commonwealth he became the only military musician to be knighted. He was succeeed by Lieutenant Colonel Paul Neville in 1968.

Further honours were bestowed upon senior members of the corps by their appointment to the Captaincy of Deal Castle – General Sir Norman Tailyour in 1972 and General Sir Ian Harrison in 1979. Councillor 'Nobby' Sargent was the first Royal Marine to be elected Mayor of Deal (in 1982) and Corps Drum Major Charles Bowden - the longest serving Drum Major in any service - was awarded the British Empire Medal in 1957.

The Depot at Deal has been used exclusively for the basic training of recruits throughout its long history. Probably the most important event that took place during the First World War was the formation of the legendary 4th Battalion for the daring raid on Zeebrugge on 23 April 1918. Training was intensive under the Commanding Officer, Lieutenant Colonel Elliot, who was killed in action. This memorable attack, which succeeded in scuttling German U-boats, took place on St George's Day. Royal Marines of the 4th Battalion stormed the Mole while the Royal Navy blocked and destroyed the harbour. There were such terrific casualties that the Admiralty decreed 4th Battalion should never be reformed. The Royal Marines won two VCs for collective gallantry awarded by ballot in this audacious raid.

The training of 4th Battalion was the occasion for a visit to the Depot by King George V in March 1918. After his tour of inspection he directed that the senior squad should in future be designated the King's Squad. In addition the best all-round recruit should be styled the King's Badgeman and wear the royal cypher on his shoulder throughout his service.

From the outbreak of the Second World War an emergency organisation came into existence and a holding battalion was formed. During 1940, hit and run raids by German aircraft became so frequent that they were a serious harassment to wartime training. At St Margaret's Bay the Royal Marines Siege Regiment manned two huge cross-Channel guns christened 'Winnie' and 'Pooh'. The first shells directed on France from this country were fired by this unit which remained operational for the duration of the war. Also coastal defence guns at Deal Castle were manned initially by Royal Marines. Numerous Royal Marines units were trained at the depot, including the revolutionary 40 Commando before the epic raid on Dieppe on 19 August 1942. The Honorary Freedom of Deal was conferred on the Royal Marines in 1945.

After the war a change in defence policies affected reorganisation of the corps. In 1950 the Chatham Division was disbanded leaving only the Portsmouth and Plymouth Divisions. Further adjustments were made in 1970 when Portsmouth and Plymouth Groups became Training Group and Headquarters Commando Forces, respectively. In 1977 Deal Depot, renamed Royal Marines, Deal, hosted

102

the reformed 41 Commando which was actively involved in internal security duties in Northern Ireland. The Royal Marines ranks were reduced to 8,000 while at the same time the corps retained its amphibious role and remained a formidable force of highly-trained soldiers fiercely proud of their history and traditions.

The links between town and corps were never more evident than when the IRA detonated a high explosive bomb in North Barracks on Friday 22 September 1989. At 8.25am, just as members of the Staff Band were changing into uniform prior to early morning practice, a time bomb exploded. This was considered the worst bomb attack in mainland Britain after the bomb which targeted Prime Minister Margaret Thatcher and members of her cabinet during their annual conference at Brighton in 1984. Eleven bandsmen died.

Emergency services were instantly alerted and launched a massive rescue operation. Ten powerful cranes were commandeered from the Channel Tunnel site at Folkestone to lift tons of rubble from the shattered buildings; 100 firemen with fifteen fire engines searched the debris with thermal imaging cameras while a fleet of ambulances ferried casualties to Kent hospitals. These rescuers were joined by policemen, clergymen and military personnel plus members of the Junior Band who had been practising on the adjacent parade ground. The Duke of Edinburgh, Captain General of Royal Marines, accompanied by Countess Mountbatten, visited the scene of devastation and comforted the survivors in hospital. The prime suspects for the atrocity were two Irish men posing as holiday fishermen who had rented a terraced house in neighbouring Campbell Road. They have never been apprehended.

Gaps in the band after the IRA bomb © Gregory Holyoake

One week to the day - without formal notice - the Royal Marines marched through the town. Crowds lined the route to cheer the proud procession of musicians dressed in their familiar blue uniform with red sashes and white helmets. The sun glinted on polished instruments as they turned into the seafront past Deal Castle. The salute was taken by Commandant General Sir Martin Garrod at the Timeball Tower. Bravely, gaps had been left where the murdered bandsmen would normally have been positioned. The eleven musicians are commemorated by an elegant bandstand on Walmer Green where an annual concert performed by the Band of Royal Marines Portsmouth attracts a vast audience born out of long affection for the corps.

When Mrs Thatcher later toured the devastation at the barracks she made the famous pronouncement that a proposed transference of the Royal Marines to Portsmouth would 'tear the heart out of the town'. Sadly, this earned the Depot only a temporary reprieve. Inevitably, the obvious difficulty of maintaining the security of such a vast site with depleting numbers resulted in the decision by the Defence Secretary, Michael Soames, to close Walmer Barracks on 31 March 1996. Before they moved the Royal Marines School of Music performed a public Massed Bands Beat Retreat ceremony on the green at South Barracks. A final parade along the Strand ended when the Staff Band marched through the clock gate of East Barracks at sunset thus closing more than three centuries of association with the Royal Marines at Deal.

ST GEORGE'S CHURCH

'A marvel of construction'

ST GEORGE'S CHURCH, intended as a chapel-of-ease to St Leonard's, is a handsome Queen Anne structure which graces the High Street. Building commenced in 1707, but after a short time funds for the new church ran out and for ten years the four walls stood open to the sky.

The community of Upper Deal and the rapidly-expanding population of Lower Deal that had risen alongside the seashore, had for centuries attended divine service at St Leonard's. A narrow, secluded lane known as Church Path, which commenced at Primrose Alley – once called Primrose Hill – opposite the present pier, led from the beach directly to the parish church. This mile-long trek was a great inconvenience to those whose livelihood depended upon the sea, particularly sailors who might be stationed for a few hours only in the port while awaiting a favourable wind to carry their ship on a long voyage.

Chief advocate for a new church was a former mayor, Thomas Powell, who found, it would appear, an equally zealous opponent in the person of Tobias Bowles, Deal's second mayor. Their conflict was satirised in a witty poem entitled *Deal In An Uproar*:

> Powell by whose activity and care
> The town got leave to build a house of prayer,
> Spar'd neither cost nor pains to bring about
> What those against him labour'd to fling out . . . '

According to this lampoon the main objection by Bowles, 'that lump of Magistracy', was that 'the Pile' would cost an estimated £1,300.

> Toby was loth to spend so much in heaven,
> But gave his vote to have it done for seven.
> Accordingly the drunken Corporation,
> Who prized their liquor more than their Salvation,
> Decreed that out of reverence to the chair,
> Seven should be given to God, and six elsewhere.

It may well be that this anonymous poem is every bit as libellous as the one it imitates (Defoe's *Deal In A Storm*). Far from being a member of a 'drunken Corporation', Tobias Bowles was pious, generous and responsible. Certainly, he was an important benefactor of the town because he had built a gallery at his own expense over the chancel at St Leonard's. Moreover, his name appears on the committee formed to petition the Archbishop of Canterbury to build a new chapel and his family gave freely to the project. Admittedly, the erection of the chapel was fraught with difficulties and the election of the mayor and corporation hinged upon this issue for the ten years it took to complete.

A petition was drawn up in May, 1706, to present to Archbishop Thomas Tenison to erect a chapel-of-ease and the committee appointed to oversee the building comprised the rector, the Reverend Henry Gerard, the mayor, Benjamin Hulke and members of the first Corporation of Deal. Land purchased for £80 was described as 'lying on the west side of the town, near the beer pump'. The foundations were laid by a local builder, Samuel Simmons, on 21 July, 1707.

Admiral Sir Cloudesley Shovell
© Rochester Guildhall

A subscription list was opened so that townsfolk might contribute towards the expense of their chapel. The Admiralty was approached - naval seamen, after all, would be the principal beneficiaries - and their Lordships agreed to subscribe once the walls had reached nine feet in height. Champion of the cause was Admiral Sir Cloudesley Shovell, who owned lands at Ham and Poulton and whose fleet frequently anchored in the Downs. He was the finest seaman and fighting admiral of the reign of Queen Anne, and had come to national prominence in the wars against pirates on the Barbary Coast. Shovell's reputation has been eclipsed only by that of Nelson. Alas, he was shipwrecked because of the imprecision of early eighteenth century navigation and drowned with 2000 men off the Scilly Isles in the winter of 1707. Sadly, interest in the project by the Royal Navy waned after his untimely demise.

The chapel remained in this unfinished state for the next ten years 'an object of pity waiting for a roof'. Subscription funds were exhausted and fresh donations were not forthcoming. Thomas Powell worked diligently to raise money and the Archbishop generously presented £100. Powell promised the townsfolk that, should he be re-elected mayor, he would endeavour to finish the building. He secured the position - but by only a small majority. Clearly, the inhabitants of Deal were disheartened.

Parliament was approached in order that public money might be secured to complete the project. An Act of Parliament, which received the royal assent on 22 May 1712, authorised a tax to be levied on all coals entering the Port of Deal for the next twenty years. The wording of this Act is particularly interesting since it gives an insight into the town at that period:

> Whereas the Parish Church of the ancient Town of Deal is a full mile from the Sea-side, where the Rendezvous of the Royal Navy in the Downs hath of late years so encouraged building Houses on that shore that a large and spacious Brick Town, well inhabited with all sorts of Tradesmen and Artificers, now stands on the Beach and is commonly called the Town of Lower Deal, the numerous inhabitants whereof finding many inconveniences by the Distance of the said Parish Church to themselves and families, which has also been an Encouragement to the Meeting of Dissenters from the Established Church, have often attempted by their own Subscriptions and the Charity of others (some whereof are yet unpaid) to erect a Chapel of Ease in the Lower Town, and have several Years since purchased the Inheritance of a convenient Piece of Ground sufficient for said Chapel and a Burial Place, and have raised the walls of a Chapel ready to receive a roof, but are not able to finish the same without the Aid of an Act of Parliament by laying some small duty on coals to be consumed in the said Town, Parish and Parts adjacent . . .

St George's Chapel, Deal

St George's viewed from the churchyard

Immediately, the corporation mortgaged the coal dues (two shillings on each chaldron entering the port) in order to raise money so that work on the chapel might recommence. A contract was entered into with Richard Card to complete the roof and construct a cupola. Originally, it was intended to erect parapet walls but upon the advice of the architect, John James of Greenwich, the plans were altered in favour of mondillion eaves.

Eventually the chapel was completed at a total cost of £2,559 12s 5d. The building was consecrated on 16 June 1716 by Dr William Wake, the new Archbishop of Canterbury, as 'a Chapel dependent upon the Parish Church of Deal' and dedicated to St George-the-Martyr. At the same time it was agreed that:

> . . . the Mayor, Jurats and Common Council should keep the said Chapel and the whole fabric thereof, with the pulpit, desk, font, communion table and the wall of the burying place in repair, and at all times provide decent ornaments, utensils, vestments and books for the same and maintain a minister, the churchwardens to be chosen by the Mayor, Jurats and Common Council.'

Controversy regarding the new place of worship had not ended with its construction but raged over the choice of its first minister. As early as 1714 the people of Deal had concerned themselves with the question of a suitable cleric. The rector of St Leonard's was assisted by his curate, John Benson, who was generally considered a capable and worthy man. Naturally, it was felt that he would make an ideal curate for St George's.

But the Reverend Mr Benson was not without enemies - despicable folk who slandered him as a Jacobite sympathiser. As this was the time of the first Jacobite

Rebellion the seriousness of these allegations could not be overlooked. It was in vain that he repudiated all charges against him - the odium attached to the mere suspicion of being a Jacobite destroyed all young Benson's chances with the highest authorities.

A petition was sent on Benson's behalf to the Archbishop of Canterbury testifying to his good character. It had been signed not only by the mayor and jurats but by leading inhabitants of the town and several captains of the king's ships stationed in the Downs. It was to the shame of the Anglican Church of that time that the young curate was vetoed. Instead a compromise was reached. The mayor and council, accepting defeat, requested Dr Wake to appoint them:

> . . . a good minister who may reside in the place to preach two sermons on every Sunday, the situation of this place being such that great numbers of ships are frequently detained in the Downs by contrary winds, which causes a vast resort of persons of all sorts to be here often for several weeks together, who will fill our Chapell and be apt to be very nice in their remarks on the preacher.

Dr Wake's choice for the first perpetual curate of St George's was William Squire. Although he remained for two years at the chapel he did not succeed in avoiding disputes with the council. The new incumbent complained bitterly to the Archbishop that he did not receive his correct stipend. The council replied that, although Mr Squire was:

> . . . a person we all have regard for, being recommended to us by your Grace, and we believe him to be a very good man and one who takes a great deal of pains in discharging his duties; but he hath the misfortune to be not well understood in his delivery by many people to their edification.

The next appointment was Nicholas Carter, who was inducted on 26 March 1718. He remained incumbent for an incredible fifty-six years. Dr Carter was a highly-learned man and many of his sermons were published. He preached in several other towns and held the living at Ham and Tilmanston. His residence was at Deal, however, in a house in Lower Street which was demolished when Park Street was constructed. He was the father of Elizabeth Carter, the celebrated 'blue-stocking', author and benefactor of the town.

Despite being such a learned man, he was intolerant of other people's opinions. To his discredit he did not welcome John Wesley, the famous Methodist preacher, although the occasion of his visit proved to be a great blessing to worshippers at St Leonard's. Nor was his character shown in the best possible light when he refused to accept a new chapel clerk appointed by the corporation - which was members' prerogative. The churchwarden was an excellent choice, Carter readily admitted, but since it had not been his own choice, he declined to accept the man's services. Obstinacy, indeed . . .

A far greater dissension between curate and council arose when Dr Carter admitted he disagreed with certain tenets of the Athanasian Creed. He refused to recite the creed in church and this omission was reported to the Archbishop.

St George's Church surrounded by historic tombstones

Later, at a service to celebrate the election of the new mayor and corporation, Dr Carter took the opportunity to preach a sermon in his own defence. The council was contrite and the breach seemed healed. Alas, the dispute found its way into print which culminated in Dr Carter publishing the text of his vindicating sermon – *A Sermon preach'd in the Chapel at Deale in Kent before the Mayor and Corporation, August 9, 1752, upon a particular occasion*. Dr Carter's brother, James, settled the dispute amicably by employing a new curate to read the offending creed.

The third incumbent was Robert England who stayed eight years before resigning the living to the Reverend Philip Brandon in 1786. Mr Brandon was the Deal representative in the band of Cinque Ports Fencibles raised by Prime Minister Pitt against a possible invasion by the French. During his ministry the Deal Charity School was formed under the auspices of St George's in 1792. President was the Reverend ME Benson, curate of St Leonard's, who also championed the building of St Andrew's Church for the boatmen of north Deal.

Children were admitted to this school from the age of six - twenty-five boys and twenty-five girls - their education being paid for by private subscription. The master, William Child, was appointed at an annual salary of fifty guineas although his fee included the provision of a schoolmistress (his wife), a schoolroom, coals and materials such as pen, ink and slate pencils. Boys sported a uniform cap while the girls wore 'leghorn hats tied and bound with dark green ferret'. Pupils were treated to cakes four times a year and the boys were given a free haircut. The school frequently moved sites but when it expanded it was transferred in 1814 to the present St George's Hall where it became known, because of its location, as Deal Central School.

An Annual Charity Sermon was preached at St George's to assist the finances of the school and this tradition continued for more than 100 years. Elizabeth Carter was prevailed upon to subscribe to this educational establishment. When she died her interest was continued by her nephew, the Reverend Montague Pennington. In 1814, Montague, too, was appointed curate at St George's, thus following in his grandfather's footsteps. Unlike his illustrious aunt, he showed sympathy for reformed smugglers who, deprived of their traditional livelihood after the successful campaign by the Royal Navy Coast Blockade, were destined for the workhouse. He could not fail to notice that numerous inhabitants were already reduced to selling their boats and pledging their furniture. He therefore wrote to the Admiralty on 8 August 1819 championing their cause and requesting urgent consideration of their appointment as Channel pilots.

Pennington, who had rejoiced in the title of Commissioner of Salvage for Deal, died in 1849 and he remains the only incumbent to be buried in the churchyard.

A terrifying incident occurred one Sunday evening in 1832. A loud crack was heard during Divine Service which sent the congregation fleeing for their lives. The organ gallery had sunk three inches and the east end of another gallery parted from the wall. Montague Pennington was forced to abandon his sermon and for some time the church was closed for repairs. In November 1836 a tremendous storm rose up in the early morning and raged with unabated fury the whole day. At that time there were about 400 merchant vessels riding at anchor in the Downs and these suffered the full brunt of the gale. In the town nearly 100 chimneys were overturned, including the one at the Town Hall. Pritchard asserts: 'The vane of St. George's Church was blown away, and the lead turned up as if it had been writing paper.'

Interior of St George's until recent renovations

Henry Honywood D'Ombrain, inducted as perpetual curate in 1849, became first vicar when St George's became a parish church in 1852. He was celebrated as an amateur rose grower and he founded both the Royal National Rose Society and the Royal Horticultural Society. He was followed by the Reverend David Bruce Payne who served for forty-six years. Canon Payne was a greatly-respected clergyman and when he died in 1913 the town expressed deep mourning.

St George's was immediately hailed as a decided ornament to the town – although, rather surprisingly, one guide published in the nineteenth century, comments upon its 'extreme hideousness'. Its interior is best viewed from the heights of the Boatmen's Gallery. Light, spacious, dignified . . . the abundance of wood as opposed to stone gives the church an air of 'comfortable solidarity'. Galleries were added on three sides to accommodate the increasing population. The north gallery was built in 1717 at a cost of £60. Immediately it was reserved for the mayor and corporation who still attend on ceremonial occasions - traditionally the first Sunday following the election of a new mayor. A rest for the mace is provided on the balcony where Deal's coat-of-arms appears carved in oak, the work of a technical class held at St George's Hall. It was intended as a belated tribute to Queen Victoria's Diamond Jubilee. The old Mayor's Chair, a cumbersome affair dating from 1759, has been moved to another corner of the church.

Further galleries were added on the north and south sides at a cost of £120. The west gallery accommodated the first Lewis organ paid for by subscription in 1815 when the corporation voted twenty-one guineas towards providing a musical instrument. It was later rebuilt by the famous Deal firm, FH Brown, as a three - manual instrument with thirty-two stops, and removed to its present position on the south side of the chancel. Two further galleries nearer the roof above the main western gallery were intended exclusively for members of the sea-faring community who, because of the nature of their work, might arrive late or depart before the termination of a service. It was thought they might disturb the rest of the congregation as they came and went and therefore they were provided with their own staircase which once resounded to the tramp of heavy sea boots.

Major alterations were carried out in 1869. The main entrances were changed from the middle of the north and south walls to the western side. Formerly a passage had traversed the church linking these two doorways. In the centre of the church, where the passage crossed the central aisle, stood the original font. When its position was changed to the western entrance a new font was donated by HA Brassey, the last Member of Parliament to represent the united boroughs of Sandwich, Deal and Walmer. At the same time the large, ungainly three-deck pulpit (comprising clerk's desk, reading desk and pulpit) was removed from the chancel. In 1876 the old high box pews were taken out and the present pine seats substituted.

The tiny vestry was reached by a door south of the chancel. North of the chancel existed a corresponding doorway which led to the exterior belfry. Since the sexton who rang the bell was also the pew opener he was kept busy darting from one task to the other. A replacement vestry with a porch to protect the new entrances and exterior staircases leading to the galleries was erected in 1884. Modern vestries were built in 1924 and extended in 1980.

The foundation stone, which displays the Rose of England, has been removed from the floor behind the choir stalls and is now set low in the south wall. Oak panelling which adorns the chancel was the gift of Mary Hougham, founder of the Boatmen's Almshouses that once stood in Beach Street. The spectacular brass eagle lectern commemorates Victoria's Jubilee; the communion rails her Diamond Jubilee.

The chancel contains an unique memorial tablet erected in recognition of the loyal service of a dedicated sailor by his sovereign, William IV – 'the Sailor King':

> This tablet is raised
> by
> King William the IV
> To the memory of
> Commander David Ross, R.N.
> As a Testimonial
> Of His Majesty's sincere regard
> For a meritorious shipmate
> Whose Welfare and Promotion
> Had been objects
> Of his solicitude
> Born Sept. 16th 1758. Died Jan. 18th A.D. 1836

Friendship between the two sailors had arisen when Ross was a fellow midshipman with Prince William, then Duke of Clarence. They served together in Admiral Hood's flagship, HMS *Barfleur*, in the famous victory when Rodney and Hood defeated the French under De Grasse in 1782, thus restoring England's credit when it had sunk to its lowest ebb in the war between America and France. Later in this naval warfare, Ross was posted to the Baltic for the Continental Blockade where he gained his promotion by rescuing one of His Majesty's ships.

Commander Ross joined the distinguished company of naval and military officers who welcomed Prince William and his German bride, Princess Adelaide, when they landed at Deal in 1818. Further, Ross became acquainted with Lord Nelson when he was made officer-in-charge of the transports that sailed from Deal. Wellington, too, delighted in his company. Apparently, he would often ride over on horseback from Walmer Castle to converse with Commander Ross in his home in Middle Street.

On the east wall is the memorial tablet to Elizabeth Carter, eldest daughter of the Reverend Nicholas Carter, famous for her erudition and command of languages. 'In deep learning and extensive knowledge she was equalled by few', reads the legend, 'in Piety and the practice of every Christian duty excelled by none'.

The original east window had been presented in 1867 by Dr George Redsull Carter, doctor, poet and philologist, in memory of his father. It beautifully portrayed Faith, Hope and Charity but it was shattered in 1942 by enemy action. The word HOPE alone survived and this has been incorporated into the present stained-glass window which fussily depicts the Ascension of Christ. A striking feature is the lowest panel which depicts Walmer lifeboat returning to shore after

Walmer lifeboat returning to shore, and the word HOPE

a rescue. The coastline is faithfully represented stretching from Deal Castle to the Time Ball Tower, but this and the word HOPE are reversed as the window is intended to be seen from the exterior.

Earliest recorded marriage is that of Henry Alexander Primrose and Margaret Bowles, a young couple from Deal, who were married on 'May ye 5th, 1717'. Two of the first eight names in the burial register, started in 1737, were each described as 'reputed smuggler'. A later entry reads: 'William Spence shot instantly dead by an officer of the Customs' (14 June 1774).

The church roof has been hailed by builders and architects as a masterpiece. It is held by a massive unsupported beam which spans a phenomenal 80 ft and this can be viewed through a trapdoor in the ceiling. In 1924 it was mentioned as being 'a marvel of construction and workmanship'. The weight of this slate roof, which rests on a complicated structure of timber supports, tie beams, purlins and ridge poles, must be colossal.

Originally, St George's Church was approached by a semi-circular recessed wall with posts and chains, a wrought-iron gate and tall railings. Here the market held sway - with a weighbridge housed in an adjacent shed - and stalls were again set up in the immediate postwar period. The church itself stood above ground level and it was entered by a flight of stone steps (they still exist although buried) through the north and south doorways, since bricked up.

Before the church stands a large stone Celtic cross erected in 1916 to commemorate the fallen of the First World War. The roll of honour includes the names of the two brilliant sons of the Reverend William St Clair Tisdall. A learned cleric, Dr Tisdall had been a missionary in India and Persia; he was an authority on comparative Eastern religions and the author of numerous books including a Persian grammar. Within a year of his appointment as Vicar of St George's war broke out and in the course of its duration he sustained this double personal grief.

Sub-Lieutenant Arthur Walderne St Clair Tisdall, a prodigious scholar who held a double first in classics, was killed at Gallipoli and posthumously awarded the Victoria Cross. Born in India on 21 July 1890, Arthur was described as tall, broad-chested, strong-limbed and having a finely-poised head crowned with wavy brown hair and arresting deep grey eyes. He was an accomplished athlete and a supporter of the suffragette movement. When the situation in Europe deteriorated during the early years of the twentieth century he was caught up in the patriotic fervour which gripped the nation and he enlisted to fight for King and Country. A faded photograph shows him smoking a pipe and wearing the uniform of an able seaman at Walmer Barracks where he trained with the Royal Naval Voluntary Reserve. After accompanying the Allied Expeditionary Force to Antwerp he was commissioned into the Anson Battalion of the Royal Naval Division where sailors were trained and deployed as infantry throughout the First World War.

Arthur was a friend of the poet Rupert Brooke, whom he met at

Arthur St Clair Tisdall

Chatham, trained alongside at Betteshanger and accompanied on his luxurious voyage aboard HMS *Grantully Castle* to the savage Turkish peninsula. Allied British, French and Indian forces landed on the narrow, heavily-defended beaches of Gallipoli on 25 April 1915 (later named Anzac Day to commemorate the courage demonstrated by combined troops from Australia and New Zealand). After he had transferred to his tender, the steam collier SS *River Clyde*, Tisdall witnessed the abortive landing of the Munster and Dublin Fusiliers on V beach where they were exposed to the merciless battery of enemy guns positioned overhead on the cliffs. Immediately, he responded to the desperate cries of stranded soldiers on the river bank by diving overboard and swimming to their rescue. Repeatedly, he returned from ship to shore, wading in deep water, to push boatloads of wounded men in front of him. This act of heroism was conducted under a continuous barrage of heavy, accurate fire from the enemy forts.

Next day this modest sub-lieutenant, who commanded the 13th Platoon, sent a postcard to his parents making no mention of his bravery:

> Have been under fire and are now ashore; all day spent in burying soldiers. Some of my men are killed. We are all happy and fit. Plenty of hard work and enemy shells and a smell of dead men . . .

Shortly afterwards, he volunteered to carry ammunition to the firing line despite intense bombardment from exploding shells. He was fatally wounded a few days later by a bullet which struck him in the chest while he was directing his men to take shelter in a trench during the advance on Achi Baba on 6 May. This occurred just two days after the death, from acute poisoning, of his companion, Rupert Brooke.

The Times published Tisdall's obituary and printed letters extolling his virtues. King George V sent a personal note to his parents who were invited to receive their son's VC at Buckingham Palace. At Deal, a memorial service in St George's Church on Ascension Day was attended by the General in Command of the Royal Marines. His wartime diary and most of his poetry – like his place of burial – are lost. The following year Arthur's brother, John, was killed in action in France. These blows greatly affected their father's health and although he strove manfully to continue his duties for several years after the war, he resigned in 1926 and retired to Walmer.

St George's Churchyard contains the tombs of countless brave soldiers and sailors who had been engaged in naval battles in the Downs. Today, most of the inscriptions are indecipherable - the ancient weather-beaten stones are so worn with age and shrouded in lichen - yet enough remain legible to allow a tantalising glimpse into turbulent times of the past when men in one way or another gained their living from the sea.

There are graves of coastguards, pilots, pursers, ships' masters, captains' clerks, officers of the East India Company and the Navy Yard. The oldest stone, dated 1727, stands near the west door of the church. Many of the seamen who lie buried here were victims of shipwreck, such as William Follett, aged twenty-three, master of the schooner *Tryphina*, of Dartmouth, wrecked on the Goodwin Sands on 11 December 1827. Death by drowning was common. One stone reads: 'In memory of Paul Mace, of Weymouth, late Midshipman of the Dublin Indiaman, who was drowned the 23rd day of March, and buried here the 19th of May, 1788, aged 18 years.' The long gap between his demise and interment is explained by the fact that his body lay buried for weeks in the soft sand having been thrown up by the waves in the vicinity of Sandown Castle. But there are tragic incidents even in the calmest seas. One luckless teenager, Thomas Hayton, lost his life 'by the upsetting of a boat in which he was returning to Deal from a visit to his father, then at anchor in the Downs, the 8th June, 1808.'

There are also the victims of pirates and smugglers:

> In memory of Thos. Cundy of Truro, late Master of the Gertrude Brigantine, who fell when gallantly defending his vessel from being boarded by a French Privateer off Dungeness on the 19th Oct., 1810.

In memory of John Ellbeck, a private in the Westmoreland Militia, aged 27 years, who was shot in Beach Street, the 26th Sept., 1794, by a person unknown in the execution of his duty assisting the officers of the Customs.

References to the Navy Yard are to be found in odd corners of the churchyard: 'George Lawrance, Esq., 31st Oct., 1807, in the 81st year of his age. Twenty-eight years Naval Storekeeper at Deal.' 'Lancelot Burton, Naval Officer of the Place, died Oct. 12th, 1756.' Another important dignitary of former times is recorded: 'Richard Canny of Deal, one of the Pilots' Wardens of the Cinque Ports, died May 1st, 1789.' Nearby stands a memorial recalling the gallant services of the Deal boatmen, exemplified by George Philpott who died on 22 March 1850, aged seventy-four:

> Full many lives he saved
> With his undaunted crew;
> He put his trust in Providence
> And cared not how it blew.

Numerous monuments relate to the fearful wars with France which ushered in the nineteenth century. The disastrous expedition of the Duke of York against Dunkirk in 1793 was matched by the appalling Walcheren invasion in 1809 when hundreds of victims perished (Pritchard says more than 1000). Men were brought in boatloads, horribly injured and without either nursing or lodging. Those who died were buried in a common grave. A single epitaph remains:

In memory of Henry Witherington, Esq., Lieu. 63rd Reg. of Infantry, here intered, who on his return from Walcheren, severely afflicted with the disease of the climate, departed this life at Deal on the 15th of Sept., 1809, in the 31st year of his age.

Memorials of the naval engagements of the Napoleonic wars are located in the south-west corner of the churchyard. Principal of these is the imposing square monument to Captain Edward Thornbridge Parker, Nelson's closest companion, wounded in the daring midnight raid on Napoleon's flotilla assembled off Boulogne. After prolonged suffering resulting from an horrendous operation involving the amputation of

Edward Parker's tomb

his leg (buried separately in a common grave) Parker expired and was laid to rest on 27 September 1801. Nelson attended his funeral for which he paid considerable expense. During the interment Nelson wept bitterly while leaning against an adjacent tree. Years later, Prime Minister William Gladstone, on one of his frequent visits to the town, asked to be shown this very tree. Traditionally a mature oak has been pointed out to interested visitors as Nelson's Tree. But when it was felled by council workmen because it was deemed dangerous a Forestry Officer declared that it was less than a century old.

After the disastrous Battle of Boulogne Napoleon's shipping remained to be defeated. Two further attempts that were made are recorded in the churchyard. In October 1804 an engagement known as the Catamaran Expedition met with little success. A tablet on the south wall, erected by the crew of HMS *Immortalite*, which took part in it, commemorates those shipmates who fell in action.

Eventually the enemy fleet was destroyed. This achievement is recalled by a later stone: 'Sacred to the memory of John Ross and James Draper, seamen, who were killed on board HMS *Naiad*, in defeating the French flotilla off Boulogne, 21st Sept. 1811.'

The churchyard - formerly known as the Chapel Field - was closed to burials in 1855. In the last century it was transferred to the care of the borough council as a garden of rest. The ancient tombstones were lined up against the walls (some were removed for safety to the nearby Maritime Museum) and a lawn was laid out in the centre. Several historic trees were preserved, including the fine oaks planted by the mayor and corporation to celebrate the coronations of Edward VII and George V. A noble avenue of limes once lined the pathway on the southern side leading to St Leonard's where the townsfolk have claimed a right of way since time immemorial.

More recent vicars of St George's have proved colourful. They include the Reverend OT Jones, a Welshman who had previously been employed by a perfumery company in Croydon and the Reverend George Lings, in whose time a baptistry was sunk for complete immersion and the chancel was drastically altered to accommodate an informal style of worship. Present vicar is the Reverend Christopher Spencer.

HENRY D'OMBRAIN

'Rose-growing vicar'

HENRY HONYWOOD D'OMBRAIN was a parson with a passion for roses which culminated in his founding both the Royal Horticultural Society and the Royal National Rose Society. Apart from being a celebrated amateur rose grower, D'Ombrain was a distinguished lecturer on horticultural subjects and he penned numerous articles on gardening matters under the pseudonym 'D Deal'.

This curious *nom-de-plume* can be accounted for by the fact that the Reverend Mr D'Ombrain was the perpetual curate of St George's Church. When it was elevated to the distinction of a parish church in 1852, Henry D'Ombrain was appointed first vicar.

Concurrent with his pastoral duties, this stocky, keen-eyed, benevolent cleric, who in later years sported a snowy-white beard, pursued his hobby of gardening. Many of his parishioners benefited from his considerate advice and were inspired to create their own imaginative cottage gardens. Among the flowers the vicar raised locally with enviable success were gladioli and ranunculi; but he was also astonishingly successful with roses, lilies, herbacious and alpine plants.

Although Henry D'Ombrain had been born in Pimlico in 1818, both his parents originated from Canterbury. His father was Admiral Sir James D'Ombrain who for thirty years occupied the post of Inspector-General of the Coastguard in Ireland and he was knighted for his distinguished service. The D'Ombrain family were descendants of the Huguenots (French Protestants who fled from the religious

The Reverend Henry Honywood D'Ombrain, first vicar of Deal

persecution of Charles IX and settled in Sandwich, Dover and Canterbury as highly skilled jewellers, silk weavers and market gardeners). Heroically, their ancestor, Jacques D'Ombrain, had escaped from France by crossing the English Channel in an open boat after the massacre of St Bartholomew's Day in 1572.

Henry, it seems, never forgot his French heritage because he took every opportunity to visit the land of his ancestry. An added incentive for his frequent trips abroad was his passion for roses and the fact that during the first half of the nineteenth century France was the breeding ground for the world's finest specimens. Since the days of the Empress Josephine, the rose had been fashionable and the French hybridists, who relied mainly on nature to do their cross-pollination, vied with each other in producing new strains - many of which were introduced into this country at vast profit. Henry D'Ombrain travelled extensively in France in search of the latest varieties, reporting upon these in his articles, and he was described by his clergyman friend, Dean Hole of Rochester, as 'the Consul for French Roses in England'.

Marechal Niel © The Rose Society

During one excursion to the Verdier nursery near Paris in 1864, D'Ombrain chanced upon a discarded seedling in a box of trial grafts. He persuaded the nursery to give this particular experiment another try and the result was the enormously popular *Marechal Niel*. This famous Noisette climbing rose with its rich shade of yellow, its powerful perfume and profusion of bloom reigned supreme in Victorian times when it was regarded as 'the Prince of Roses'. It makes an appearance in Oscar Wilde's *The Importance of Being Earnest*. Yellow had proved an elusive colour but its discovery pioneered the way for brilliant flames. Still obtainable, *Marechal Niel* has the merit of flowering early in a cool house and making fresh growth rapidly but it is nowadays not considered hardy enough for growing in the open-air.

In addition to introducing the Noisette rose into England, Henry D'Ombrain was instrumental in popularising the Bourbon rose, one of his own particular favourites. This delightful species, which originated from the Isle of Bourbon around 1825, is noted for its sweet scent and its excellent autumnal qualities - true Bourbons generally give superior blooms in the second crop. Eventually, D'Ombrain was rewarded by having a Bourbon named after him - an early, reliable, vigorous, bright carmine rose.

For more than fifty years Henry D'Ombrain was a prolific writer on gardening topics and hardly a week passed without an article by him appearing in one of the national gardening newspapers. His first contribution to the horticultural press was in the *Cottage Gardener*, the title of which magazine was later changed to the *Journal of Horticulture*. Dean Hole commented that his colleague 'writes as he talks - pleasantly, freshly, simply, as he thinks and knows'. But much of his success should be attributed to the fact that he wrote as an experienced amateur horticulturist for amateurs, and he was therefore in complete sympathy with the many difficulties that attended their efforts.

From 1860 until 1876 Mr D'Ombrain was editor of *The Floral Magazine* in which were fine coloured illustrations by such accomplished artists as Fitch, Andrews and Worthington-Smith.

The Bourbon rose named for D'Ombrain
© *The Rose Society*

At one time he compiled a *Life History of The Rose Society* which appeared in the programme distributed annually at the society's Metropolitan Exhibition. In 1876 he produced and edited an admirable little volume, *The Rosarian's Year Book*, fore-runner of *The Rose Annual*, containing particulars of the society's activities and featuring excellent articles by leading rosarians.

By the middle of the nineteenth century a number of flowers - the dahlia, the carnation, the chrysanthemum, the tulip and even the humble pansy - were awarded annual shows but the rose could not boast this particular distinction until July 1858 when Deal Hole created the first Grand National Rose Show at St James' Hall in London. 'No words can describe the infinite variety of form, colour and odour which belonged to the field of roses spread before the visitor,' trilled one contributor to *Gardening Chronicle*. This show was widely publicised, prizes were generously donated and the Coldstream Band was hired to provide live entertainment although this turned out to be a mistake since, Dean Hole commented wryly, 'their admirable music proved to be too loud for indoor enjoyment'. This novel event was such a success that future shows were held at a larger venue - the newly opened Crystal Palace.

Reynolds Hole was by all accounts a humorous character, a keen botanist and an able sportsman (he was a skilled archer). Yet he was a gentle giant for he was author of the widely acclaimed *A Book of Roses* which appeared in 1869. His enthusiasm was boundless and he would drive miles with his horse and carriage to inspect a recommended rose garden. He soon persuaded prominent rosarians that it was not sufficient for the rose to have a show of its own but that a society was required to foster its interests.

Consequently, the Reverend Henry D'Ombrain, universally hailed as a promoter of old-style floristry, called a meeting of enthusiasts in the winter of 1876 at the Adelphi Terrace in London where the National Rose Society was formed. Dean Hole was elected its first president and Mr D'Ombrain its secretary, a position he held for the next twenty-five years. The aim of the society was clearly defined: 'The extending and encouraging by every means and power the cultivation and exhibition of the rose and of uniting all who are interested in it in one bond and union'.

Apart from its annual show, the society organised lectures and discussions and issued pamphlets proffering advice upon the cultivation of the rose. Part of the appeal for the clerical gardeners was that the rose, no matter how intensely bred, never acquired the apparent artificiality of a florists' flower. D'Ombrain, then approaching sixty, quickly established contact with rose growers overseas and soon had correspondents all over the world who formed their own societies based upon the National Rose Society and adopting their own rules. A high point of honour came in 1888 when Princess Alexandra agreed to become patron of the Rose Society which immediately added the prefix 'Royal'.

Although both D'Ombrain and Dean Hole loved the exhibition rose best they strove to encourage the growing of decorative and old-fashioned varieties. After all, one of the prime objects of their society was to encourage rose-growing in all its forms, in all places and in all seasons. Remarking upon the scarcity of new roses in 1887, D'Ombrain sensibly declared:

> There can be little doubt that novelty is a great necessity to rose-growing, and if the time ever comes when new flowers are not produced it will be a bad thing for the rose.

When, owing to infirmity and old age, Henry D'Ombrain was forced reluctantly to retire as secretary, he left the society in a flourishing condition. He had worked with selfless devotion to promote interest in its aims and had delivered countless lectures on the art of growing roses to enthusiasts throughout the country. He was a fluent speaker, possessing a clear, pleasant voice, and his gentle humour, tact and good judgement endeared him to his audience. In 1897 the Victoria Medal of Honour was instituted by the Royal Horticultural Society (which had originated from a club he had founded) and by popular assent Henry Honywood D'Ombrain was one of the first recipients of this prestigious award. Earlier, in 1871, he had been appointed secretary of a fund-raising organisation formed to aid French horticulturists ruined by the Franco-Prussian War.

In 1868 D'Ombrain exchanged his incumbency of St George's for that of St Mary's at Westwell near Ashford. He remained vicar of that church for thirty-seven years. When he died in 1905 a brass plate was erected to his memory under the tower arch of this lovely church sometimes termed a 'village cathedral'.

Also commemorated there is the death of his soldier son, Lieutenant RD D'Ombrain, who died fighting in South Africa in 1879 in the bitter conflict between the Zulus and the Dutch Boers. A remarkable link between the churches of Deal and Westwell is that the fine organ commemorating the D'Ombrain family was built by the firm of FH Browne whose original factory was at North Deal.

Westwell is a tranquil village which even today boasts a Victorian school, an overshot watermill, a farm with oasts and an inviting pub, The Wheel. The original vicarage remains a grand Gothic affair with a profusion of gables decorated with intricate barge boards, tall twisting chimneys and mock Tudor timbering. It is blessed with spacious grounds stocked with blossoming trees and flowering plants that border a trim lawn traversed with inquisitive blackbirds and industrious bees.

Despite heavier demands upon his time in a larger parish, Henry D'Ombrain continued his hobby of gardening, ably assisted by his wife and daughter. Shortly before his demise a contributor to *The Journal of Horticulture* (July 1898) visited Westwell vicarage to write a feature on D'Ombrain's colourful garden. The writer travelled along the fragrant lanes from Ashford early one summer morning and arrived in the village which he was delighted to find 'rich in pastoral charm'. While the vicar was absent paying a charitable call, the journalist was conducted around by the stalwart head gardener, Edward Clements, whose fame as a vegetable grower had extended far beyond Kent.

The modest garden appeared a riot of colour: there was a sturdy colony of gladioli, an array of columbines, a mass of auriculas in glazed pots within weathered wooden walls and a splendid collection of pelargoniums including the delicate salmon tinted *Mrs D'Ombrain*. A neat path wandered among hardy rock beds and broad plant borders (the sight of which was breathtaking in spring on account of the bulbs) intersected by a hedge of pungent sweetbriar. The garden was at once both practical and decorative, noted the correspondent, with beds of tea roses sandwiched between rows of potatoes and celery, while fruit trees and rambler roses shouldered each other close to the vicarage windows.

After an hour or so D'Ombrain appeared, a sprightly octogenarian with a genial smile, feeling his way along the familiar path with an outstretched stick to aid his sight. While Clements disappeared to the greenhouse to battle with an erratic flue, the vicar took time to point out the special features of his garden. There was to be admired a glorious bush of *Madame Chedane Guinoisseau* rose, a line of horizontal cordon apples laden with summer fruit and a row of Sutton's Early Giant Pea 'with eleven great fat peas of marrow flavour in the pod'. Roses, naturally, were his principal pride and joy and about these the writer waxed lyrical.

> I have seen larger beds, but never more beautiful ones. There are probably few collections fuller of interest, I mean as regards vigour, excellence of culture, and choice of variety . . . The collection is representative, it is being kept up-to-date with meritorious new varieties, and in respect of quality of bloom it suffers nothing in comparison with many others that send out prize stands. Tea roses, particularly, presented a marvellous sight for they

seemed to contend well with the brisk hill breezes. One immense bed appeared, according to the journalist, 'a picture of chaste and delicate beauty'.

The vicar, apparently, regarded his country garden with great modesty but the correspondent for the *Journal* was ecstatic:

Mr. D'Ombrain's garden is full of interest, full of beauty, full of lessons . . . It is a garden of which the memory is to be placed amongst beautiful, sweet and cherished possessions, not alone for its own charm and fragrance but from the impulse and inspiration it has given to the venerable figure which has played so large a part in developing British horticulture.

Today, Henry D'Ombrain's achievements are largely forgotten by the local populace although the two roses he introduced into this country - *Marechal Niel* and the Bourbon - are portrayed on the sign of the Rose Hotel adjacent to St George's Church.

SMUGGLING

'A plain, practical sin'

IT WOULD BE FOOLISH to deny that Deal's prosperity in times past was founded upon smuggling. Almost everyone was involved in the 'midnight trade', from the common boatmen who were the carriers, to the magistrates who not only sympathised with the smugglers, but often funded their nocturnal activities.

The Customs was established in the reign of King Edward I in order to collect duties on both imported and exported goods. Immediately, it was centralised, with Collectors at prominent ports, including Dover and Sandwich. In 1374, Geoffrey Chaucer, author of *The Canterbury Tales*, was appointed Controller of Customs on exported wool and leather in London. Excise, which deals exclusively in the taxation of home commodities, was introduced during the Civil War but the two Revenue services were not combined until 1909.

Customs officials were primarily concerned with collecting duties on the export of raw wool, which was discouraged in order to foster the manufacture of woollen garments in this country. English raw wool was regarded as the best in the world and so it was greatly desired by the highly-skilled Continental weavers. The clandestine export of wool was organised on a grand scale by Huguenot and Walloon communities at Canterbury. Free traders who specialised in smuggling raw wool were termed 'owlers' – since they worked by 'owl-light' – and their efforts were concentrated mainly on the lush sheep grazing pastures of Romney Marsh.

Earliest recorded incidence of smuggling in this locality concerns wool. One dark February night in 1617 the owlers were busily engaged in transporting fifteen packets of raw wool from Sandwich to the shore to be loaded on to a Dutch vessel waiting in the Downs. Two law-abiding citizens raised the alarm (a rare occurrence), the owlers were apprehended and their goods confined in a storehouse in Deal. Unfortunately, the Lord Warden's officer, John Clark, who was in charge of the storehouse in Beach Street, was in the pay of the Dutchmen and he connived at the owlers' escape.

Customs officials who targeted the owlers were met with violent opposition after the introduction of the death penalty for wool smuggling in 1662. Later deterrents for smuggling were impressment for five years into the Army or Navy and transportation first to Britain's plantations and colonies in North America but afterwards to Australia. For three centuries wool smuggling was the main

*Smuggling in High Life, a cartoon of contraband leaving the
Dover road © National Museums and Galleries of Merseyside*

'nocturnal trade' but inevitably 'run' goods switched to luxury items as duties were imposed by the Treasury to pay for a succession of wars. High taxation made smuggling profitable and the experienced Kentish owlers turned their attention from wool to brandy and silks, and then tea, which was first brought to England in the mid-seventeenth century by the East India Company.

In 1699 the Landguard of Riding Officers was formed under the direction of its founder, Captain Henry Baker, who acted as Surveyor-General. Eight Riding Officers - armed with pistols and sabres - had tentatively been appointed for Kent, charged with patrolling the coast on horseback day and night, gathering intelligence concerning owlers. Once the alarm was raised they could summon the assistance of either cavalry stationed at strategic towns along the coast, including Dover and Folkestone, or dragoons (infantry who rode on horses but who dismounted to fight with muskets) posted inland at Canterbury and Ashford. Baker soon reported woollen bales being shipped out from Deal despite a complement of ten soldiers and 'Notwithstanding all the Sea Guards in the Downs'.

Additionally, the Waterguard had been formed to deploy armed sloops which cruised between the North Foreland and the Isle of Wight with orders to board any vessel suspected of carrying wool. This primitive marine force, which flew 'a jack and red ensign with the seal of office (a castellated portcullis) thereon', was later extended to include a fleet of cutters and cruisers, and marked the first combined effort in preventing smuggling by the Customs and the Royal Navy. Commanders of Revenue vessels were reminded by the Customs Board that they were to patrol ceaselessly and not to return to port other than to revictual. Further they were to maintain close cooperation and communication with the Landguard along the coast. *Nimble* and *Scourge* were the two Revenue cutters permanently based at Deal.

Optimistically, Captain Baker reported to the Exchequer in 1703 that the owling trade had been curtailed, but by that time the Kentish smugglers had turned their attention to alternative contraband. John Collier, a solicitor for the Customs Commissioners, noted the number of boatmen in 1713 who had 'no visible means of livelihood' apart from smuggling which had reached such a height 'that there were up to two or three hundred persons concerned in it at Deal'. Tea and brandy illegally imported became the top priority for Customs officials after 1730. Masters and crews of homeward bound East and West Indiamen, Chinamen and Turkeymen had been permitted to bring in 'private investments' free of duty until 1674, after which abuse of this privilege led to restrictions. Deal boatmen transacted illegal business on the pretence of putting pilots aboard, while these noble vessels avoided official searches by passing through the Downs at night, in 'Blowing Weather'.

Customs officials and Royal Naval personnel were not, themselves, exempt from dabbling in contraband. Richard Watts, Surveyor of Customs at Deal, was dismissed from office shortly after the Restoration and the disgraced officer brought a counter-complaint against his successor, Bartholomew Marsh, accusing him of buying excisable goods from ships in the Downs. Captain Gregory of HMS *Bideford*, after escorting George I across the Channel on his state visit to Hanover in 1720, returned to take aboard tea, chintzes, muslin and arrack from a homeward bound East Indiaman, *Queen of Peace*, and landed them on the Kent coast. Two Riding Officers were caught redhanded at Folkestone in 1806 as they were deviously unloading goods from the Revenue cutter *Nimble*, and they, too, were suspended.

The Treasury was alarmed by the developing market for contraband in shops and alehouses in the towns and villages of East Kent and decided the problem was best tackled at sea, so it placed four sloops at the disposal of the Customs at Deal and Sandwich. William Hickey witnessed a transaction between an East Indiaman and a smuggling vessel in the English Channel in 1770 and was appalled that the Customs vessel was powerless to intervene since it took place just outside the legal limit. Andrew Read and his officers tracked *Valentine* upon her return from China in June 1774 and watched several boats and a cutter run alongside as she slid behind the Goodwins under cover of darkness. There he observed senior officers passing tea chests over her poop deck and out of her gunports on the starboard side. When the Excise Commissioners subsequently sent their crack team of officers, supported by twenty-two dragoons and forty-six infantrymen, to search for an abundant store of tea at Deal, they were met with such hostility they were forced to retreat, retrieving only a few chests. A Parliamentary Report on smuggling noted the transportation of 21,442 lbs of tea between London and Deal over a three-month period in 1783. Permits issued by the Excise for the transference of this stock 'for the convenience of trade' was actually a scam, disguising fraudulently-landed goods transferred in the opposite direction - from the coast to the capital. Little wonder Deal was regarded as an emporium.

Intervention by the Revenue men was always fiercely resisted by local people. On 25 February 1767, James Heard, a Customs Officer from London, came to Deal escorted by 200 dragoons to carry out a search for goods from an East

Indiaman. A vast quantity was found and stored in the warehouse at the Navy Yard. Heard was pelted with stones by a mob as he rode back to Canterbury while Sergeant Lock of the dragoons was threatened with hanging up from the Hoop and Griffin signpost. Thomas Hayman and Thomas Mockett, 'dextrous and audacious' smugglers, were held responsible for this instance of mob rule.

In August 1771 a boat from the sloop *Cruizer* chased a pair of suspected smuggling galleys on to Deal beach. A mob gathered and attacked the retreating crew with 'Cricket bats, Stones and Staves' while they were struggling to launch their boat from the shingle. John Winder accidentally discharged his musket into the crowd when tackled from behind by Gideon Chitty, a Deal pilot, and he was hauled before the mayor. Whilst he stood trial for attempted murder, three of his colleagues were recovering from their wounds in the Naval Hospital, but Richard Hornsby and Deliverance Little, who had incited the mob, were let off scot free. Captain Cummings, commander of *Cruizer*, called for a permanent military force at Deal.

The following summer a Customs boat tracked a suspicious lugger visiting a flotilla of East Indiamen in the Downs before heading for North Deal. Thomas Sharp fired a warning shot when he was bombarded by a hail of stones from the beach. This so incensed the boatmen that they launched three galleys in hot pursuit. The Customs men reached the safety of their watch house but were besieged by a huge mob wielding clubs. The crowd included Robert MacMurray and Richard Middleton - Constables of Deal.

On 4 August 1784 a midshipman was beaten up outside Deal Post Office simply because he was recognised as belonging to the Revenue cutter *Nimble*.

Launching a Deal boat

Captain Lindsey of *Scout* and Captain Hills of *Wasp* harried the smugglers relentlessly as they traded illegally with East Indiamen in the Downs. The ruffians became so exasperated that they brought down 'a Carriage Gun upon the Beach opposite the Middle of the Town' and aimed it at the boats belonging to these two Revenue ships.

One instance of a bloody skirmish at Deal was reported in the *Morning Post* of 31 October 1781:

> Just before daybreak four Irish independent companies and two of the Middlesex Militia arrived from Dover, conducted by two Customs-house officers armed with extraordinary powers who began to break into the houses. A large quantity of uncustomed goods were soon found and many waggonloads conducted to Deal Castle. You will hardly imagine that this was done with much tranquility and, lest nine companies should not be sufficient, above one hundred of Lord Sheffield's Horse came into town during the affair. I can not describe the scene, but it gave me the tolerable idea of the sacking of a town. Some flint and many stones came at the windows and many shots were fired by the soldiers but most miraculously nobody was killed and only one man considerably wounded who, having thrown a mattock-iron from a garden at the officers, a Middlesex militiaman fired at him as he was scrambling over a wall. We passed a most remarkable day and night, every moment upon the brink of mischief . . .

Incredibly, despite the presence of this vast number of troops the townsfolk, warned in advance of the ransacking, had managed to ship the bulk of their loot across to France. For it was estimated that the goods recovered were valued at a mere £10-15,000 whereas the amount originally lodged was nearer £100,000.

Punishments of the greatest severity were inflicted upon convicted smugglers although generally the men were executed only if guilty of murder or of violently resisting arrest. The penalty for warning smugglers of the presence of Revenue men was one month's hard labour while gaolers who facilitated the escape of their prisoners were themselves incarcerated. Samuel Harris and John North were charged with fatally shooting John McNier, Receiver of Customs, when he attempted to board a smuggling boat off Deal in April 1784. Both men were found guilty and sentenced to death, their bodies afterwards 'to be cut down and anatomified'. George Hubbard, a Deal publican, was transported for life for arranging the escape of prisoners-of-war, including a French general, although local magistrates tended to sympathise with smugglers since they had a vested interest in their trade.

Heyday of smuggling was from the mid-seventeenth century to the early nineteenth century when the expansion of world trade was coupled with the necessity to finance wars both in Europe and America. Concurrent with the start of the three Dutch Wars in 1688, when taxation rocketed, was the invention of the fast, sleek yacht which assisted Customs officials in their pursuit of Kent boatmen as they transported their illicit cargoes across the Channel. At the commencement of the American War of Independence in 1775, the whole country was bereft of fighting men, which opened up further opportunity for

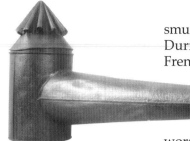

Smuggler's hooded lanthorn
© Dover Museum

The term smuckellors, to describe importers and exporters of proscribed goods, was first used during the Civil War, but there is a suggestion that the word derives from the Old English, smuga, meaning 'hidey-hole'.

The Revenue cutters were armed with light, short-barrelled guns called carronades that were so effective at point blank range that they were nicknamed smashers.

Smuggled brandy was easy to detect since it was imported white, but caramel, which gave it a honey tincture, was added by Customs officials once duty had been paid.

smuggling gangs to operate along the south coast. During the Napoleonic Wars the importation of French goods was prohibited while at the same time Revenue cutters were required for the war effort. Local boatmen turned to the illicit trade and soon Deal had the dubious reputation of being the worst smuggling town in the whole kingdom.

Taxation escalated as these wars intensified. Initially, duties were restricted to the importation of wine but they were soon extended to the main commodities of tea, tobacco, spirits and eventually Lyons silk, Valenciennes or Chantilly lace, French, Spanish and Portuguese wines. During the reign of Elizabeth I, cannons cast by the ironmasters of the Weald were smuggled to Spain and were eventually fired against the English at the Armada. Bibles, crucifixes, statues and relics blessed by the Pope were smuggled into England during times of Catholic persecution. King James I's abhorrence of tobacco resulted in the imposition of an excessive duty and any seized by the Revenue was publicly burned. After the Restoration there was a tremendous trade in tea between China and Europe and it remained expensive until the tax was dramatically slashed by Pitt in 1784. Curiously, he replaced it with an increased window tax.

At the accession of George III in 1740 there were 800 items on which duty had to be paid but over the next fifty years hundreds more goods became taxable. Wines and spirits which attracted high duties included brandy, rum, whisky, port wine, cordials and Dutch Geneva (gin). Luxuries which were taxed - and therefore smuggled - included coffee, chocolate, cocoa, ivory, perfume, gold rings, pearls, damask, velvet, calico, cambric, satin, tiffany, gold and silver brocade. There were several oddities, such as starch, soap, straw, salt, pepper, vinegar, paper, dice, wire, dried fruits, hair powder, sealing wax, scented snuff, coffin nails, currants, coconuts and counterpanes. Contraband followed fashion, which resulted in smuggling becoming romanticised, particularly among the ladies who were able to sport cheap purchases of fine goods – ribbons, laces, shawls, caps, lappets, shoes, silk slippers, leather gloves, bead purses, mousseline handkerchiefs and ostrich plumes for their hats. At the height of the wars with France there was a specialised trade in spies, newspapers and despatches.

Attention focused on the Kent coast - and in particular Deal - which was regarded as 'a nest of smugglers'. A lonely, shingle beach three miles long situated close to the Continent - what more might the smuggler require? Fishing boats guided by silent flashes from flink pistols, signal fires and hooded lanterns slipped silently onto the foreshore on misty, moonless nights. Contraband was swiftly unloaded and disappeared into the myriad streets of the North End. At a convenient hour it was packed on to wagons pulled by ponies with felt horseshoes and rope traces and conveyed in secrecy and silence to distant inns - The Jolly Sailor and Noah's Ark - where it was stored before being whisked away by coach to stately homes and to the fashionable shops of London or Tunbridge Wells. The port prospered from the clandestine trade, which was patronised, encouraged and even romanticised by people of fashion and fortune.

One of the few people who dared to criticise smugglers was Deal's blue-stocking author, Elizabeth Carter, who wrote:

> I hear nothing here but tea and brandy, and prohibited clothing; which is bought up with a scandalous degree of eagerness by people of fashion and fortune.

Her friend, Dr Samuel Johnson, an inveterate tea drinker, defined the smuggler in his 1755 *Dictionary* as 'a wretch who in defiance of the laws of his country, imports or exports goods without payment of customs'. John Wesley, the Methodist preacher who passed through the Downs when he returned from America, called smuggling 'the accursed thing' and declined to drink tea altogether. Tea, or 'tay', which first arrived in Britain about 1657 from China, was served by the gentry at almost every meal. The price was exorbitant since more than half represented duty and so caddies were kept locked. Cheap black tea, known as Bohea, was welcome especially when sweetened with smuggled sugar.

Elizabeth Carter, who lived a stone's throw from the seashore at Carter House, deplored the prevalence of smuggling locally and denounced it as 'a plain, practical sin'. She was particularly critical of those who might have set a better example, for it hurt her to see the carriages of 'people of the first rank in the land' leave Deal laden with every kind of contraband. She would have been incensed to learn that the nobility frequently paid for regular orders of goods by banker's draft or cheque rather than hard cash. Her complaint fell on deaf ears, however, for gentlefolk regularly travelled from London to buy contraband.

Lady Mary Coke, the youngest daughter of the Duke of Argyll, described as 'a tempestuous petticoat', paid a fleeting visit to the Lord Warden, the Earl of Holderness, at Walmer Castle in the summer of 1768. Lady Holderness obligingly escorted her friend round the town in search of contraband and Lady Mary recorded their escapades in her journal:

> Friday 17 June – After breakfast Lady Holdernesse and I walked to Deal where She carried me to three of the Houses that smuggle Indian goods. I saw several pieces of very pretty silks; I shall certainly buy one before I go. Tea and musline is extremely cheap; the former seven shillings the pound, the same you pay sixteen for at London. We came back in the Coach.

Lady Mary scandalised the other castle guests by her determination to buy smuggled goods although she probably did not mention this to Mrs Carter whom she found an amiable woman. Alas, when she returned for the silk she was disappointed to learn that it had been reserved as a gift so she came away with only five pounds of tea and some china. Lady Mary had, in any case, lost most of her pin money playing cards the night before and she feared she had no money left for the contraband goods.

Fanny Burney, diarist, author and member of the Georgian court circle, recorded in her journal of 7 September 1778 a letter from Lady Hales, at whose country seat, Howletts, her daughter Susan, was staying. They drove to Deal, 'a sad smuggling town' where Lady Hales purchased run goods and she wrote to Fanny begging her to accept a very small part of her purchase - namely, a roll of chintz.

Homeward-bound vessels of the East and West India Companies had anchored in the Downs laden with spices, opium, sugar, silk and ivory since their inception in the mid-seventeenth century. Their captains and crew were not averse to selling 'over the side', which was a constant source of iritation to the Revenue men. Tall ships were escorted by Revenue cutters along the Thames estuary, which meant that it was far too risky to carry contraband into the Port of London. Therefore they welcomed the longshoremen of the Kent coast who rowed out to collect quantities of 'uncustomed tea'. Deal bumboats, too, arrived to provide fresh meat and vegetables in return for Chinese silk, Bandana handkerchiefs, Indian and Cashmere shawls. These desirable commodities were ferried over to Dunkirk where they were stored temporarily in vast warehouses until they might be conveniently returned to England. Undoubtedly, smuggling was a highly profitable joint English/French commercial venture.

A 'centipede' smuggling galley © Dover Museum

Admiral Vernon (known as Old Grogram after the material from which his boat cloak was made) complained to the Admiralty in 1745:

> I can't but think 'tis a seasonable time to suggest to your Lordships that there are said to be in the town of Deal no less than two hundred able young men and seafaring people who are known to have no visible way of getting a living but by the infamous trade of smuggling, many keeping a horse and arms to be ready for all calls . . . This smuggling has converted those employed in it, first from honest industrious fishermen to lazy, drunken, profligate smugglers, and now to dangerous spies on all our proceedings, for the enemy's daily information . . . I can't but think it a national reproach upon us, to have let their villainy & treachery run to such extensive lengths.

Old Grog's estimate of the fishermen's involvement around Kent was conservative for it is known that at the beginning of the eighteenth century about 200 open boats were used for smuggling between the North and South Forelands. Deal galleys, it must be remembered, were built with smuggling in mind. Cheap and dispensable, they paid for themselves after only a couple of runs. Nonetheless, they were 'a beautiful description of boat' - slender, robust, elegant and capable of being rowed across the treacherous waters of the Channel in all weathers in a matter of hours. Galleys were fitted with about five seats or thwarts because they were rowed by from four to twenty oars, although they were sometimes driven by a square lug sail stretched across the hull. They were steered by means of an oar when rowed and a rudder when sailed. Owing to their narrow beam, shallow draft and large sail they required nearly half a ton of ballast which had to be shifted quickly to the weather side at each change of tack. Two galleys which have miraculously survived are *Undaunted* and *Saxon King*, which are displayed in Deal Maritime Museum.

Galley punts were larger craft measuring seven feet wide and from thirty-five to sixty feet in length. (Galleys were boats which were rowed but could be sailed while galley punts were sailed but could be rowed.) All Deal boats were clinker -built allowing maximum strength, increased speed and greater flexibility. They were manned by athletic young oarsmen who, because of their valuable piloting skills, were provided with 'tickets' exempting them from impressment into the Royal Navy. Perhaps for this reason Deal had only a lieutenant whereas Dover, a less important port, had a captain in charge of its three or four Press Gangs. Incredibly, galley punts were capable of making a dash from Dunkirk to Deal in five hours. One dodge, when chased by the Customs, was to land on the Goodwins, drag the galley over it and land at Deal before the Revenue cutter could sail round the sandbank.

Free traders experimented with longer craft manned by about thirty-six oarsmen, and nicknamed 'centipedes'. Deal centipedes, apparently, were between fifty and seventy feet long, and could reach Calais under oars in two hours. There is an entry in *Old Townsman's Diary* concerning the crew of one gargantuan vessel actually named *Centipede* which surrendered a terrific haul on 2 September 1806. This was such a cumbersome boat that the crew found her difficult to manoeuvre so she was easily surrounded by Customs officers assisted by a strong party of mounted dragoons when she attempted to land.

> The novelty of the circumstances produced a great sensation . . . The smugglers were taken by surprise, for heretofore no interference with their trade was ever attempted, and it was done in open day without fear or mistrust whatever.

Giant galleys were declared illegal since they could have no obvious purpose other than smuggling. Various laws were introduced to limit their existence. A rowing boat with four or more oars found near the coast could be burnt; vessels exceeding twenty-eight feet were forfeit to the Crown. Those revealing a secret compartment were sawn into three after which the pieces were often converted into a curious beach house. A Deal resident remembers seeing these upturned beach boats, one with a door cut into the hull and a chimney pot coming out through the keel, lining the beach between Walmer Castle and Kingsdown in the early years of the last century. Occasionally, captured boats were sold at auction but usually were regained by their original owners for a pittance since boatmen declined to bid for rivals' crafts.

Afloat, galleys were notoriously difficult to catch and often managed to evade the Revenue ships with consummate ease. This was surprising since the Revenue cutters, which were often built in the same dockyards, were regarded as the thoroughbreds of the sea. They were the epitome of fine sailing vessels and reigned supreme from 1785 to 1845. Nonetheless, they found their match in Deal galleys. One Naval officer despaired: 'Sending a cutter after one of those was like sending a cow to catch a hare'.

Luggers were preferred for smuggling larger cargoes. They were known as

Smugglers' Death galley, shown on a cigarette card © Dover Museum

'forepeakers' because of a small cabin which accommodated their crew of seven or eight men forward of the mast. These famous craft were two- or three-masted and rigged with a huge lug sail allowing them to ride closer to the wind. Luggers were always launched bow first sliding on greased skids down the steep beach where they gathered enough momentum to slice through the breakers and sail swiftly away from the coast. Their lute stern provided further lift when the boat was launched into a convenient wave. French versions of luggers were magnificent vessels with several decks and sails developed for privateering and known as *chasse-marees*. Luggers and galleys were often employed in tandem - a lugger towing a galley, both heavily laden with tubs, across the Channel, thus doubling the contraband. When challenged by Revenue officers, it was a simple matter to cut the accompanying boat free and deny all knowledge of the seaborne contraband . . . bobbing along with the tide.

All these boats were custom built - whether in England or France - with hollow masts or oars for storing tobacco and false forecastles, bulkheads, bows or keels for hiding barrels of spirits. The most favourite place to store contraband was in the cargo hold. Cabins held secret compartments behind panelling, under floorboards and above ceilings. When 'rummaging', Customs officials often failed to notice that boats were smaller inside than out. Skeins of tobacco were artfully coiled to resemble lengths of rope. Fishing nets, ballast bags and beach huts provided further concealments. Whenever goods were seized, details of their hiding places were carefully recorded and passed to all serving Customs officers along the Kent coast.

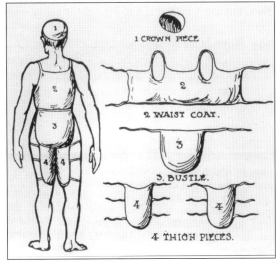

Concealments for tobacco in seamen's clothing © Dover Museum

An artful stratagem was to rope tubs of spirits together - with a heavy stone positioned between each one - and place them on the gunwale. Should the smugglers be chased it was a simple task to ditch the cargo overboard and retrieve it at a later date. It took only two or three minutes to sink a cargo of 300 tubs. Spirits and tobacco wrapped in oilskin could remain underwater for a month without deterioration. Another ruse was to sink the tubs close inshore attached to a recovery line marked by a cork buoy or feather. One of the regular duties of the Revenue boats was to patrol the shore with grappling irons which were pulled along the seabed in the hope of recovering sunken goods. This tedious task, called 'creeping', was hopeless, surely, without a precise location.

The seamen's clothing demonstrated further subterfuge. Pockets might be stitched inside their clothes so that jackets, waistcoats, trousers and underwear held tea or tobacco. A 'duffer' might walk with these padded garments all the way to London where he found a ready market. In 1851, John Cottle was discovered with six pounds of 'segars' packed in 'a pair of stays very ingeniously made' while his companion, John Osborn, had a further six pounds stowed in his hat and boots. By this time the extended run to London might be conveniently made by steam train.

Ownership of the craft employed for smuggling was dominated by the landlords of seafront inns who regularly financed expeditions across the Channel to restock their depleted cellars with illegal spirits. Cousin Jack, the smugglers' rhyming slang for cognac, was almost pure spirit and conveyed in vessels supplied by French distillers. Between runs crews slept in the taprooms and passages of inns awaiting the opportunity for a smooth crossing but also, at times, to recover contraband seized by the Customs. In December 1801 Customs officers captured a smuggling lugger near The Three Kings (the Royal Hotel) but as they were about to make off with their prize about 150 men

135

stormed from the public houses and retrieved the boat. A reward of £100 was offered for the apprehension of the men but it was never claimed. A similar reward was offered in July 1819 for the identification of the hovellers who violently obstructed the arrest of a notorious smuggler, Joshua Mocket, landlord of the Scarborough Cat.

During the French War, there was a specialised trade in smuggling gold across the English Channel – Deal smugglers were never inhibited by feelings of patriotism. After the Revolution the French currency had collapsed and the price of gold soared through devaluation at the height of hostilities with England. The French Empire remained solvent by purchasing English sovereigns and guineas, which were made of pure gold. Deal boatmen exploited the situation and were notorious guinea smugglers. It was estimated that gold worth £10,000 was smuggled out of the country each week. English guineas were conveyed to Paris under military escort and from thence to Spain to pay the troops engaged in battle against Wellington during the Peninsular Wars.

Napoleon boasted that for his final conflict at Waterloo a great part of the money was raised in London. He actively ecouraged Kent smugglers and allowed them to land unhindered at Dunkirk since not only did they convey intelligence from spies, but repatriated French prisoners-of-war. After his capture, Napoleon boasted to his gaolers:

> During the war all the information I received from England came through smugglers. They are people who have the courage and ability to do anything for money.

'Death' galleys were ingeniously constructed to provide an express service for these lucrative 'guinea runs'. Built cheaply in France, they were sixty feet long, carried two small auxiliary lug sails and bore minimum keel. They were exceedingly fast and dangerous to handle. Cunningly, they were painted white so that they merged with the surf, rendering them difficult to pursue at sea. Moreover, they lacked cargo space: there was no need of any since coins were secreted in leather purses strapped round the waists of the oarsmen. Death galleys were deemed expendable. They were required for one trip only - a night-time dash across the Channel.

An exciting chase occurred on 17 June 1811. The *Beagle* sighted a convoy of ten rowing boats heading for Calais. Immediately, it opened fire as the boats drew into line and attempted to defend themselves. At the same time the French brought field armament on to the sands to assist them. Most of the boats managed to land safely but the *Beagle* captured a galley, a catamarin and two punts. One Deal man was killed and eleven arrested. The boats were carrying not only gold but escaped French prisoners-of-war. In desperation the following year the government ordered the seizure of all galleys on the south-east coast considered suitable for guinea traffic. Seventeen galleys were confiscated at Deal, ten more at Folkestone. This trade died a natural death after the Peace Treaty of 1814.

William Pitt realised upon taking up office as Prime Minister that drastic measures needed to be taken to halt the smugglers, and he declared himself their chief foe. He resented the fact that a tremendous amount of duties required to

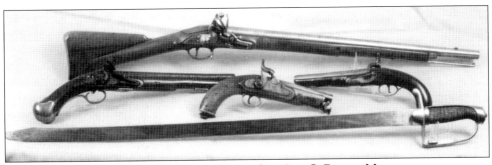
Weapons of the Preventive Service © Dover Museum

fund coastal defences at a time when Napoleon's invasion seemed imminent was lost through contraband. The instant he became Lord Warden he caused the extensive path to be built on the sea-ward side of Walmer Castle to assist the Preventive men. And it was while Pitt was in residence that he devised a devilish plan for which his name has become anathema among the fishing fraternity. From the ramparts he observed the fleet of luggers drawn high and dry upon the foreshore during the stormy month of January, 1784. Secretly, he contacted the War Office to request that a regiment of soldiers be despatched to Deal.

Rumours of the Prime Minister's malicious intentions towards the smugglers were rife. The landlord of the Fig Tree Inn at Kingsgate overheard the conversation of troops of the 13th Light Dragoons quartered nearby and he sent notice by carrier pigeon to his brother who kept the Drum Inn at Walmer. Consequently, a force of 300 smugglers turned out to prevent the troops from riding into the town, and a violent skirmish took place along the Sandwich Road. The 38th Foot marched swiftly from Canterbury to act as reinforcements.

All the landlords in Deal removed their signs - which meant that they were no longer obliged by law to billet troops - and lodging houses were inexplicably full up. The quartermaster secured a barn at a preposterous rent on the outskirts of the town to provide the troops with shelter. Subterfuge was required on both sides. Pitt ordered Captain Bray to patrol the Downs with Royal Navy cutters so that the following morning, when the soldiers arrived with loaded muskets on the foreshore, the townsfolk, who had gathered on the scene in numbers, assumed that a military exercise was about to take place as a precaution against invasion.

Instead, the troops set the entire fishing fleet ablaze. The boatmen stood helplessly by. The most they could do was to burn effigies of Pitt that night on their beach bonfires. While the Lord Warden expressed satisfaction that he had taken his revenge on 'this infernal town' the true effect on the economy of the port was disastrous since several gallant seafaring families were forced to enter the workhouse. 'Great indeed,' comments Laker, 'must have been the mortification of the men at this wicked and wanton destruction of their only means of livelihood.'

The Annual Register is the principal contemporary source for this incident. A report written by Captain Gabriel Bray gives an alternative account. According to Bray, he was assigned six Revenue cutters to assist him confiscate thirty-eight Deal luggers, many of which were:

So stove by the Smuglers that they sunk and went to pieces, about Forty more (some very large ones) were destroyed by the Smuglers before the Troops were drawn up, suspecting our design.

Surprisingly, Bray makes no mention of Pitt's terrible retribution which one recent researcher (Pat Muskett) has even ascribed to folklore. Whatever the circumstances, the destruction of Deal luggers knocked back smuggling for a short time only. Soon it was business as usual. Ironically, war leaders themselves frequently made use of intelligence supplied by sailors from the French ports. Pitt, personally, received news of the victory of Camperdown from a Deal smuggler at Walmer Castle. Wellington welcomed reports from smugglers while Nelson, too, employed them as pilots because of their expertise. And it should be remembered that during the ill-fated Walcheren expedition in 1809, a complete fleet of Deal luggers transported British troops to Holland free-of-charge, guided by smugglers familiar with these dangerous waters.

Generally, conflict raged between the authorities and the 'midnight men' of Kent. Captain Bray, who commanded the cutter *Nimble*, asserted that it was common practice for Deal smugglers to fire on Revenue boats: 'They have Carriage Guns at many Avenues or Streets, to cover their large boats, when landing Goods in the Night', he claimed. Once his crew came under artillery fire from the beach but they were assisted by dragoons, one of whom was shot by John Pettit. He was arrested but during his examination Pettit was rescued by his brother, George, who entered the courtroom with a brace of pistols tucked under his greatcoat.

A Preventive man © Dover Museum

Worse, when Bray's crew tried to seize a lugger beached at the North End in April 1784 they were hindered by smugglers firing muskets. His men retreated with only a few chests of tea and bags of cocoa, currants and rhubarb. They were lucky to escape with their lives because the smugglers 'drew down four Pounders very near the spot, which must have swept all our Men off', he reported. One crewman was captured, his head was shaved and there was talk of spiking him to a warehouse door for target practice until the smugglers decided he was more useful as a hostage.

A bloody clash at sea between

smugglers and the preventive men under Captain Bray was reported in a most unlikely newspaper, *The Lady*. On the night of 30 April 1784, Bray encountered the contraband-laden *Juliet* lugger, commanded by Thomas Brown, near the Goodwin Sands. He directed boats from both *Nimble* and *Scourge* to give chase and his men finally caught up with the smugglers as they hastily landed spirits on the beach near Deal. The vicious fight was graphically described: 'Brown presented a blunderbuss to Bray's breast, both of them not being half-a-yard distance from each other, the captain was not daunted. One of his men seeing his brave master in this situation, with a cutlass cut Brown's cheek clean off. Bray seconded the stroke, and with his cutlass severed his head from his body and put a period to this pirate's life.' Brown's death was not lamented since he was still wanted for the murder of Thomas Baxter, Customs officer, six years earlier.

The Gentleman's Magazine described a full scale assault which raged on 8 February 1783. Excise officers received a report that 1500 casks of smuggled spirits were being secreted in warehouses at Deal. They decided to investigate and travelled from Canterbury accompanied by a contingency from the 38th Regiment of Light Dragoons commanded by Captain Pennyman. The smugglers, having received intimation of their approach that evening, made preparations to repel the authorities.

A pitched battle ensued. The smugglers divided themselves into two groups. First they attacked the soldiers from a place of concealment and afterwards fired from behind windows and walls. Ropes were

Deal's Customs House seal

drawn across the streets to prevent the horses from advancing. Despite such determined resistance the troops stormed one warehouse which was found to contain twenty-two gallons of brandy, 304 gallons of gin and 225 lb of raw coffee. Casualties were light – two dragoons were injured and three horses were killed, but the smugglers concealed their wounds, fearing prosecution. A Royal pardon and a reward of £100 was offered for information regarding the offenders.

Early efforts to combat smuggling involved the military. In 1737 the Scots Greys were stationed at Deal while patrolling the Kent coast; in 1776, the 13th Dragoons were posted to the town at which time landlords protested that they lacked sufficient stabling while in 1784, a troop of 1st Dragoon Guards were despatched to control 'a partial state of anarchy and rebellion' which stemmed from smuggling at Deal.

When the regular army was required for more important duties the Militia was raised to fight the smugglers. The War Office recruited regiments from the furthest distance possible in an attempt to counter collusion with coastal inhabitants. This explains how a soldier from the north country met his untimely fate in Deal in 1794. On 25 September Customs officers discovered a lugger laden with contraband and called upon the Westmoreland Militia quartered in Deal to assist them in their seizure. A guard of soldiers was left to watch the prize on the foreshore overnight, but a midnight marauder shot at point blank range and fatally wounded Private John Elbeck. His tombstone has been removed from St George's churchyard to Deal Maritime Museum.

Violence against revenue men continued to escalate.

At first smugglers used oars, boathooks, handspikes, whips and scythes to defend their cargoes but they soon resorted to cutlasses and firearms. In 1732, Richard Hill, a Customs boatman from Deal, was shot dead at St Margarets Bay. In 1774, George Hughes and George Peake, Customs boatmen, were fired upon by horsemen when they attempted to seize tea and brandy. Francis Stubbers, another official, was threatened and stoned by forty riders who made off with their confiscated contraband. The Customs Commissioners concluded that smuggling at Deal 'was carried on by open force and violence . . . to a greater extent than at any other port in the kingdom'.

Charles II had appointed the Board of Customs in 1671 and the Board of Excise in 1683 to oversee the collection of duties and prevent evasion by smugglers. Uniforms for Customs officials were not introduced, surprisingly, until the late eighteenth century and only then for officers serving aboard cutters who were obliged to purchase their own naval style rig (although the Customs Board generously supplied their first set of buttons free). Customs officials were invested with immense power but met locally with firm opposition. The Collector of Customs at Deal commanded nineteen serving officers including landwaiters responsible for imported goods, tide surveyors who rummaged vessels and tidesmen who were put on board vessels until loading was completed. The Customs House stood half way down Custom House Lane at the south end of Middle Street. Nearby was the Tidewaiter's House (the official who boarded a ship upon arrival to enforce customs regulations) while at the top of the lane stood the boat station in Beach Street. The Customs House seal, which was stamped on legal cargoes that had passed through the port of Deal, was made in the Georgian period. Cast in silver, it carried the royal coat-of-arms and was inscribed *Honi Soit Qui Mal Y Pense*.

In 1717 the Customs Officer was John Gould. He was so diligent in the execution of his office that the smugglers contributed towards a common purse amounting to an incredible £200 to finance a dastardly scheme to ruin him by character assassination. In 1810, the Collector at Deal was William Rickords who appears to have been an elderly, timorous man. The smugglers intimidated him by threatening to blow up him, his house and the storehouse with gunpowder. Rickords applied to the government for protection and he was granted a military guard. Soldiers patrolled the vicinity and a sentry box was placed adjacent to his house. Pritchard asserts that, despite these precautions, an attempt was indeed made upon his life.

Customs officers constantly worked in danger of their lives. In January 1818 a seaman from the frigate *Severn*, detailed for duty in the Downs to support the Customs, attempted to board a suspicious lugger in the North End. He was seized, bound and gagged by the crew, then carried to a secluded alley where he was severely beaten. On another occasion, a coastguard was suddenly pounced upon, trussed up in a sack and dumped in St Georges churchyard. A third terrified victim was left to dangle on the end of a rope over the moat at Deal Castle. And it was quite usual for Customs officals, when attempting to board a suspect vessel, to be pitched headlong out of the boat. There are further tales of a Preventive man being pushed over the cliffs at Kingsdown to be dashed to pieces on the rocks below; of another being bashed over the head with a tub-filled sack and of a third whose hand was severed by a sweeping blow from a cutlass as he tried to board a boat. In wartime it was a simple matter for the smugglers to highjack officers wearing the King's uniform, ship them to France and land them on foreign soil where they might be incarcerated in prisons or executed by a firing squad.

Collisions between the smugglers and the authorities eventually reached such violence that ordinary people were afraid to walk the streets of Deal in safety.

In the midst of such hostility a tale is told of extreme kindness. Admiralty House, a grand mansion built about 1740, which stood in Queen Street until the middle of the nineteenth century, was the residence of the Port Admiral. Here was stored the fleet's pay plus gold bullion landed at Deal and guarded by Royal Marines. There was said to have been a secret room near the safe deposit where the wife of the chief official kept a wounded smuggler. Secretly, she nursed him back to health until he was able to make his escape . . .

THE COAST BLOCKADE

'Flogging Joey's Warriors'

AFTER THE FINAL DECLARATION of peace with France, smuggling soared to new heights with the surplus of demobilised sailors who sought profitable peacetime employment. These were daring seamen who had been trained to sail, fight and shoot aboard warships. At the same time the Admiralty made still more strenuous efforts to stamp out the 'National Evil' in Kent and Sussex and to this purpose deployed the now drastically curtailed Royal Navy.

The extent of smuggling in Deal has always been impossible to judge. One indication of the scale is from the list of goods which were actually seized although this can have been only the tip of the iceberg. While cruising for one month off Deal in 1786 *Nimble* captured and conveyed to the Customs House 1020 gallons of spirits, 7000 lbs of tobacco and 2000 yards of silk. On 14 February 1798 two Excise officers halted a post chaise leaving Deal by the Dover Road. It contained 14000 yards of French lace and 246 pairs of French gloves. In February 1805 the most notorious Deal lugger, *Diana*, was intercepted by Customs officials and revealed a consignment of 665 casks of brandy, 118 casks of rum, 237 casks of gin, 119 bags of tobacco, 43 lb of tea and countless bottles of wine. In June 1807 the cutter *Mosquito* seized more than 1000 kegs of spirits and sixty bags of tea while the following winter a total of 1890 kegs of spirits was brought into the Custom House. In May 1813, seventy casks of spirits were discovered under the nets of a mackerel boat which was being hauled up the shingle. And in September 1814, 420 bandana silk-patterned handkerchiefs were recovered from the rear of the Hoop and Griffin. Early in 1825, *Fly* surrendered to the Customs 1249 yards of silk, 2845 yards of ribbon and 461 handkerchiefs - all fashionable items in Regency days.

Smugglers vigorously defended their contraband. In 1801, when two Revenue vessels had driven a smuggling lugger ashore near Deal, the crew jumped overboard and went in search of assistance. Then, while the revenue men were struggling to refloat their prize, they were set upon by a horde of armed boatmen intent upon recovering the valuable cargo of fashionable fabrics, tobacco and playing cards. (Playing cards were taxed by Charles I - the exorbitant rate soon rose to half-a-crown per pack - and duty was not abolished until 1960)

In 1808 *Nimble,* supported by *Asp*, sighted two large galleys at dawn and chased them ashore at the North End. When the Revenue officers attempted to land themselves, they were assailed by heavy fire from the smugglers, who used beached boats as a barrage. They kept the officials at bay for half an hour until a detachment of soldiers arrived from the barracks. Finally, the smugglers fled leaving behind their booty – 400 tubs of gin.

In 1809 the Preventive Waterguard was formed to fill the gap between the Riding Officers ashore and the Revenue cutters which operated far out to sea. This amphibious, nocturnal force was charged with the pursuit of smugglers either afloat or on land. Preventive men were Royal Navy veterans whose shore bases were watch houses, also furnished with life-saving equipment to assist ships in distress. The Treasury, resigned to the fact that it was almost impossible to convict a smuggler unless caught in the act, proposed a new method whereby Preventive men would attempt to capture boatmen when they were actively engaged in running goods at sea. The Admiralty, therefore, provided the south coast with twenty-three cutters and forty-two rowing boats for this purpose. Each vessel was suitably armed and equipped with spying glasses, dark lanthorns and rummaging tools, including iron rods or prickers for thrusting into bales while searching for contraband. A Preventive boat manned by a Chief Officer, a sitter (coxswain) and a crew of six was now permanently stationed at the North End of Deal.

A sensational trial took place at the Old Bailey of two Deal men charged with wilful murder on the high seas in November 1815. John Gillam and William Brockman, alias Billy Rock, were accused of killing four seamen from the Revenue cutter *Fox*. The chief witness was John Atkins, keeper of a lodging house at Walmer, who had bravely turned King's evidence. He expressed repulsion at the prisoners' heinous crime even though he had been paid handsomely for his part in the smuggling expedition that had such horrific consequences.

Atkins had provided the smugglers with a crew for his own centipede galley which had ventured across the Channel overnight to collect 200 tubs of spirits from Boulogne. On 8 August the rowing party left the French coast in the early morning, taking firearms on board as a precaution. At noon they were spotted by the boat belonging to *Fox*, whose eight-man crew hoisted her warning sail and made toward the galley, firing a gun as a signal that she intended to board.

When the vessels were within hailing distance the Revenue men perceived they were outnumbered and decided to retreat. Gillam deliberately ran into the government boat, cutting her down to the water's edge. The smugglers then opened fire. Four of the officers sprang into the galley where they were met with a hail of bullets. One of them was shot in the chest and, after being clubbed on the head, was thrown overboard. *Fox's* boat turned over and her remaining crew hung desperately to the wreck. Gillam and Brockman waved their hats mockingly at the doomed seamen as they turned for the shore. Luckily, the four surviving officers were rescued by a passing Deal lugger.

Twelve hours later the smugglers successfully landed their goods at Herne Bay. They took their galley further along the shore where they had nothing to fear, even when approached by the Revenue cutter *Scorpion*. Gillam proffered Atkins an extra guinea on account of the affray and the smugglers went their separate ways. Later they were identified by oyster fishermen who had witnessed the brutal incident mid-Channel.

At their trial Gillam and Brockman were convicted almost entirely upon the evidence of the informer, Atkins, for whom afterwards they magnanimously declared no malice. The pair were found guilty and hanged at Execution Dock.

Smugglers were, in truth, ruthless and aggressive. A £500 reward was offered in June 1816 for the capture of the audacious gang who not only violently obstructed Stephen Smith, sitter of the Preventive boat, and his assistants who had seized a vessel laden with spirits near Sandown Castle, but had daringly rescued one of their members when he had been detained in the guard house by a sergeant of the 39th Regiment. It was remarkable that there was no informant because the reward offered was far in excess of the combined value of the boat and its cargo.

Revenue men faced constant danger. In 1811 an officer aboard the Excise cutter *Lively* was killed in a skirmish with smugglers at North Deal. In 1818 William Soames, Searcher of Deal, attempted to apprehend two boatmen strolling through Middle Street apparently carrying a tub of spirits concealed in a sack. Soames gave chase but while he stopped to examine the burden which one of the men had dropped he was stabbed in the back with a large clasp knife.

The Times reported an appalling incident involving two Excisemen - Smith and Payne - in the summer of 1821. Deal smugglers were pitiless in their treatment of these diligent officers who had actively pursued them and almost brought them to justice. They were surprised while on duty by armed men who carried them away by force to a lonely place where they were stripped naked, daubed with tar and covered with feathers. They were then paraded through the streets in a cart until their merciful release.

It must be admitted that the authorities were not always successful in holding their prize. In 1813 carousers spilling out of the Port Arms drove off Customs officials who had that moment seized a smuggling boat and regained its contraband. That same summer the boats' crews of *Rattlesnake* and *Scourge* made a capture in the sandhills and were conveying their wares to the Customs House when they were violently attacked by smugglers near Sandown Castle. In 1814 two boats' crews from *Scourge* chased two smugglers ashore at the North End but were instantly ambushed by a mob from Beach Street.

Nor did they always have success in retaining their prisoners. In 1817 four smugglers were confined in the four cells at the newly built Town Hall which comprised Deal Gaol. Their friends came to the rescue, made a hole in the wall and carried them off in triumph. A similar event occurred the following year when the smugglers cut through the roof of the gaol and carried off another prisoner leaving the blade of their saw behind.

Pritchard notes an incident when the members of a gang of smugglers charged into the Council Chamber to rescue their comrades brought before the Magistrates. Brandishing pistols, the ruffians broke up the court and ordered the authorities to leave forthwith. 'One of the justices fainted, another was seized with cramp, and the whole of the bystanders dumb,' he asserts, 'with wonderment and fright.' Prudently, smugglers afterwards brought before the Deal magistrates were surrounded by an armed guard.

The Admiralty's determination to combat smuggling on the south coast culminated in the formation of the Royal Navy Coast Blockade for the

Prevention of Smuggling in 1816. Its command was entrusted to Captain James William McCulloch RN, who, because of his brutal discipline, earned the sobriquet Flogging Joey. Previously McCulloch had spent much of his time in service with the Channel Fleet blockading the French ports, before crossing the Atlantic to distinguish himself fighting in the American War. Returning from the West Indies, Captain McCulloch was appointed to command HMS *Ganymede* and charged with patrolling the English Channel in pursuit of smugglers, which task inevitably brought him into the Downs. At the same time, Revenue cutters came under the control of the Navy and commanders of a small fleet of vessels stationed on the south coast - *Rattlesnake, Scourge, Seagull, Swallow, Nimble, Asp, Lively* (Excise) and *Lively* (Customs) - were obliged to report directly to Captain McCulloch.

Captain William McCulloch

Deal, by now, had become the country's most notorious centre of smuggling and McCulloch's avowed intention was to restore law and order into the town and to make the grass grow in its streets. He practically realised this noble objective in a short period of time by his systematic harrying of smugglers by land and sea.

Certainly, the arrival of this dedicated young commander in the Downs was tantamount to a declaration of open warfare between the government and the criminal fraternity of Deal and Walmer. Almost immediately after he accepted his appointment, Captain McCulloch intercepted a Dutch schooner, *Celeritas,* out of Antwerp, as she prepared to offload kegs of gin onto a Deal galley which ran casually alongside. He was astonished by the audacity of the crew who attempted this illegal transaction in broad daylight.

McCulloch received reliable intelligence from a paid informer that there was a programme of massive boatbuilding in Boulogne and Dunkirk in preparation for a renewed campaign of organised smuggling on the Kent coast. Consequently, he rowed out armed seamen nightly from his three large, locally-built galleys, to form a cordon on the land around Deal and Walmer. His novel method of employing armed shore parties proved far more effective than the outmoded Waterguard and Landguard, although he was careful to liaise with Customs Collectors at Deal and Dover.

Captain McCulloch acted entirely upon his own initiative. The Prime Minister, Lord Liverpool, was so impressed by his laudable efforts that he offered his full support by ordering the despatch of fifty marines from Chatham to assist. Unfortunately, when the marines arrived at South Barracks, they found that not only had the military stores been robbed but the new recruits were soon infected with 'the Itch'. Further they were met with such hostility from the natives that after one affray at Kingsdown three marines were admitted to the Naval Hospital.

Captain McCulloch could not relax his vigilance for one moment. Believing that he had achieved instant results by forcing Deal smugglers to operate further west, he ordered the commanders of *Scourge* and *Asp* to concentrate their offensive on an area between the South Foreland and Dungeness. His complacency was soon shaken when he tried to land shore parties from *Ganymede* in a strong gale on the night of 12 December 1816. One galley was sunk, attempts to launch a sailboat from the Navy Yard failed while the Revenue cruisers were forced to seek shelter in the Downs. Next morning he was dismayed to learn that at the height of the storm 2500 kegs of brandy were landed from ten boats, completely unhindered.

OGDEN'S CIGARETTES

HMS Ramillies on a cigarette card

Deal smugglers soon became accustomed to working elsewhere. On 12 August 1817, Midshipman Doulton chased the *Hope* from Deal as its crew attempted to land tubs of spirits at Broadstairs. That October, Deal luggers *Salus*, *Ox* and *Po* towed seven galleys laden with tubs from Boulogne and offloaded them on the North Kent coast. *Nancy* and *Ox* frequently crossed the Channel laden with gold to pay for further supplies of contraband, and their skilled crews easily evaded pursuit by Revenue cruisers. The infamous *Po* was repeatedly seized but she obstinately continued to operate. After ten years' fruitless pursuit the Coast Blockade teamed up with Customs officers to seize her as she attempted to land twenty-four bales of tea from an East Indiaman on Deal beach. The men pounced as her crew manned the capstan but the smugglers escaped and presumably bought back their boat at a ridiculously low price at a later date. On 18 November 1828 *Norfolk* was seized after a chase, although devoid of contraband, as she left Calais. This lugger was impounded for contravening the licensing law, introduced in 1820, which forbade a sailing vessel to operate beyond twelve miles from port.

McCulloch was tenacious in his pursuit of Deal smugglers wherever they operated, and so the Admiralty extended his territory in the autumn of 1817 to between the North and South Forelands. Resolutely, he took total command of the Revenue cutters and organised boat patrols to row out from a succession of vessels - *Ganymede* (a sixth-rate frigate captured from the French) *Severn* (a fourth -rate frigate built experimentally of pitch pine rather than oak, which soon rendered it unseaworthy) and HMS *Ramillies* (a redoubtable third-rate sloop of the line which had distinguished herself fighting alongside Nelson at the Battle of Copenhagen and now served as the main floating headquarters of the Coast Blockade from 1823 to 1831) - stationed in the Downs.

Smuggled kid gloves found under floor boards of a house in Golden Street

In addition, Captain McCulloch instigated night-time surveillance of the cliffs and beaches. Crews were landed in their galleys a little after sunset and returned to their ships before dawn. All boats in local waters were ruthlessly watched, followed and searched directly they landed at night. The Captain's repeated requests for increases in manpower - officers and marines - were readily granted by the Admiralty who enjoyed the novelty of the Royal Navy acting for the first time as an effective law enforcement on land. They even authorised the purchase of a private schooner, *Flying Fish*, to act as McCulloch's tender and assist in recruitment around the coast. Later tenders based at Deal included *Pioneer, Industry, Antelope* and *Grinder*.

Captain McCulloch's district was extended from the Isle of Sheppey to Chichester Harbour in 1820. Wisely, he organised the Coast Blockade into three manageable divisions - Left, Centre and Right (looking seawards) - which were then subdivided into four districts. The divisions were each supervised by a senior lieutenant, a midshipman and two petty officers, while the districts were overseen by junior lieutenants. Men were grouped into parties of ten - five were to be on duty at any one time - who patrolled a stretch of the coast and were stationed in guard houses situated about four miles distant from each other. Deal was in Central Division and the Blockade Headquarters eventually moved from ship to shore into South Barracks when the service became more land orientated.

In 1869, a Lloyds correspondent observed: 'Deal might have been built for smuggling . . . The streets run parallel to the beach, and close to it, and are connected by numerous narrow alleyways, out of which open doors leading into yards and sheds. The beach extends some miles, and at various points of it, on the shingle itself, stand roomy wooden sheds, belonging to the boatmen. The cargoes of a whole fleet of ships, once landed on the beach, might be so effectually disposed of in these yards and sheds, in a few hours that not a trace of them would remain.'

Skirmishes intensified along the line and major affrays reached unprecedented savagery. The first murder of a member of the Blockade occurred on 20 October 1818. Customs officers secured the assistance of Blockade officers from *Severn* to arrest two hovellers, suspected of smuggling, hiding in the King's Arms in Beach Street. It was surrounded but as the smugglers made their escape through the door John Nelson barred their way and was shot dead. The murderer was identified as William Dowers and a reward of £500 was offered for his capture. The landlord was arrested for complicity and brought before our timid Mayor. Meantime, Dowers made his way to Ramsgate from whence he obtained a safe crossing on a merchantman bound for America. In the summer of 1823 Lieutenant Jay and Sentinel Williams were ambushed by three smugglers and beaten with cudgels, reputedly six feet long.

Two Blockade officers from HMS *Severn* who died young are buried at St Mary's Church, Walmer: James Nicol, an assistant surgeon, aged twenty-seven (presumably from accidental blood-poisoning) and Godfrey Springall Finch, Master's Mate, aged twenty-nine.

At first, the strength of the Coast Blockade comprised 1300 men who were drawn from naval personnel discharged from service after the French Wars. This tremendous independent fighting force was trained in the use of the fearsome cutlass and sea-musket and it soon became the scourge of Channel smugglers. It was accommodated in a variety of buildings which ensured 'a complete cordon of sentinels posted within hailing distance of each other along the entire coast of Kent and Sussex on the brink of the tide'. Walmer Barracks, Sandown Castle, No 1 and No 2 Batteries on the sandhills were requisitioned locally, and Watch Houses were built at North Deal.

Captain McCulloch occupied a suite of rooms with his secretary and clerks inside the Port Admiral's office, a bleak, exposed building facing the grim foreshore. At least it was convenient for him to draw stores from the nearby Navy Yard and to contact the adjacent Royal Signalling Tower. In 1820, a series of signalling stations employing Popham's two-arm land semaphore was established along the south coast linking Deal with Beachy Head. This provided rapid visual communication between Revenue ships, the Royal Navy and the Coast Blockade.

Flogging Joey's Warriors, or 'Sentinels', received fierce resistance not only from the smugglers but local dignitaries who secretly supported free trade. For instance Captain McCulloch identified a public house, Good Intent, near Sandown Castle, as a centre for smuggling but he was thwarted in his attempt to close it down since the chief brewer, Edward Iggulsden, was both mayor and magistrate.

Once, Captain McCulloch detailed two midshipmen from the *Severn* to watch the movements of a pair of boatmen, suspected of handling contraband, in Middle Street. One of the suspects was recognised as the notorious scoundrel Will Worthington. The midshipmen gave chase and pursued the men through Lower Street to the Fish Market where they were surrounded by a hostile crowd who had gathered in support of the smugglers. One of the midshipmen, James Taverner, panicked and fired a shot before retreating to the safety of a nearby shop. He was promptly arrested by Mayor Iggulsden, and committed for trial - bail refused - on a capital charge.

Midshipmen David Peat and John Robilliard, recently promoted, were put in charge of search parties at North End Watch House. The first time they went to search luggers an angry mob tried to overturn a boat and crush the two men. Peat, while further investigating the beach near the Hoop and Griffin, was attacked by a total stranger who broke a stick over his head. When he fired his pistol to summon aid, Peat was cautioned by the parish constable that he was in breach of the peace and hauled before Edward Iggulsden. Robilliard apprehended three men carrying a tub but he was knocked to the ground and drew his cutlass in defence. The same parish constable arrested him on a charge of wounding and brought him before Iggulsden, who, predictably, imprisoned him in Deal Gaol.

David Peat, the first officer appointed by the Blockade, was also the most distinguished and rose swiftly to become Commander. The epitome of the dashing young naval officer, he sustained terrible injuries in the course of his duty and earned praise for his courage from Captain McCulloch. His tenacity was demonstrated when he captured a boat attempting to land 180 tubs of spirits at No 1 Battery, north of Sandown Castle, and warded off ten armed men until help arrived. Two nights later he discovered stow holds in the sandhills containing twenty-eight tubs of brandy and 121 of gin, which infuriated the local smugglers who had jealously guarded their secret location.

Once they were caught, McCulloch had extreme difficulty keeping his prisoners. George Gard escaped from the guardhouse of the 39th Regiment at North End in June while another miscreant, named Foreman, was snatched from an escort of soldiers and Customs men in August 1816. Each time a mob of 300 or more - mainly women and children - assembled throwing stones. They closed in so tightly around the soldiers that firearms could not be employed.

Even seized vessels were likely to vanish. On 6 June 1817 a smuggling galley was handed over to the Excise but that night its owners broke into the boathouse and spirited it away. McCulloch's revenge was swift. He ordered a routine search of all the boats on the beach - two revealed false bottoms and a third contained dry goods - discoveries which inflamed the crews. Next morning the missing galley reappeared, hard by the Excise boat shed. More successful was the retention of a newly built giant galley discovered on the beach near Walmer Castle and requisitioned by the Blockade in September 1817.

The Sentinels remained relentless in their pursuit. One Deal report records:

Lugger Active came on shore at night, was searched but nothing found. A sentry was placed on board and in daylight a further search revealed the hollow masts to conceal 20 pieces bandanas and 655 French silk. (22 May 1820).

Next day *Snipe* and *Fly* revealed equivalent cargoes artfully concealed. Similarly, *Hero* was later found to contain 15 tin cases in her hollow keel each containing a quart of spirits.

A triumph for Captain McCulloch came when he learned from his informer that his arch enemy, Harry Stokes, the notorious Deal smuggler, had announced his retirement and removed to Brighton.

Captain McCulloch's miniature shows him to be a handsome Scot with alert eyes, determined mouth and short black hair. He sports a royal blue jacket, cream waistcoat with gold buttons and a black stock tied round his high collar. A flash of lace at his neck presents him as a dandy. He was certainly a wealthy man since his annual salary rose to almost £600. Surprisingly, he was capable of showing compassion towards the Deal boatmen when his campaign against the smugglers began to bite. He petitioned the Admiralty to foster their former skills as Channel pilots in order to prevent them from being admitted into the workhouse after the loss of their illegal trade.

The Blockade Service was divided into two counties in 1825 with Captain McCulloch in charge of the Kent Coast Blockade. Deal remained at the centre of his activities so it was natural that he took up residence in the town with his wife, Jane, whom he had married in 1810 in the West Indies. They had a large family and the parish registers record the burial of eight children in Deal and Walmer. Initially, they occupied an empty house in the Naval Hospital but later were forced to retreat into South Barracks after McCulloch received death threats and his pregnant wife had been stalked.

McCulloch's death is a mystery, for after 'a long and afflicting illness', he died prematurely, aged forty-five on 25 October 1825. He had been nursed at Admiralty House, the imposing residence of the Port Admiral in Queen Street, where Dr McArthur, an eminent surgeon of the day, treated him for spasmodic asthma.

His widow retreated to Harbledown near Canterbury where she lived on her pension from the Admiralty. The Captain received only a brief obituary in the

Deal lugger in the Downs, from a painting by Clarkson Stanfield

local newspaper and his memorial tablet in the burial ground of St Leonards Church adds scant information. The log of *Ramillies* recorded his funeral: '29th October 1825, Capt. McCulloch interred 12.30 hrs., Lieuts. Searle and Williams attending'. Clearly, the service had taken a toll on his health for he tirelessly patrolled the line in his private coach, often in foul weather, at night and in winter. Yet he remained unmourned by either his serving officers or Deal inhabitants.

'In a perverse way this lack of recognition serves only to underline the man's achievements', opines Roy Philp in *The Coast Blockade*. This successful service had evolved from such humble beginnings when Captain McCulloch initially proposed his *Suppression of Smuggling between North Foreland and Dungeness* to the Admiralty. Before his untimely death he commanded an unprecedented preventive campaign involving 2600 men on 130 stations along 200 miles of coast, despite minimal support from Revenue authorities and open hostility from communities. 'At a time when a desperate government wanted action he showed what could be done by a naval commander endowed with imagination, enthusiasm and persistence'.

Certainly, smuggling never attained such mammoth proportions after the active intervention of Flogging Joey.

His post was taken by Captain Hugh Pigot, an heroic sailor who proved far more popular among the townsfolk. This was no doubt because he instigated the first Deal and Downs Regatta where galleys and luggers competed off-shore from Deal, Dover and Folkestone. Yachts entered from as far away as Cowes on the Isle of Wight. Signal guns for the eight races were fired from HMS *Ramillies* on Regatta Day, 10 August 1826. The event concluded with a grand ball previously advertised in the *Kentish Gazette*:

Tickets, Ladies 4s, Gentlemen 5s. Dancing to commence at Nine.

Prizes were distributed by the mayor, Edward Iggulsden, for once displaying affability towards members of the Coast Blockade.

Pigot's career as a Commander of the Coast Blockade culminated in the capture of George Ransley, leader of the vicious Aldington Gang whose field of operation stretched from Walmer to Rye. His crew were also involved in several heroic rescues of ships trapped in violent storms in the Downs including the brig, *Mountaineer*, which had a Deal pilot aboard, on 24 November 1829. The Admiralty provided Captain Pigot with a new depot ship, *Talavera*, named after the great sea battle, which was towed to her moorings off Deal by two steam vessels in 1830.

The Coast Blockade was abolished in 1831, largely as a cost-cutting measure by the new king, William IV, by which time it had been superseded by the Coast Guard as the principal anti-smuggling force. This was commanded by Captain William Bowles, and it became the Royal Navy's first reserve charged with the duty to 'search and examine all suspicious vessels coming within the limits of their stations . . . and to seize all goods prohibited to be imported or exported'. The Coast Guard, which had been formed ten years earlier, was divided into two divisions - a marine section and a land section that consisted of a Mounted Guard of young cavalrymen armed with pistols and sabres. The advantage of the

An old-world nook, DEAL - KENT.

The Fountain Hotel at Deal, a centre of smuggling

new service was that it could not only authorise military assistance but also the county police force which had recently been instigated by Robert Peel. This arrangement still exists with the modern Coastguard.

Sam Hellard, a veteran of the Coast Blockade, was appointed Commander, Deal District Coast Guard, in April 1831. Coast Guard officers wore a distinctive blue uniform with gilt buttons, and a glazed black hat encircled by a ribbon, and they lived with their families in commodious stations. They were heavily armed with a brace of pistols, cutlass, musket and bayonet, and were equipped with a telescope, lantern and stool known as a one-legged donkey. The new method of routing free traders involved constant vigilance rather than chasing smugglers by land at sea. For a time there was rivalry between the two services - the Naval Blockade was directed by the Admiralty while the Coast Guard was formed by the Customs - and there are reported instances of both attempting to impound the same illicit cargo. The Customs resumed control of revenue vessels and when *Talavera* was requisitioned as a depot ship for the Coast Guard it signalled the end of an era for the Coast Blockade.

By the middle of the nineteenth century the Coast Guard could justifiably claim that it had substantially curbed smuggling in the English Channel. The introduction into the Revenue service of steam cutters powerful enough to pursue the fastest sailing vessel, coupled with the standard issue of the Colt revolver to all officers, resulted in far fewer cases of smuggling reported in the official station log books. In 1856, the Admiralty took control of the Coast Guard, which began to concentrate on its secondary priority of saving lives at sea – which laudable role it continues to this day. Consequently, the Customs service was reduced to a smaller, unarmed force. In 1867, smuggling had so far diminished that only three cases were brought before Deal magistrates: George Reed, discovered with 3lb of tobacco; John Holloway, 5lb of tobacco and Robert Norris, a North Sea pilot, who dared to land his galley punt with 13lb of tobacco concealed in his personal luggage. Norris was fined, despite his plea that the tobacco was a gift from the captain of a ship he had piloted.

Queen Victoria's Prime Minister, Sir Robert Peel, vastly reduced or abolished the import duties on tea, wine and spirits so that tobacco remained the only worthwhile commodity in the nineteenth century to interest the Kentish smugglers. The government's main source of income had been duties collected by the Customs and Excise services until this time, but Peel re-introduced income tax first levied by Pitt, but abolished after the French Wars. Peel's bold act actually increased revenue and fostered trade, particularly for the manufacturing industries, and in consequence Victorian Britain prospered. Smuggling was mainly confined to spirits, watches and tobacco.

In 1851, James Dawes was convicted of attempting to smuggle 24 lb of cigars and his boat was confiscated while he was imprisoned in Sandwich Gaol. Cigars were often carried into the country by women who tucked them into their crinolines or muffs, while fishermen's giant seaboots were a further source of concealment thus enabling tobacco to be marched past the most vigilant Customs officers and giving rise to the term bootlegging. A far greater seizure was made the following year by the Customs at Deal when 1200 lb of tobacco was discovered aboard the lugger *Earl Grey*. John Foster and his crew surrendered but, amazingly, prosecution of their case collapsed in court through insufficient evidence.

Stories concerning The Chequers Inn at Sandown strike a gruesome note. Mr Marsh, the landlord, supposedly constructed chambers in the sandhills where run goods could be temporarily stored. His cart shed served as a makeshift mortuary when bodies were washed ashore at North Deal. In 1872 the corpses of two men drowned when they were swept from the lower foreyard of the brig *Mercy*, of Poole, were laid out on a bench there. A suspicious Coast Guard dared to disturb the sailcloth shrouds which, strangely, reached to the floor. Underneath were hidden sixteen tubs of brandy.

A trap was set to catch the smugglers. Early the next morning Coast Guards kept watch as a cart approached, drawn by mournful mariners intent on removing both the bodies and the brandy. A looker's son alerted the smugglers by his wild cries and the men made off towards the town. The Coast Guards gave hot pursuit. When they returned to the cart shed, having failed to capture their prey, they found the bodies - but no spirits.

From the mid-nineteenth century onwards smuggling was definitely in decline. In future Deal boatmen tended to desist from their illegal pursuits and turned to the nobler yet dangerous career of 'hovelling', which included taking out supplies to ships, dredging for lost anchors, providing pilots and salvaging wrecks. The days of the big organised runs seemed over although from time to time the boatmen were tempted by an opportune moment.

'Handsome Georgian houses built during this era in many otherwise poor areas testify to the wealth brought by the smuggling industry', says the modern historian, Roy Philp. Deal's boatmen's quarter boasts an abundance of imposing houses built from illegal profits, while vast attics and cellars, hidden rooms and secret passages reveal the extent of the trade. Occasionally, smuggled goods come to light when builders renovate period houses. One intriguing discovery concerned a batch of two dozen early eighteenth century white French kid gloves found wrapped in oilskins and concealed under floorboards in a house in Golden Street.

Hidey-hole at 13 Silver Street

Houses reluctantly surrender their secrets. That at 13 Silver Street has a trapdoor in a recess to the left of the fireplace on the first floor, where a wooden ladder leads down to the spacious hide behind the ground floor room. At 2 Farrier Street there is an enormous storage space hidden by rafters in the pitched roof. A trapdoor leads to a hidey-hole beside the chimney breast on the second storey of 151 Middle Street and the former Seven Stars Inn, at 142 Middle Street, has a tunnel filled in with shingle in the cellar, which is a sure indication of discovered smuggling pursuits.

Renovation of 94 Middle Street revealed a vertical drop behind the fireplace inside a ventilated cupboard on the first floor. Demolition of 36 Beach Street caused excitement when the verandah was discovered to have a double skin most convenient for storing a lifetime's supply of tobacco. The tiny porthole at Porthole Cottage in Exchange Street and the minute window high on the wall of 127 Middle Street are said to have been lookouts with an uninterrupted view of the sea.

Try as hard as they might Revenue men were unlikely to discover one extensive run which stretched almost the entire length of Coppin Street leading directly from the beach. So artfully concealed, in fact, was this particular hide that the 'gentlemen' might well have been engaged in their illicit pursuits, undisturbed, while a careful search took place below.

Start of the run was at the Three Compasses Inn at the head of the street facing the sea. A three feet square shaft - still existing - led from a small back room on the ground floor upwards through two storeys to the attic. Smugglers hauled barrels of brandy through this shaft and stored them temporarily in the rafters. From there it was possible to travel in a westerly direction under the eaves to where a hatchway concealed a small circular opening. Along this narrow passage, now bricked off, it would have been possible to push the contraband one barrel at a time. Audaciously, this short tunnel passed through Coppin House and its adjoining coach house, built for Joshua Coppin, Mayor of Deal, and out through a trapdoor on to the rooftops.

It is still possible to trace the tail end of the run as it winds its way over three houses where the smugglers deftly conveyed their wares. A narrow gully served as a footpath and where the height of the roof varies convenient footholds were set into the walls. All the time, the sharply rising rooftops concealed the smugglers from view at street level.

Every so often openings were set into the roofs allowing contraband to be stored in spacious attics. Occupants of these houses did not have internal access to their own top rooms because they could be reached only from the outside. Number 7 is an exception since a trapdoor gives access to an extensive loft. Here the treads are incredibly thick, to prevent barrels crashing through the ceiling. On the ground floor a flagstone lifts beside the fireplace to allow a further place of concealment in the cellar.

At the end of the rooftop run, No 5, a trapdoor is set into a traverse wall through which more barrels might be passed. To the right is a small attic having a sloping ceiling yet in which there was room to store a dozen or more barrels. Should the smugglers be disturbed a room one floor below contained a secret compartment. A slim cupboard cunningly leads to a wide recess behind the chimney. There the smugglers might wait in comfort until the danger had elapsed. Thus the craft of the Deal Smuggler had reached its zenith.

Over the years local inhabitants had learned that they disturbed the smugglers at their peril. William Hulke, the apothecary, who lived at Comarques in Lower Street, was often called upon to attend the Duke of Wellington when in residence at Walmer Castle. Late one night while making a call upon a humbler patient he interrupted a gang of smugglers unloading contraband on the beach below the castle. Three pistols were fired in rapid succession and one bullet whistled past his head. Elvin relates an interview with an elderly resident who recalled attending a supper party at Beach House, adjacent to Walmer Lodge, in the late nineteenth century. A gang of smugglers burst into the room and ordered their host to extinguish all the candles while the Preventive men rode past.

Customs and Excise merged in 1902. Twenty years later the Coastguard was transferred from the Admiralty to the Board of Trade when it assumed an exclusively life-saving role. Today HM Customs and Excise at Dover is responsible for preventing smuggling via ferries and pleasure boats across the English Channel. Smuggled goods now number alcohol, tobacco, drugs, pornography, firearms, ammunition and counterfeit items such as Swiss watches, designer clothes, CDs and motor parts, which are secreted in cars or lorries. The main system for identifying possible smugglers is by profiling – a complicated analysis of individual passengers developed at Dover after the withdrawal of internal frontiers in 1993. Smuggling, indeed, remains a complicated business.

TELEGRAPHS AND TIME BALLS

'The phenomenon of the age'

DEAL'S TIME BALL TOWER, which stands prominently on the seafront, was the earliest means of making Greenwich Mean Time known to shipping in the Downs. Its purpose was to signal accurate time - essential for mariners to determine longitude - to fleets passing through the English Channel. Originally, this building had been a Royal Signal Tower. It is the last remnant of the thriving Navy Yard established in the reign of Charles II to provide light repairs, stores and provisions for warships anchored in the Downs.

Deal had been the last in a line of telegraph stations across the county by which the Admiralty in London communicated with Royal Navy ships during the Napoleonic Wars. Trials in passing urgent messages by telegraph had begun in 1794 after a drawing of a T-type mechanical system invented by Claude Chappe had been discovered on a French prisoner-of-war. It showed how a revolutionary telegraph system superseded beacons and horsemen for long-distance communication on the Continent.

The Reverend Lord George Murray, fourth son of the third Duke of Atholl, devised a similar levered telegraphic system which was hastily adopted by the Admiralty. Messages were transmitted by means of pivoted shutters mounted on the roofs of a string of stations placed on prominent positions across Kent and the Isle of Sheppey. The *Picture for London* for 1808 states:

> On the top of the Admiralty are erected two telegraphs, one communicating with Deal, and the other with Portsmouth, the inside of which may be seen, on proper application, or very small interest with the porters, or persons who work the machines.

Murray's machine consisted of six shutters, each three foot square, arranged in a double column on a twenty-foot high vertical frame. These square - sometimes octagonal - shutters were pivoted horizontally and could be opened or closed by a complicated system of cranks, ropes and counterpoises. The combination of open or closed shutters corresponded with a recognised code thus enabling messages to be passed from one station to another. In this ingenious manner it was possible to receive, check and transmit instructions within minutes from the Admiralty to ships lying at anchor in the Downs.

This revolutionary device was capable of sixty-three changes corresponding with letters of the alphabet, numerals and pre-selected codes. Numerous arbitrary phrases included 'Deal', 'the Downs' and 'Port Admiral in the Downs'. Curiously, the key is revealed on a lady's fan dating from the late eighteenth century displayed in the National Maritime Museum at Greenwich. This was not an inappropriate pattern, since fashionable ladies operated their own telegraph system, employing fans to convey clandestine messages across the crowded ballrooms of the eighteenth century. A central illustration depicts operators of the shutters inside the hut - a foreman attending to the ropes, a midshipman looking through his telescope and a disabled officer copying the message into a ledger.

Murray's model shutter telegraph
© National Maritime Museum

George Roebuck, surveyor, was contracted to set up an experimental line of twelve timber-built telegraph stations between London and Deal with a branch line of a further three stations to Sheerness. The telegraph line was completed by January 1796. It ran from the roof of the Admiralty building in London across Kent to the terminal station at Deal. Cornilo's map of *c*1800 identifies the telegraph station as a wooden hut actually on the beach, although a less reliable report asserts that the shutter frame surmounted the Admiral's office adjacent to the gates of the Navy Yard. *The Kentish Travellers Companion* of 1799 notes:

> At the south end of Beach Street, close to the sea, stands a telegraph, being the first of the series communicating with each other, for conveying intelligence from the Downs to the Admiralty office in Westminster.

An 1829 plan of the Naval Yard at Deal places the telegraph station at a curious angle and this puzzling orientation is explained by the fact that it corresponded with the second station in line four miles westwards at Betteshanger. This ramshackle building remains alongside the Roman Road at Telegraph Farm on a slight eminence affording a clear view of the Downs. Built of brick with chalk rubble the historic station is in a truly derelict state but adjacent stables are

Fan showing the shutter telegraph © National Maritime Museum

constructed of strangely scored timbers which may be the actual shutters rescued from the original telegraph. Potential building land next to the Deal station was purchased by the Admiralty for the use of the telegraph and was retained as a garden presumably to prevent obstruction of the sightlines between the two shutter stations which crossed it.

The overland telegraph stations each consisted of an operations room and two small apartments heated by an iron stove; the cost, including furnishings, was £215. Each station was manned by a crew of four - a lieutenant, a midshipman and two seamen acting as watchers - who were generally retired or disabled naval veterans. They were supplied with free furnished accommodation, coal and candles, but additional requirements such as beds, linen, tables and chairs were to be bought privately. Essential equipment included a timepiece and a pair of telescopes supplied by Dollands. A foreman employed to supervise the Kentish stations received a weekly wage of 24s 6d.

The crew soon acquired tremendous skill. Swiftly, they manipulated the complicated system of shutters in a style which resembled bell ringing. Two men were required to work the shutter ropes; one man kept watch through the forward telescope while another peered through the rear telescope. When a signal was received by one of the watchers the telegraph frame was altered appropriately by the shutter men to forward the desired signal one step further along the line. A preparatory signal alerting the stations that a message was about to be sent could be relayed from London to Deal and acknowledged in two minutes. A complicated message between London and the ports, however, might average fifteen minutes. Obviously, bad weather, such as fog or even heat haze, delayed communications. Damp caused the shutters to stick and high winds presented further difficulties. Nevertheless, Murray's system was robust, reliable and hailed as the phenomenon of the age.

Rapid telegraph was celebrated in song by Charles Dibden in his *Great News, or a Trip to the Antipodes,* first performed in London in October 1794. Although his rhyming couplets referred to the Continental system, his witty observations applied prophetically to Murray's simplified British version:

> If you'll only just promise you'll none of you laugh
> I'll be after explaining the French Telegraph.
> A machine thats endowed with such wonderful powr
> It writes, reads and sends news 50 miles an hour.
>
> Adieu, penny posts, mails and coaches, adieu.
> Your Occupations gone, 'tis all over wid you.
> In your place telegraphs on your houses we'll see
> To tell time, conduct lightning, dry shirts and send news.

Later lines were developed linking the Admiralty with Portsmouth, Yarmouth and Plymouth. All the same, the shutter telegraph was regarded solely as a wartime requirement and after the decisive Battle of Waterloo it was abandoned. The Admiralty complained that the Kent line actually cost £2950 a year to operate and argued that it was far too expensive to maintain. Laker mentions that immediately after the escape of Napoleon from Elba the East Kent ports were put on red alert. A telegraphic chain of ships was formed between Ostend and Deal, so that news from the seat of action could quickly be conveyed to the telegraph at the Naval Yard and sent on to London. Probably this was the last time that the shutter telegraph operated, for shortly afterwards Roebuck, who had assumed the role of Inspector of Telegraphs, was ordered to dismantle the sixty-four stations, taking care to return the telescopes.

By the time the Admiralty recognised the need for a permanent peacetime communication between London and the home ports, the shutter telegraph had been superseded by semaphore. This was the invention of Sir Home Riggs Popham (1762-1820) who, as a post captain in 1798, had command of the Sea Fencibles stationed between Deal and Beachy Head. He rose to become a Rear-Admiral, despite the hostility of Lord St Vincent ,who opposed him politically, and the disturbing fact that he was court-martialled after an 'excess of zeal' in Buenos Aires. Popham's elaborately carved tombstone in Sunninghill Church, Berkshire, displays a globe, compass, sextant, telescope, flags and semaphore. He became famous for his Telegraphic Signals or Marine Vocabulary, an innovative signalling system whereby numbered flags corresponded with an Admiralty code book, prudently adopted by the Royal Navy for communication between battle ships shortly before the Battle of Trafalgar.

Admiral Popham had already perfected a sea version of semaphore. Inspiration came once more from a Frenchman, Depillon, a former artillery officer, who had invented a jointed three-arm visual signal for ship-to-shore communication in 1801. Popham's clever adaptation comprised twin 12ft posts, each having a single arm, mounted on a trolley which could be wheeled about the ships' decks. His modified version for use on land was soon adopted by the Admiralty to communicate with their coastal naval stations.

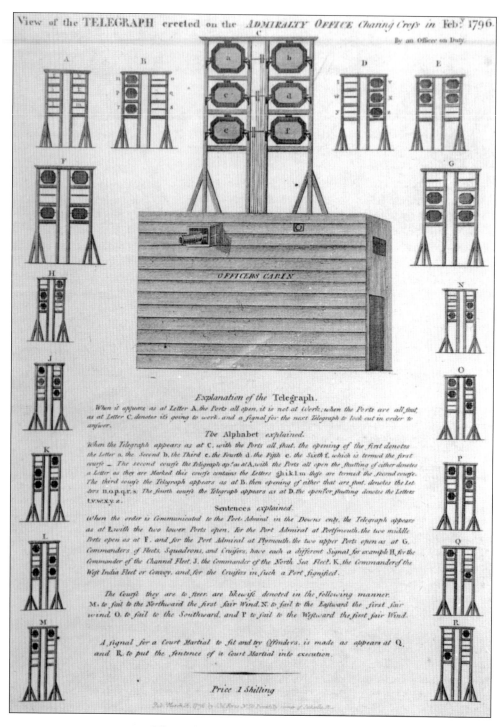

The telegraphic shutter system

160

Popham's mechanical semaphore was considered a vast improvement on the cumbersome shutter system. It consisted of two 8ft moveable arms, set one above the other, mounted on a single 30ft high hollow mast, which were capable of revolving to produce forty-eight different combinations. These symbolised letters of the alphabet, numerals and arbitrary phrases such as 'Commander-in-Chief', 'fog' and 'closing down'. This method proved to be swifter, cheaper and more efficient than rival inventions since it could be read easily at far greater distances. Stations would still be closed down in inclement weather and, naturally, at night. In May 1816 *The Times* informed its readers that the old telegraph apparatus communicating with Deal and Sheerness had become obsolete and was to be dismantled while the new semaphore for Sheerness would be erected within a few days.

John Barrow, Secretary to the Navy Board, ordered an experimental semaphore telegraph line to be established between the Admiralty and Chatham. New stations were permanent constructions rather than adaptations of rented buildings and their pattern was almost identical: three sub-basement rooms with three rooms above at ground level. There were two more rooms, one above the other, in the central tower, the lower one being the operations room. The flat roof, reached by a ladder and a trap door, was leaded and it had a low parapet all the way round. This plan was later adapted for the construction of the Deal Station.

Semaphore stations were manned by just two men - a Royal Navy veteran lieutenant and his assistant who needed to be a reliable glass man - paid just 3s 0d per day plus half-pay, and 2s 4d respectively. Attendance was from 10am until 5pm in summer or 3pm in winter. One man was to remain permanently at his post to prevent plunder and there were strict orders that spy glasses were not to be left unattended for more than two minutes at a time. All mechanical apparatus was supplied by Maudslays and the telescopes were ordered from Dollands. The London-Chatham line was fully operational by summer, 1815.

Meticulous regulations were drawn up for operating and maintaining the signal stations. The machinery was to be kept clean and well oiled. The station was to be swept once a day and washed once a week in winter and twice a week in summer. Sixpence per day was allocated for coals and candles. Each station was to keep a journal signed by the officer and sent to the Secretary of the Admiralty at the end of each week, It had to state the time every communication was received, with the position of the arms, so that, by comparison, the origin of any mistake which might occur could be determined.

Five years later the Admiralty decided to make their Chatham line permanent and extend it to Sheerness, Deal and Dover. When this additional line was proposed Thomas Goddard, Surveyor of Telegraphs, was commissioned to investigate suitable sites across Kent. Their Lordships had clearly been impressed by the successful demonstration between the first two stations on the London to Deal line at West Square (Southwark) and Nunhead (New Cross). A transmission rate of ten words a minute was a fair average, while a complicated message might take fifteen minutes to pass along the complete line. (Semaphore, as with the earlier telegraph, often contracted words leaving out certain vowels when the meaning was obvious.) Results were indeed impressive. Lieutenant

George Pace, Superintendent of Telegraphs, advised the Admiralty that not only was the system faster but he could distinguish the movements of the semaphore arms at a distance of three miles without the aid of a telescope. Popham pocketed £2000 for his invention.

Goddard acquired sites that almost followed the identical route of the former shutter stations, apart from a diversion at Barham Downs and Malmains to connect London with both Dover and Deal. Deal was to be the terminal station for the Kentish telegraph, and to link the country with the coastal semaphore, providing countywide communication. Goddard reported to the Admiralty in 1819:

> If a semaphore was placed upon the Admiral's Office at Deal, having the floor of the room at a corresponding height with the upper part of the frame work of the old telegraph, which now stands thereon, the station at East Hill will be brought into full view.

This seems to indicate that the redundant telegraph shutter station stood at the side of the Admiral's Office. The proposal to place the new semaphore on the roof was based upon the fact that it would give greater height for the benefit of the next station along the coast at Kingsdown.

Evidently, this projected line was never completed because there was a decline in the concentration of Royal Navy ships in the Downs after peace was declared with revolutionary France. In 1822 the Admiralty also abandoned the London to Chatham line in favour of an important link with Portsmouth and Plymouth. Peacetime communication was considered far more important between these distant dockyards under development along the south-west coast. Meanwhile, smuggling had increased alarmingly after the cessation of the Napoleonic Wars, affecting trade and providing a tremendous problem for the Admiralty.

The Coast Blockade was established by the Royal Navy expressly to combat smuggling in 1816. At first the service was assisted by a primitive coastal signal system previously introduced by the Admiralty for the purpose of 'conveying intelligence of the approach of an enemy and for the protection of commerce'. Gradually, coastal communication progressed from a rudimentary ball and flag device to a complicated three-arm semaphore copied from the French. Popham's land pattern semaphore, which employed two arms, was universally adopted by the naval stations around 1820 and this new system of signalling proved so successful in the pursuit of smugglers that it was expanded along the entire coastline from Yarmouth to Land's End.

When Captain William McCulloch assumed command of the Coast Blockade he had soon convinced the Admiralty of the cost effectiveness of establishing a rapid system of communication between the Channel ports. Blockade Divisions, Districts and Stations would further be able to receive intelligence from revenue cutters patrolling the English Channel. Thomas Goddard was again appointed to survey a possible semaphore line between Beachy Head and Deal. He made a careful note of all the existing towers and buildings - Martello towers, forts and batteries - and purchased those suitable for conversion into signal stations. The seventeen stations were to be auxiliary to the system adopted for the prevention of smuggling, and held in reserve in the event of renewed war.

Deal station, which would be crucial to the line, was purpose-built although work was inordinately slow to start. The semaphore tower must have been complete by December 1820, however, for Goddard mentions the 'lofty building' lately erected on the site of the old telegraph house which stood just outside the entrance to the Navy Yard. Indeed, Captain McCulloch notified his officers on 10 December that the coastal semaphore stations were now in operation and mentions 'the tall building known as Semaphore House at the south end of Beach Street, near the Dock Yard'. In anticipation, the Captain placed an order for instruction manuals and spy glasses for Deal's Royal Signal Tower.

Ten years later the Coast Blockade was disbanded and replaced by the Coast Guard. The Royal Signal Tower may have been retained for a short period although the semaphore system was abolished in 1842. Stripped of its mast, the signalling station proved ideal accommodation for two families of Coast Guards. Certainly the remaining apparatus would have been dismantled when land semaphore was superseded by the electric telegraph. This newly-discovered 'electric ether' had distinct advantages since remote stations might be contacted at a moment's notice in any weather, at any time of the day or night. Generally, the new electric wires

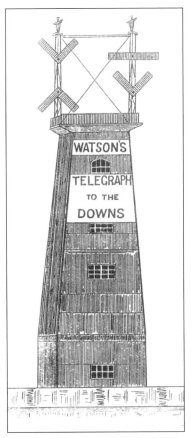

Watson's semaphore telegraph at Topping's Wharf, Southwark

followed the tracks of the railway companies which began to criss-cross the country in the middle of the nineteenth century. One telegraph line was installed by the Post Office between Deal and Dover in 1865, and part of its route is marked by the present Telegraph Road.

Another commercial venture, Watson's Telegraph to the Downs, connected London Bridge with the South Foreland. Bernard Lindsay Watson was a resourceful inventor who arrogantly signed himself Lieutenant RN. His improved semaphore employed three pairs of rotating arms working on three pivots mounted on a single mast providing an incredible 999 changes. A surviving sketch of the first signal station along the line at Toppings Wharf, Southwark, shows an alternative system employing twin 50ft masts. There the tower advertised the head office as '83 Cornhill, London'.

Watson published his own code of signals, which was printed in numerous editions between 1827 and 1842. His system of eleven stations across the county rendered the Admiralty's semaphore stations obsolete. Mainly, it was employed to serve merchant vessels waiting for wind and tide in the Downs. Watson's telegraph must have been a conspicuous landmark locally but references to it are scant. Confusingly, contemporary references mention The Downs, Deal and even Dover. The actual site of the terminal station is therefore difficult to determine but it is thought to have been near the present golf course on Kingsdown Cliffs.

Watson's advertisements in 1842 emphasised that he enjoyed the patronage of the British Government, the East India Company, Lloyds and Trinity House. Queen Victoria often resorted to Watson's telegraph and thanked him for forwarding a report on the arrival of the King and Queen of the Belgians in HMS *Ariel* off the North Foreland in June 1842. On 20 August Watson reported that the royal yacht, *Royal George*, which was shadowing her progress through Kent, had passed through Dover Straits. The Admiralty made use of the company's services and paid ten shillings for each message, although it could not be prevailed upon to make an annual grant for which the self-styled Lieutenant Watson repeatedly applied.

On Saturday 19 August 1843 a disastrous fire engulfed Watson's principal station at Toppings Wharf. Alas, the station might have been saved but help arrived too late - owing to a lack of communication! Watson's General Telegraphic Association proved too expensive to replace and so fell into obscurity. The Admiralty had, in any case, been experimenting with its own improved communications system - the electric telegraph - which would follow the line of the London and South Western Railway. By the mid-nineteenth century the Admiralty could send messages from the heart of the metropolis to the coast within moments.

Meanwhile, the Royal Signal Tower at Deal fell rapidly into disrepair until a proposal was made for a novel visual time signal device that gave it a new lease of life . . .

Captain Robert Wauchope invented a time signal ball to signal the precise time for ships to set their chronometers at Portsmouth Harbour in 1829. The ball was dropped manually upon receiving a visual signal from the nearby Royal Naval College in the Dockyard. Captain Wauchope interested the East India Company in his device, which resulted in its erection at random stations across the world –

Mauritius 1833, St Helena 1834, Cape of Good Hope 1836, Bombay 1840. He repeatedly wrote letters to the Admiralty proposing that time signal balls for the purpose of regulating chronometers should be made available for the Royal Navy.

Eventually, their Lordships responded by adopting his novel idea at the Royal Observatory, Greenwich, where accurate time has been determined since 1675. An experimental time ball was positioned there in 1833 to enable masters of ships to check the accuracy of their chronometers while in London River. Previously a temporary fixed ball had been tried to ascertain its visibility from various reaches of the Thames. The Greenwich time ball therefore became the world's first public time signal.

In 1855 a similar time ball was installed on a square mast atop the redundant semaphore station adjacent to the Navy Yard at Deal. It was a hollow sphere made of wood, covered with zinc and painted black. At 12.55pm

Astronomer Royal Sir George Airy depicted as a time ball in Punch
© National Maritime Museum

each day the ball was raised manually half-way up the mast and at 12.58pm it was further elevated to its highest position at the summit. At 1pm precisely the ball was brought down by a galvanic (electric) impulse direct from the Greenwich Observatory. This signalled the precise time for ships' masters to adjust their chronometers before setting off on a precarious voyage across the Atlantic.

The Greenwich time ball was erected under the supervision of John Pond (1811-1835), sixth Astronomer Royal. It was constructed of wood, filled with cork, covered with canvas and painted black. It was a hollow sphere, 5ft in diameter, sliding on a deal mast surmounted by a weathercock, and had letters pointing to the four quarters of the compass. It cost precisely £180. This curious contraption was positioned on the eastern turret of Flamstead House, a splendid Palladian building designed in 1675 by Christopher Wren. At one time it was both the Observatory and the living quarters of the Reverend John Flamstead (1675-1719), first Astronomer Royal.

The time ball, together with its operating mechanism, was designed and made by Maudslay, Sons and Field, the Lambeth marine and general engineering firm. The ball was cranked up by hand and dropped manually by an assistant standing below consulting a clock. Except for a few days when the wind was too strong for the ball to be raised, or while undergoing repair, the ball functioned daily until World War Two when the Observatory was evacuated. Apart from a slight modification made by Pond's successor, Sir George Biddell Airy (1835-1881),

The Time Ball Tower at the entrance to the Navy Yard

seventh Astronomer Royal, the mechanism remains as originally constructed, although from 1852 onwards the ball was triggered automatically by an electric signal from Shepherd's Mean Solar Standard Clock.

The intention had been that the ball should drop at midday but the Admiralty decided in favour of 1pm. Pond's limited staff would then be engaged in *finding* the time by observing the noon transit of the sun at the meridian. 'The ball will be hoisted half-way up the pole, at five minutes before One o'clock, as a preparatory signal, and close up to two minutes before One,' explained John Barrow, Admiralty Secretary, in his Notice to Mariners.

> By observing the first instance of its downward movement, all vessels in the adjacent reaches of the river as well as in most of the docks, will thereby have an opportunity of regulating and rating their chronometers.

Quite early in its existence (25 November 1833) the ball was one minute late. *The Times*, in ponderous journalese, drew prompt attention to 'the most scandalous results' which might arise to shipping if there were an error of even one second. It was 'of the utmost consequence that the ball should act at an invariable time'. The writer had overlooked the fact that the signal had been available for only a few weeks and that navigators had managed before without it.

Over the years the Greenwich time ball kept remarkable time. Occasionally, snow, ice and blizzards interfered with its smooth operation. Once, the ball was blown down into the courtyard and took months to be repaired. At the start of British Standard Time in 1916 (an economic measure calculated to save light and fuel by gaining an extra hour of daylight during wartime) the ball was dropped at 1pm Mean Solar Time, and therefore in reality fell at 2pm. Another exception was made when the ball was lowered at 11am on 11 November upon the cessation of the First World War.

Greenwich's time ball was an overwhelmingly successful innovation. A correspondent to the *Nautical Magazine* in 1835 sketched its design and called for similar devices to be installed in ports around the country. The Admiralty took the hint and eventually time balls were constructed at various points around the coast including Edinburgh, Glasgow, Falmouth, Liverpool, Devonport, Portland, Portsmouth, Southampton and Sheerness. Greenwich provided the electric impulse to drop all these time balls or, in certain places, to fire time guns, although these were less precise – sight travelling faster than sound. Subsequently time balls were put up worldwide and several remain in working order (Lyttleton on South Island in New Zealand; Adelaide, Sydney, Newcastle and Williamstown in Australia). Novelty timeballs were erected at seaside resorts such as Brighton and Margate.

Commercial time balls were also to be found in numerous cities. Crowds gathered to watch the hesitant fall of the ball located atop one of the twin 'pepper pot' towers surmounting the offices of the Electric Telegraph Company in London's Strand. The facade of John Nash's elegant building survives opposite Charing Cross Station, although there is now no trace of the time ball. Jewellers frequently displayed time balls connected by telegraph to Greenwich. The one in Manchester has long disappeared but another survives in the centre of Leeds. Deal's time ball, however, was the first to be activated at a distance from Greenwich, and to disseminate accurate time to ships in the English Channel.

In 1850, Charles Walker, Telegraph Superintendent of the South Eastern Railway, mentioned to Airy that a timeball might drop at Dover.

Advanced technology would enable an electric impulse to be relayed by means of overhead telegraph wires direct from the Observatory. His idea was modified by Commander Thomas Baldock, who proposed a timeball at South Foreland Lighthouse to serve shipping in the English Channel. This visual time signal would be linked to the firing of a gun at 8am, noon and 4pm. A time signal gun activated by a current from Greenwich was actually installed at Dover Castle. The Admiralty assented and plans were drawn up marking the position of a mast and a ball attached to the lighthouse. Airy was sent to investigate but he discovered that neither signal could be noted by outward-bound vessels anchored in the Downs. He suggested a superior site when he travelled around the coast and chanced upon the abandoned Semaphore Tower at Deal.

Airy, one of the few scientists in government service at that time, has been hailed as a Victorian visionary for he resolutely championed Standard British Time. A meticulous adminstrator, he grasped the concept that national distribution of accurate time would be essential as travel progressed from relays of horses to steam locomotives. The Great Exhibition of 1851 caused a great increase in passenger traffic and heightened the need for uniformity of time for public transport. The illogicality of local time was clearly demonstrated where, for instance, Ramsgate was five minutes ahead of Deal!

Airy astutely realised that Deal's timeball might be remotely controlled from Greenwich. An impulse could be sent via the newly invented railway electric telegraph whose mainline conveniently passed within half a mile of the Observatory. He supervised every detail of the installation of the new time ball atop the 40ft square Signalling Tower at Deal. He visited the town in early May and insisted upon being rowed around the Downs to test the view of the building from every angle. His helmsman was a young Robert Wilds, later to gain fame as coxswain of the first Deal lifeboat.

Airy duly reported to the Admiralty in 1853:

> On proceeding to Deal for the purpose of examining the locality I was struck by the appearance of the Semaphore House . . . a few yards north of the gate of the Navy Yard . . . It is a lofty building of four storeys . . . It is impossible to imagine a building more favourable in its form for the erection of such machinery.

The Admiralty approved Airy's proposed site and the Astronomer Royal commented on their Lordships decision in a further report:

> I have the satisfaction of stating that the Lords Commissioners of the Admiralty have decided on the erection of a Time-Signal Ball at Deal, for the use of the shipping in the Downs, to be dropped every day by a galvanic current from the Royal Observatory. The construction of the apparatus is entrusted to me. Probably there is no roadstead in the world in which the knowledge of true time is so important.

Deal's time ball was constructed in March 1854, again by Maudslay and Field, at a total cost, including work by telegraph companies, of £886 3s 9d. The black sphere, 5ft in diameter, was mounted on a 14ft mast surmounted by cross arms and a weathercock above the old telegraph tower. It stood 76ft above high water, 65ft above ground level. The connection of the electric current from the Royal Observatory was by underground line to Lewisham Junction, thence to London Bridge railway station, Ashford, Minster and Deal stations, from where it travelled via government line to Semaphore House. The new time ball was fully operational by New Year's Day, 1855.

Airy's report for 1854 states:

> I alluded in my last report to the erection of a Time-Signal Ball at Deal, to be dropped every day by a galvanic current from the Royal Observatory. The ball has now been erected by Messrs. Maudslay and Field, and is an admirable specimen of the workmanship of these celebrated engineers. The galvanic connexion with the Royal Observatory (through the telegraph wires of the South-East Railway) is perfect. The automatic changes of wire communications are so arranged that, when the Ball at Deal has dropped to

its lowest point, it sends a signal to Greenwich to acquaint me, not with the time at the beginning of its fall (which cannot be in error) but with the fact that it has really fallen . . .

Occasionally, the signal failed due to weak current or high winds. A system was organised whereby a black flag was hoisted and the ball kept up for ten minutes, then slowly lowered, the signal being repeated by hand at 2pm instead. The time was taken from the two-day chronometer kept in the instrument room and frequently consulted in person by captains of vessels stationed in the Downs. The alternative time signal was recorded in a rating book although its accuracy could not be guaranteed within two seconds. At all other times the performance of the time ball at Deal was prompted by a revolutionary battery-operated, galvano-magnetic clock made for twenty guineas by Charles Shepherd of London.

Shepherd was one of the pioneer electrical clockmakers. Yet he was not consistently successful since a showpiece clock displayed at the Great Exhibition in Hyde Park proved to be unreliable and had to be removed, causing him acute professional embarrassment. He persevered in his experiments, however, being determined to harness electricity for the measurement of time not only as a source of power to drive an accurate clock, but as a means of transmitting signals from one master clock to a number of slave clocks so that all might indicate identical time.

The Astronomer Royal was convinced of his abilities and realised the potential of regulating public clocks and time balls by means of electrical impulses. In 1852 Shepherd's motor clock (later called mean solar standard clock) was installed in the North Dome of Greenwich Observatory and that summer the timeball was dropped electrically for the first time. Soon afterwards Airy commissioned four electrical clocks for the Deal time ball system, to be installed at the four railway stations through which the telegraph line carrying the signal to drop the ball passed. The clock at Deal station was soon afterwards removed to the time ball tower. Shepherd was late in supplying these and he was ticked off by Airy who threatened to have the work 'begun afresh by another person'. Luckily, the clocks were delivered in August 1854. The total cost was £197 12s 6d.

Shepherd's magnificent clock, with its 24-hour white enamelled dial, is today contained in a mahogany longcase at Deal. Its main purpose was to act as a gate to prevent a signal operating the ball at any other time than 1pm. Its accuracy was recorded in a log book, still extant, which normally shows some seconds difference from the infallible Greenwich signal. Consequently, it was regularly corrected by the keeper who was strictly charged that 'if any part of the machinery fails, or if no current is recorded at 1h, or if the ball is dropped at the wrong time, communicate directly by letter to the Astronomer Royal'. The clock is no longer in working order, although its identical master, linked to its slave prominently displayed on the gate, still beats accurate time in the Time Gallery of the Royal Observatory at Greenwich.

Failures for the precise dropping of the time ball were rare, though, as Airy's report for 1855 states:

The Time-Signal Ball at Deal was brought into regular use at the beginning of the present year. In a short time, however, its action was interrupted, partly by derangement of the apparatus, and partly by the severity of the weather, which froze the sulphuric acid to the state of jelly. I sent an assistant and workman to put it in order, and since that time it has generally acted very well. Since March 2nd there have been three failures: one of these arose from the Ball hanging on the clips, which were not properly oiled, and one from the turning off of the current on the railway line; the cause of the third has not been traced with certainty. The success or failure of the drop is known at Greenwich immediately . . .

Deal's telegraphically-released time ball had an important secondary role in that it provided standard time for clocks ashore, including privately-owned clocks and watches. For the first time it was possible to have standard time over a wide area. Prime examples are the churches of Eastry and Woodnesborough which were supplied not only with a tower clock, but also a telescope by which the fall of the ball at Deal could be observed.

By 1863 the Admiralty had decided to close the Navy Yard at Deal, to remove the stores to Chatham and to sell the ground. The next year the whole property was auctioned and the land was partly cleared for building. On the advice of the Astronomer Royal, the Admiralty bought the old Semaphore Station for £600.

William Curling Newby was appointed warden of the Tower at a fee of one guinea per week. He was assisted by a local clockmaker named Pegden who received £15 per annum. Newby was a naval veteran who had served on a whaling ship before being appointed to the Navy Yard. A widower, with three children, he moved into the Tower and, in 1871, married again. He continued to reside there until long past his eightieth year.

A later warden, Isaac Gammon Hayward, fireman and watchmaker, commenced duties in 1899. He was the founder member of Deal Fire Brigade and secretary of the neighbouring Oddfellows Hall. Gammon lived in the cramped apartments of the Tower, now with a water closet, with his family of thirteen children. His salary included living accommodation although an iron shaft descending through the top two floors may have proved a trifle inconvenient. In 1904 Mr Hayward was superseded by Mr Jermyn.

The last occupants were George Cutcher, retired marine lieutenant, his wife and two children, George and Peggy, who took up residence in 1921. For the keeper and his family the time ball tower made an intriguing home. The Cutcher children recalled romping on their parents' massive four-poster bed, exploring the machinery room and listening to the band playing in the bandstand in front of the tower on sultry summer evenings. One afternoon a most distinguished visitor called to take tea - Sir Frank Dyson, ninth Astronomer Royal. On the day of the Tower's closure the Cutchers climbed to the platform beneath the time ball to have their photograph taken for posterity.

In 1884 the Astronomer Royal surrendered the telegraphic wire from Greenwich Observatory to London Bridge. Instead, the time current was relayed through the clockwork chronometer housed in the Post Office's Central Telegraph Office in London. Once the Post Office assumed responsibility for the

The Cutcher family on the roof on the day the Tower closed in 1927

time signal, maintenance of the apparatus came under the charge of the Royal Engineers Telegraph Corps. The Astronomer Royal reported the success of the alterations to the system: 'After various delays the arrangements . . . for sending a current to Deal, and receiving a return signal through Post Office telegraphs, was brought into operation on February 29th, and has worked well since . . . There have been 16 cases of failure in the dropping of the Deal time ball owing to the interruption of the telegraphic connections, 12 under the old system, and four since the new arrangements'.

At the beginning of the twentieth century the days of time balls were clearly numbered. Marconi's inventions made it possible to send much more reliable wireless time signals across the sea. Nevertheless, Greenwich's time ball remained operational until 1939, when the Observatory was bombed at the outbreak if hostilities. The practice of dropping the ball was resumed in 1952, mainly as a tourist attraction. In 1960 the Ministry of Public Buildings and Works assumed responsibility for its maintenance and today it continues to function automatically. Yet for all practical purposes the signal had been superseded by aural signals.

The pips signal broadcast at specific times by the BBC was introduced in 1924, while the Rugby Time Signal was inaugurated in 1927 for the benefit of shipping worldwide. The GPO speaking clock (known as TIM) was introduced

171

in July 1936 and featured the voice of the telephonist Ethel Cain, who had won a national competition for switchboard operators judged by John Masefield and Sybil Thorndike.

Deal's time ball went out of service on 25 February 1927 when the last telegraphic circuit carried the 1pm time signal from Greenwich. During the Second World War its mechanism, including the original mast and ball, was removed but lost. The top floor of this four-storeyed building, with its exposed brick and timber construction, retains an old fireplace across one corner of the room, sash windows in each of the four walls and a step-ladder leading to the trap door in the ceiling which gives access to the time ball. Part of the original machinery remains, including the central iron shaft fitted with the capstan employed to raise the ball. This still bears the plaque displaying the royal coat-of-arms and the legend Maudslay, Sons and Field, Engineers, London, 1853.

The Time Ball Tower has become an unique Museum of Time, Telegraphy and Maritime Communications, funded jointly by Dover District Council and British Telecommunications. Inside are displays relating to the history of signalling - everything from bonfires to satellites, from homing pigeons to the transatlantic cable. Exhibits include a curious Tuba Stentora Phonica – a seventeenth century brass speaking trumpet that conveyed messages between Deal and Walmer Castles.

A replica time ball - once raised by compressed air and activated by a quartz clock - is now dropped automatically every hour purely as a tourist attraction. For more than seventy years the time signal ball gave a daily time signal to shipping passing through the English Channel when it was regarded as the most important signalling device in the country after Greenwich.

Today, the Tower is a museum of time, telegraphy and communication

RAILWAYS

'Take away the horses!'

THE OPENING OF THE RAILWAY brought an influx of holidaymakers which greatly added to the prosperity of the town in the Victorian and Edwardian eras. Charles Dickens travelled on the first train to Deal and later distinguished passengers included Lord Kitchener (in life) and the Duke of Wellington (in death).

Kent had the first regular steam-drawn passenger train service in the world. The Canterbury to Whitstable line opened on 3 May 1830 when twenty carriages were hauled along the tortuous six-mile track by a sturdy locomotive, *Invicta*, built by George Stephenson and now displayed in Canterbury Heritage Centre.

By the middle of the nineteenth century a complex system of railways crossed Kent connecting London with the south-east coast. Their progress was chartered in *Bradshaw's Railway Guide*, a monthly timetable, innovatively showing Greenwich Mean Time rather than local times; it first appeared in 1841. Indeed, *The New Official Guide to the South-East Railway and Its Branches* by George Meason, published in 1858, plainly announced: 'London Time is observed at all stations'. Kentish seaside resorts flourished from the constant flow of visitors, particularly after the Bank Holiday Act of 1871 ensured regular day's off for all labourers.

Kent railways were operated by rival companies – The London, Chatham and Dover Company and The South-Eastern Railway Company. The SER brought its line from London to Ashford in 1842, to Folkestone in 1843 and to Dover in 1844. The Ashford, Canterbury and Margate line, owned by the same company, reached Canterbury West on 6 February 1846, Ramsgate Town on 13 April and Margate Sands on 1 December. An eight mile branch of that line across flat farmland was opened the following year from Minster via Sandwich to Deal.

Transportation of the first steam locomotive to Deal was an eventful occurrence. An engine was needed for essential work between Deal and Sandwich before a bridge had been constructed over the River Stour. During the winter of 1845-1846 an engine mounted on a wagon was conveyed by a team of horses along the winding road between Dover and Deal. This extraordinary procession almost came to grief as it slipped down a frosty hill at Oxney Bottom.

A sketch in *Rambling Recollections of the Neighbourhood of Dover*, published in 1848, shows the scene, while a lively description recalls the dilemma as the twenty ton locomotive stuck at the foot of the hill:

The snow was crushed by its broad wheels to solid ice; and, although skidded by every possible means which heavy chains would furnish, it began to increase in speed at an alarming rate. Forty horses were an unmanageable team. 'Take away the horses!' was now the cry, and at great risk many of the leading horses were detached, whipped and halloed out of the way as much as possible. With perhaps a third of them still attached the monstrous load came rushing down the hill and, had it been much longer, fearful might have been the result. But, fortunately, at the bottom of the road was rather softer and the whole was brought up, partially running the carriage on the footway by the roadside. Once here, the trouble of staying it was at an end, but that of getting forward was soon to begin.

The horses were once more attached to the wagon but as they moved forward it was without their load. Chains which had been fixed to the wheels to serve as drags were cut away. A jack was utilised to raise a wheel that threatened to become embedded in the soft earth and to cause the ponderous load to overturn. At one point the jack gave way and the carriage almost broke, but after much effort the engine was shifted to firmer ground. Several horses had cast their shoes in the strain of pulling and these had to be renewed before the main team was once more connected to the wagon. Eventually the locomotive was hauled up the top of the opposite hill.

The first steam engine en route to Deal in the winter of 1845-1846

The engineer for the Deal to Minster line was George Robert Stephenson, nephew of the celebrated George Stephenson. The extension necessitated the construction of a swing bridge over the River Stour which a correspondent for *The Pictorial Times* described as being 'built on a new and ingenious principle . . . considered a curiosity by engineers'. This bridge was swung annually, despite declining river traffic, to assert navigational rights. There were two new stations, at Deal and Sandwich. 'The

The first train passing through Sandwich

station at Sandwich', the writer continued, 'is a plain, substantial and convenient building situated just beyond the Deal Road'.

Deal Station was built with an arched canopy over the platform and railway lines to shelter passengers and protect the trains. The station building included a booking office, waiting room, and porter's lobby with accommodation above for the guard and station master. A wall marked the southern end of the station property, for Deal was regarded as the terminus of the South-Eastern Railway. When the line was continued through to Dover later that century it became necessary to build the overbridge carrying traffic from Queen Street into London Road.

A special edition of *The Pictorial Times* pictured the opening ceremony which took place on Wednesday 30 June 1847. It featured an engraving of the scene as the train – SER Loco No 37, King Lear, and its special – passed Sandwich. Customarily, the ceremonial engine would have been driven by its engineer, George Robert Stephenson. The contrasting towers of the churches of St Peter and St Clement are shown in the distance. A tall-funnelled, six-wheeled engine is depicted drawing a line of stylish, crowded carriages. One gentleman sporting a top hat, apparently the guard, is seated on the first open carriage similar to a driver on the box seat of a horse-drawn vehicle. He seems in an unenviable position where he might inhale fumes from the engine's funnel. Dense crowds are gathered on either side of the line – the ladies appear sedate in their bonnets and shawls but the menfolk vigorously wave hats and handkerchiefs.

Pritchard provides the following account:

It was a day that will be remembered by all who were old enough to be spectators. The number of strangers that visited Deal on that occasion, arriving from all parts of Kent, surpassed the powers of calculation. The town had the appearance of a swarm of bees . . . The South Eastern Railway Company came to Deal, accompanied by friends, who filled a great number of carriages, picking up as they came along the line, that such a number of living human beings never appeared before in the old town. A public dinner was provided, over which the Mayor, Henry Wise Harvey, Esq., presided. The Directors of the Company generously supplied the wines without stint or measure.

Charles Dickens
© National Portrait Gallery

Newspaper editors complained about the late notification of the opening. This was because the ceremony had been deferred several times. Various reasons were offered for the delay - the swing bridge over the Stour was not built; Minster Station was incomplete . . .

A reporter managed to attend at short notice, however, and gave a detailed account:

The stations along the new line were handsomely decorated. The whole population of the neighbourhood assembled to celebrate the event; huge flags were seen fluttering in every direction; shops were shut and business suspended; and, in fact, it was a complete holiday. At half-past 4 oclock a public dinner took place in the Town Hall of Deal.

The excellent meal for 150 gentlemen was supplied by the landlord of the Royal Hotel while the fine wines were generously supplied by the directors of the South Eastern Railway. Actually, the deputy mayor presided and welcomed guests included Daniel Maclise, the artist, and GPR James (1801-1860), a prolific author of melodramatic historical novels, who resided at The Shrubbery, Walmer.

The guest of honour at the banquet was Charles Dickens. He had arrived with his wife, Catherine, and their young family only a couple of days previously to holiday at Bleak House, high on the cliff at Broadstairs. The author received short notice by electric telegraph either from local dignitaries at Deal or railway officials from London Bridge. He prepared a hasty speech in which he was careful to mention Deal's beautiful beach and gallant boatmen.

Apparently, Dickens lodged at the old Swan Inn which stood at the corner of West Street and Queen Street. Built in 1694, this ancient hostelry was originally called Five Bells and it lent its name to Five Bells Lane (now Queen Street). The Swan was the old posting house of Deal with adequate stabling for thirty-five horses. At the time of Dickens's brief sojourn the licence was held by a landlord with the decidedly Dickensian name of Pockett.

Dickens subsequently penned a portrait of Deal's port in Bleak House. Esther Summerson visits Richard Carstone during his brief army career and stays at a seafront hotel which can probably be identified as The Royal:

> At last we came into the narrow streets of Deal: and very gloomy they were, upon a raw misty morning. The long flat beach, with its little irregular houses, wooden and brick, and its litter of capstans, and great boats, and sheds, and bare upright poles with tackle and block, and loose gravelly waste places overgrown with grass and weeds, wore as dull an appearance as any place I ever saw. The sea was heaving under a thick white fog; and nothing else was moving but a few ropemakers, who, with the yarn twisted round their bodies, looked as if, tired of their present state of existence, they were spinning themselves into cordage. But when we got into a warm room in an excellent hotel, comfortably washed and dressed, to an early breakfast, Deal began to look more cheerful . . .

When The Lord Warden of the Cinque Ports, Arthur Wellesley, Duke of Wellington, died in the autumn 1852 at Walmer Castle, his body lay for two months in his black-draped study while preparations were made for an elaborate state funeral. On the evening of 11 November a hearse, mounted on a gun carriage and drawn by four black-plumed horses, made its slow progress through the town preceded by a torchlight procession. The mournful route was

Terminus of the Minster and Deal Railway

lined by troops from the local garrison – bowed heads and arms reversed – while the minute guns sounded from the three castles. At Deal Station the coffin was received by James MacGregor, MP, chairman of the South-Eastern Railway Company, and at a quarter past nine it began its journey by rail via Ashford and Tonbridge to London. The South-Eastern Railway Company made a modest charge for the removal of the illustrious remains – £90.

Ironically, the Iron Duke had a hatred of trains all his life since he witnessed the horrific death of his colleague, William Huskisson MP, during the opening of the Liverpool to Manchester line in 1830. Nevertheless, the SER was careful to cultivate his patronage, and not only did it name its prestigious hotel at Dover The Lord Warden, but adopted Wellington brown, a dark maroon representing the Duke's family colours, as its livery. When it became inevitable for the Duke to travel by rail to the capital he rode to Dover in the early hours of the morning where his personal carriage - a first and second class composite - conveyed him on a three-hour journey via Ashford and Tonbridge to London Bridge.

The opening of the line to Deal ensured that townsfolk now had a direct link with London although their route was a roundabout one through Ashford, Tonbridge, Redhill and Croydon. The journey was laborious - almost five hours - and the return fare of fifteen shillings was exorbitant, although this was slightly less than the penny per mile stipulated by Parliament.

A proposal had been made as early as 1862 by the London, Chatham and Dover Company to continue the line from Dover to Deal but this suggestion did not come to fruition until 1874. Royal assent was then given to the scheme which was to be a combined effort of the London, Chatham and Dover Company with the South-Eastern Railway Company. A rare piece of co-operation. Their new venture would save about twenty-five miles on the journey between Dover and Ramsgate because the previous route required a roundabout excursion via Ashford. The first sod was officially turned by Earl Granville, Lord Warden of the Cinque Ports, on 29 June 1878, in a field behind South Barracks. During the progress of the excavations between Deal and Dover the following summer workmen unearthed a perfectly preserved skeleton of a Roman soldier buried with his short, broad and double-edged sword.

Surprisingly, the Dover to Deal line, which is only eight miles long, cost more than £200,000 and took three years to complete. Local artist, JL Roget, made a number of finely-detailed pencil sketches recording the progress of its construction. CF Dendy Marshall, in *History of the Southern Railway*, described the completed route:

> Leaving the London, Chatham and Dover Railway main line at Buckland Junction, 73 chains east of Dover Priory Station, the line rises for two and three quarter miles at 1 in 70. Near the top it passes through the Guston tunnel, 1,425 yards long, and then falls with varying gradients to Deal.

The junction at Buckland was the wrong way for the Chatham and Dover trains to negotiate when travelling from London to Deal and so in 1881 the company obtained powers to create the Kearsney Loop.

The Dover to Deal line was opened on Tuesday 14 June 1881, a bright, sunny day with a refreshing, cool breeze. Directors and officials of both the South-

Eastern and the London, Chatham and Dover Companies travelled from London by express trains which arrived simultaneously at Dover Town Station. Here, a special train headed by locomotives from both companies was waiting to convey visitors along the newly-completed line.

Among the 250 invited guests of the railway companies were local dignitaries from towns across Kent. Flags and banners had been hung in profusion about the station to welcome them and the whole neighbourhood wore a gala aspect.

Promptly at 12.30pm the special train started for Deal, calling at the Harbour and Priory Stations where excited crowds had gathered to cheer the procession. The train followed the London to Chatham line as far as Buckland Junction just beyond Dover Priory where the locomotive touched on the new track. Just beyond Charlton Cemetery the train passed into a tunnel, almost a mile long, before racing through the parishes of West and East Langdon, Martin and Ringwould.

A reporter from the *Deal, Walmer and Sandwich Mercury* recorded the excitement of that first ride:

> The first stop is made at Martin Mill, where a small station has been erected for the above parishes as well as that of the inhabitants of the village, who cheered slightly as the train took its departure after a stay of two or three minutes. The next stop was at Walmer where another station had been erected: and here something like a demonstration was made, the precincts of the station being thronged with people, who expressed unmistakable delight at the appearance of the first train in their midst.
>
> Dignitaries of the parish boarded the train at this point at which, almost before they were seated, it began to move on the last lap of its journey. Deal was soon in sight. The station approach had been erected over the line bearing the inscription: "All best wishes of the town of Deal to the new railway." Under the arch and into the station . . .

The Mayor and Corporation of Deal stood proudly on the platform bedecked with flags and bunting waiting to receive the directors of the railway companies. Smartly, these privileged passengers were marched into a refreshment room where a light luncheon had

The Kearsney loop came into its own during the Second World War at a time when Dover was a restricted town. During heavy shelling or bombardment trains from Deal to Dover either waited in a tunnel or were diverted via the loop to Kearsney. In the 1970s the curved track was temporarily re-layed to test safety for the cornering of 125mph trains.

The creation of a rail link to Deal resulted in the severence of the ancient Coffin Path which linked Lower Deal with St Leonards Church. This means that a public right of way across the footbridge over the railway still exists to this day.

Freight services from Deal to London involved fresh fish and farm produce, but the main commodity was coal from Betteshanger Colliery; until that time coal had been transported by sea.

179

been prepared to celebrate the success of the venture. Yet there was limited time to spend feasting and toasting for the train was timed to depart for Dover in twenty minutes so there could be no delay. This was the age of the train!

This time the Deal officials joined the travellers for the return journey. Cheers from the crowds, whistles from the guard, a hissing and puffing of steam and the train was on its way. For the first time the Deal contingent could appreciate the passing scenery glimpsed through clouds of billowing smoke - shipping in the Downs, the coastline of Thanet, gently undulating countryside near Martin Mill and finally the splendour of Dover Castle and a distant view of France. And as the train carefully circled the hills above the town there was that magnificent view across the bustling harbour . .

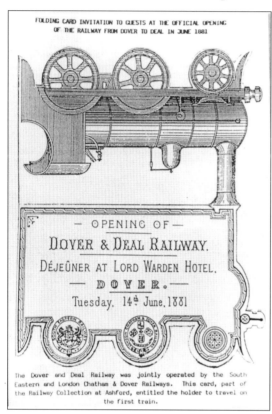

Invitation ticket for the opening of the Deal to Dover line © Alfred Minter

At 2pm precisely the train steamed triumphantly into Dover Town station where the passengers alighted and were escorted to the Lord Warden Hotel for a swish luncheon. After congratulatory speeches, those honoured guests were invited to make their way to the quayside where a steamship, *Samphire,* was waiting to escort them out into the Channel to inspect the English fleet. The Dover to Deal line opened to the public on the following day.

Extension of the line involved the demolition of Albert Terrace in Wellington Road and the construction of the over-bridge to carry traffic along the London Road. Later a weight restriction had to be imposed since this bridge was intended only for horse-drawn traffic. A handsome station building combining booking hall, parcels' office, porters' lobby and refreshment room was provided on the west side. It was built of yellow brick to match the stations at Walmer and Martin Mill. This was demolished in the 1970s. The two platforms were not at first connected, but the creation of a buffet on the west side necessitated a new footbridge complete with curved, corrugated iron canopy to protect passengers during inclement weather.

Later Deal was to have a replacement engine shed with a turntable, a goods shed with a weighbridge, a signal box, workshops and even a forge. The station master was presented with a grand detached villa but this, together with the adjacent Railway Hotel, was bombed in World War Two.

The South-Eastern Hotel, Deal

The amalgamation of the SER and LC&DR into the South Eastern and Chatham Railway (Slow, East and Comfortable) on the first day of the new century accounted for some unique timetabling. Trains would arrive direct from London at either Up or Down platforms (then in reverse of the present system). This was finally regulated in 1923 by the newly formed Southern Railway.

There were several accidents on the line, but the most spectacular occurred on 6 July 1898. At 5pm three third class coaches and two loaded goods trucks of the SER parted from their engine at Walmer Station and sped downhill towards Deal. The driver of the locomotive drove off in hot pursuit, hoping to catch up and couple the runaway coaches onto his train. The coaches, however, jumped the catch points and continued their journey where they careered into an empty LC&DR train from Dover being shunted onto the opposite track. Collision was inevitable. Broken coach bodies and timber spilled onto the track and their underframes shot into the air. The accident took place south of the railway bridge over Queen Street. Nobody was hurt. The *East Kent Mercury* commented dryly: 'When the two companies (SER and LC&DR) announced last week the probability of a fusion of interests, they doubtless had but little idea their rolling stock would so soon take the initiative'.

The London, Chatham and Dover Railway continued to be responsible for cross-Channel ferry services. The company also operated a small scheduled steamer service along the coast to compensate for the lack of rail travel between Dover and Ramsgate. A coastal ferry began to call at Deal soon after the new pier was opened and adapted with a special landing stage in 1866. This boat-rail link was continued throughout summer months, even when the railway line was completed between Deal and Dover, purely as a tourist attraction. It proved highly popular among holidaymakers in the Victorian and Edwardian eras.

In order to cater for the crowds of holidaymakers who were expected to travel from London by train to this popular resort, the South-Eastern Railway Company commissioned James Brooks, an award-winning architect noted for his church buildings, to design a sumptuous hotel on a site adjacent to Deal Castle. In 1896 the *Deal and Sandwich Gazette* published a drawing and description of the proposed edifice:

> The building, the erection of which has been entrusted to Mr James Wise, the well-known Deal builder, is of red brick, with facings of Ancaster stone, and it is being fitted throughout in the latest modern style, including electric lighting, lift to the upper floors, and every luxury and convenience that would possibly add to the comfort of visitors.

When the South-Eastern Hotel opened its doors to paying guests the following year it was recognised as being one of the chief architectural features of the town. Advertisements trumpeted: 'A first class hotel, an excellent cuisine, the best accommodation, tasteful decorations and above all comfort.' Certainly it was a grand structure with a profusion of towers and turrets, chimneys and gables. Ground and first floor windows were enlivened with curved stone balustrades, keystone heads and graceful shell hoods. The eastern elevation had a grand central doorway flanked by two elegant conservatories which were favoured by diners who appreciated their superb vistas over the Downs. On either side of this doorway were carved angels (evidently Brooks could not resist an ecclesiastical touch), one of which carried the Deal coat-of-arms and a galleon; the other supported the South-Eastern Railway Company's crest and a steam engine.

Visitors could not fail to be impressed by the sixty-two bedrooms (thirty-six with private baths) handsome staircase, tessellated tiled corridors and spacious public rooms. Immediately opposite the hotel, on the castle green, stood a prominent landmark – a First World War tank.

This grand hotel, which changed its name to The Queens, served the town for nearly eighty years, but eventually diminishing bookings marked its decline. In 1977 it closed its doors and fell rapidly into decay. In April 1981 The Queens was mysteriously destroyed by fire - arson was suspected - and total demolition soon followed. Luxury flats now occupy the site.

During the Second World War Deal was a restricted area. Every train was met by a policeman who examined everyone's identity card. He prevented entry to the town of all who could not justify their purpose. During the summer of 1940 Deal Station was involved in the transportation of troops landed along this part of the coast after the strategic withdrawal from Dunkirk. Evacuation of local schoolchildren took place simultaneously. The first train left on Sunday 2 June with 668 children and sixty-seven teachers, bound for South Wales.

Kent coast railway lines were electrified between 1959 and 1962, and electric trains were introduced to Deal in January 1961. Inevitably, this meant the

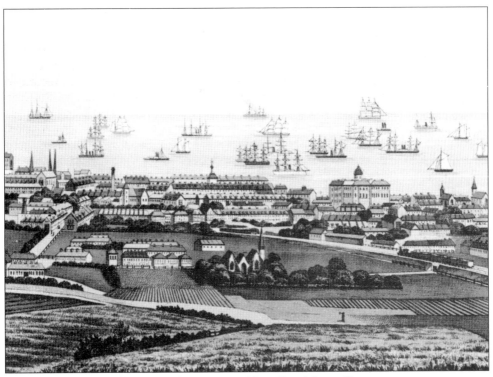

Steam train approaching Deal from Dover

streamlining of the railway complex: the goods yard was closed, the sidings were removed, the engine shed (which had become a wagon repair shop) was abandoned and the splendid west side station demolished. Deal, once an important semi-terminus station, was reduced to a partially staffed halt.

PIERS AND JETTIES

'Splendid marine parades'

FOUR PIERS AND JETTIES have graced the seashore in times past and their history has mirrored the fate and fortunes of the town.

The first pier was commenced through a chance remark by George II. He arrived from Hanover on Monday 13 October 1740 and so has the distinction of being the first King of England to land at Deal. In the absence of a jetty, George Carr, Collector of Customs, drove his open chaise down the beach, into the water and alongside the royal barge. King George scrambled aboard in an ungainly manner and received the inevitable dowsing. The King later complained to the mayor, Josiah Lane, that a landing stage was urgently required.

Lane was an astute businessman and an ardent royalist so he swiftly organised the construction of a wooden jetty which stretched a short distance out

Sir John Rennie's wooden pier

184

The Esplanade and wooden pier

to sea opposite Coppin Street. It was regularly used by passengers and crew joining their ships at anchor in the Downs. A great storm lasting two days in October 1758 completely demolished this jetty, which was never rebuilt.

Schemes for the construction of a harbour to facilitate the commercial progress of the port had been seriously considered over the centuries but none had ever come to fruition. Landing passengers and cargoes on the shingle beach in an open boat had always proved a risky business particularly in rough weather. To overcome this problem a company was established in 1838 to erect a wooden landing pier or jetty as a substitute for a purpose-built harbour.

An Act of Parliament was obtained sanctioning the formation of The Deal Pier Company with a capital of £21,000, and a plot of land was purchased immediately to the north of the Royal Hotel. The celebrated engineer, Sir John Rennie (1794-1874), who had been responsible for the construction of London Bridge, was commissioned to design a pier 445ft in length. Piling was completed for a length of 250ft at a cost of £12,000 and a further sum of £8,500 was then raised by the issue of £5 shares.

Sufficient funds to complete this ambitious project were lacking, however, and so the original wooden pier was soon abandoned. It remained for many years projecting from the foreshore, an eyesore and a constant hazard to shipping. Each year the pier succumbed further to the violence of winter gales and it was still further weakened by attacks from sandworm, peculiar to the Kent coast.

Finally, around 1857, a sudden storm brought the whole structure down - almost to the relief of everyone - and the materials when auctioned realised a mere £50. Stonework at the entrance to the pier remained upon the beach for a long time and occasionally wooden stumps which formed part of the lower construction are uncovered during the lowest of neap tides. A short alley leading off Oak Street bears the name Wood Yard, where wooden spars and seasoned timber were stored for maintenance of this first Deal Pier.

The opening of Deal's iron pier

The mid-Victorian period was the heyday of the seaside pier. The first had been built at Ryde in 1814 and this, after spasmodic extensions, reached 1250ft . It was followed soon after by piers at Brighton (1823) and Southend (1830). Herne Bay was the first coastal resort in Kent to invest in a pier and this had several novel features, including a Neptune Car which whisked passengers along the full length of the stem - almost one mile - at frightening speeds.

Effectively, Herne Bay pier shortened the travelling time between the capital and the Continent. Steamships from London were met at Herne Bay by stage coaches which transported passengers swiftly across the Isle of Thanet to connecting vessels at Deal or Dover. The advent of the railway and subsequent decline in sea traffic heralded the advent of a far smaller pier designed purely for pleasure.

Edward Hayward, editor and proprietor of the *Deal Telegram*, a weekly journal begun in 1858, campaigned indefatigably for the construction of a pleasure pier at Deal, both in his columns and among the townsfolk privately. As a result of his efforts The Deal and Walmer Pier Company was incorporated in September 1861 and, after another Act of Parliament was obtained, work on this new venture commenced. The structure was designed by Eugenius Birch, the world's greatest builder of piers, who is credited with the construction of fourteen piers in Britain including those at Blackpool and Brighton.

In the spring of 1863 Edward Knatchbull-Hugessen, MP for Sandwich, Deal and Walmer, drove the first pile of the new pier in the presence of a large number of townsfolk. Details of the construction written on a parchment were placed in a tin box and deposited in the first column. By August the abutment had been completed from stones acquired from Sandown Castle, then in the course of demolition.

Deal's Victorian pier was 1000ft long, constructed of wrought and cast iron and it was supported upon cast iron columns which were screwed into the ground. It had seating along its entire length, was illuminated by attractive globe lanterns and in the centre was a tramway for conveying luggage. There were three decks - promenade, fishing and small boat - and at the seaward end there was a cafe and concert hall.

The ceremonial opening took place on 14 July 1864 when all the troops from Walmer Barracks paraded along the narrow stem. The mayor and corporation, directors and workmen, the band of the Royal Marines and 6th Depot Battalion paraded the streets and proceeded to the pierhead where the mayor declared the structure open to the public. Mrs Fowler-Burton, wife of the Depot Commandant, was the first lady to pay the toll and pass on to the pier.

A sudden squall resulted in gentlemen losing their top hats into the sea and ladies clinging tightly to their escorts, but their alarm was dissipated by champagne and oysters served at a celebration lunch in the pavilion.

Building operations were still not complete, however, and so a further opening ceremony proved necessary on 8 November 1864. The following report, accompanied by a detailed engraving, appeared in *The Illustrated London News* on 19 November:

> There was a great concourse of spectators around the flagstaff at the pier-head to witness this ceremony, which was performed by Mrs Hugessen, wife of the borough member, who had herself, in April, 1863, inaugurated the commencement of the work. The lady took her seat in a chair which was placed on a truck and drawn along the tramway to the end of the pier. She then declared the pier opened, and congratulated the Deal and Walmer Pier Company, as well as the town of Deal, upon the completion of this useful structure. There was afterwards a banquet at the New Assembly Room. Mr John Attwell, chairman of the company, presided; and among the guests was Lord Clarence Paget, the secretary to the Admiralty, beside the county and borough members. Lord Clarence Paget highly commended the erection of the pier to give a readier access to the Downs roadstead and hinted that if the charges were not too exorbitant the Government might be disposed to use the Deal Pier for the embarkation of troops. It is expected that this accommodation will induce many persons to land at Deal from ships passing up the Channel.

Sad to relate, this new venture did not turn out to be quite the success that had been anticipated and in 1866 the Pier Company was wound up. As a large amount of money was still owing to the contractor, R Laidlaw and Son of Glasgow, the pier eventually passed into Laidlaw's hands. The constructional engineers finished, managed and improved the pier over a period of fifty-four years after which Deal Borough Council purchased it in 1920 it for £10,000.

Although some of the local mariners considered the new structure to be a danger to shipping and hoped that it might soon be 'unscrewed', the benefits from this pier were generally appreciated by townsfolk and seafarers alike. Provisions and water were supplied from here to vessels in the Downs and a fair number of passengers landed with an assortment of cargo besides. One enthusiast, commenting on 'the beauty, solidity and elegance of the structure', considered the pier to be a most charming retreat when in search of health from the penetrating effects of sea breezes.

An 1874 guide book described some of the facilities available:

> At the very entrance is a reading-room where you may read all the London papers, the local journals - for the small charge of one penny. At the end of the pier are salt baths, where those who fear to trust themselves alone in the water may with perfect safety obtain all the medicinal advantages of the sea-water bathe. The pier itself is a splendid marine parade, and here the society of Deal do congregate at all hours of the day. Everything is done to cheer them, and make their maritime pedestrian agreeable, for during the seaside season a band, paid for by the inhabitants, plays morning and evening a selection of the best airs of the Cecilian art.

Angling remained the principal attraction. *The Illustrated Sporting and Dramatic News* for Saturday, 10 December 1892, carried two large drawings of Deal fishermen in its centre pages and compared the sporting qualities of two local late autumn fish.

> The silver whiting is one of the gamest of sea fish, and much resembles the river perch in its bold biting and plucky struggles to escape . . . no prettier sport can be had. The codling, although a heavier fish, simply gives two or three plunges, and then seems to open his capacious mouth and take in as much of the surrounding water as possible to check your persuasive efforts . . . One of the best places for pier fishing on our south-east coast is Deal, here the angler will find all his wants supplied, every kind of bait necessary being furnished on the pier, under the superintendence of the genial pier-master, Mr. Lawrence.

The Pier Master, naturally, was a much respected person in the town and he cut a jaunty figure in his smart nautical uniform. One of the most jovial of the

Tolls levied on goods carried on to the first pier at Deal brought in further money for the company. Some of these old tariffs make puzzling reading – 'empty bottles, 1d per dozen; a horse or a fox, 5 shillings; turtles, 3/6d; marble tombstone, 10/6d; a corpse, £1/11/6d'.

'Here, on this Pier, one can imagine himself on the deck of some huge vessel in the Downs at anchor, enjoying the invigorating and life-giving effects of a sea voyage in the Channel,' wrote an admirer.

breed was George Rivers who, in those leisurely days prior to World War One, was often seen patrolling the stem in the company of his faithful hound.

The pier was the centre of social activity during the summer. Concerts, dances and talent contests were held in the pavilion. Pleasure steamers called to take passengers on short excursions along the Channel. And it was possible to travel as far as London on the steamer *Koh-i-Noor,* until the outbreak of the Great War.

Deal's second pier was celebrated in poetry and prose. In 1917 a book of verse was compiled by the vice-principal of Deal College, John Sparke, entitled – *The Old Deal Pier - An Autumnal Evening Dream.* The author imagines a gathering of local characters in the Concert Hall at the pier-head for an impromptu entertainment consisting of recitations, songs and ballads. Most of the verse is purely sentimental but one song of interest, *Jesse's Song,* extols the merits of the new pier:

Pier Master George Rivers and dog

> Arise, my love! the torch of Morn
> Glows on the Forelands crest,
> The frills of surf are gleaming white
> Upon the Goodwins breast -
> The Downs now breaking from nights rest;
> Tis such a sunrise, dear,
> As when at first we met and loved
> Upon the old Deal Pier:
> The Old Deal Pier,
> The Old Deal Pier,
> Can I forget the time we met
> Upon the old Deal Pier?

Tragedy struck the pier on several occasions. In 1871 the loss occurred of a Deal lugger, *Reform,* which was launched in a gale to answer a distress signal. Weather conditions were so appalling that the moment to cast off the rope could not be accurately timed. Disastrously, this splendid boat was pulled completely around into the pier where it sank between the piles with the loss of eight members of her crew of eleven.

The pier survived further buffetings from stricken vessels. During a storm in January 1873, the barque *Merle* hit and badly damaged the structure and in January 1884, the schooner *Alliance* crashed into the pier and carried away several columns. But it was the incident involving the Dutch ship, *Nora,* which signalled the end of Deal's iron pier on 29 January 1940.

Wreck of the Merle alongside the pier © Deal Library

The 350-ton motor-driven vessel was carrying a cargo of straw boards from Harlingen to London when she was struck by a drifting magnetic mine off Deal. A huge hole was blown in her stern. The cook was injured when the galley was demolished; the captain and a mate were hurt in the wheelhouse and a crewman was blown overboard by the force of the explosion. Fortunately, he managed to keep himself afloat before being picked up by a patrol boat. The same vessel rescued the remainder of the crew while salvage tugs took *Nora* in tow and succeeded in beaching her 50yd southwards of the pier.

There she lay for some while, almost completely submerged, but the rising tide lifted her from the beach and, as the flood tide gathered strength, the danger to the pier became apparent. Several stragglers who happened to be on the promenade deck raced ashore just in time to watch horrified as *Nora* crashed broadside into the pier. A heavy sea and a strong tide repeatedly hurled the crippled vessel against the shore end of the pier, which withstood the battering for some time and then collapsed. Finally, *Nora* was driven clean through the stem and came to rest on the beach slightly northwards of the pier, carrying part of the wreckage with it.

Numerous attempts were made to refloat *Nora*, without success and during the early part of the Second World War she remained a pathetic spectacle lying upside down beside the pier she had mortally wounded until strong tides and rough seas carried her further northwards. Her remains are now well dispersed '1 mile east of Deal Coastguard' but occasionally divers think this wreck is worth a rummage.

The remaining two-thirds of the pier was blown up by the Royal Engineers later that year because it obstructed the field of fire of coastal guns erected on the seafront after the fall of France. The decision to demolish the twisted remnants was probably taken by Winston Churchill when he made an inspection of the town in order to appraise coastal defences. In the spring of 1943 a brick-built look-out post was erected at the entrance, by which time all that remained of this

*The Dutch motor vessel Nora destroyed Deal's
iron pier in 1940. Top picture © Terry Williams*

once-noble structure were the twin toll houses that had featured in countless photographs of the pier throughout its eventful history.

Deal's present pier is built on the site of the one it replaces. It is the only pleasure pier to be constructed since the war (if one discounts the extension to Southwold in 2001) and it was opened on 19 November 1957 by the Duke of Edinburgh. The band of the Royal Marines, a guard of honour and a large concourse of people attended the ceremony. The silver presentation key made by Thomas Fattorini is displayed in the Town Hall. Its design embodies the ducal coronet in silver-gilt and enamel with the arms of the borough on both sides, parcel-gilt in blue and red enamel. A trident and rope border denote the town's maritime connections.

This pier was designed by Sir William Halcrow and Partners to the specifications of the town council and it was constructed by Concrete Piling. Built of reinforced concrete, it has a 1000ft stem with open seating stretching for almost one third of a mile. At the seaward end there is a three-deck pierhead set at right angles to the approach and parallel to the coast. At promenade level there is a lounge café, bar and terrace area while below is the main landing and fishing deck with angled wings to increase berthing facilities for pleasure steamers. In the early days there were frequent cruises from the historic paddle steamer *Waverley* and a trio of steamships - *Royal Daffodil, Eagle* and *Sovereign*. At the lowest level there is a half-tide small boat landing stage which is generally covered by water. The total cost was £250,000.

Deal now has the only pleasure pier in Kent – recent hurricanes have wrought havoc with rival piers at Margate and Herne Bay. It was nominated second in the National Pier Society's Pier of the Year award in 2001. An invigorating stroll along its stem – slightly longer, apparently, than SS *Titanic* – is rewarded by a spectacular panorama of the coastline stretching from Kingsdown Cliffs southwards to an extensive sweep of Thanet in the north. And in between is the townscape of Deal with its orderly row of eighteenth and nineteenth century cottages, behind which are the myriad spires and cupolas of churches and chapels. Local landmarks include the redundant Royal Marines East Barracks, the Time Ball Tower and three low, squat Tudor castles. Pleasure craft and fishing boats frequent home waters while ferries make their speedy crossings from the shelter of Dover Harbour to the coast of France.

WINDMILLS

'Shaking skeleton arms'

SEVEN MAGNIFICENT WINDMILLS, whose slowly revolving sweeps added much to the character of the landscape, were once situated in the immediate locality of Deal and Walmer. This generous number of mills was exceeded only by two other Kentish towns - Chatham and Rochester - which both had eight.

During the Napoleonic Wars constant blockades of European ports, coupled with poor harvests, caused serious food shortages in Southern England. Continental corn became increasingly scarce and eventually ceased to be imported. Consequently, the price of wheat rose sharply from £2 3s a quarter in 1792 just before the war to £6 6s in 1812. Bread, cheese and beer was the staple diet of working class families and the spiralling cost of a loaf caused considerable hardship. Fortunately, the surrounding countryside of Deal was rich in wheat fields, so poorer inhabitants learned to be self-sufficient.

The main reason for the generous presence of windmills so near the coast, however, was that ships of the Royal Navy and Merchant Marine, anchored in the Downs awaiting a favourable wind, were accustomed to take on provisions - flour for fresh bread in harbour and ships' biscuits at sea - before commencement of a voyage. Unscrupulous millers took advantage of this opportunity for brisk trading and sold their wares at extortionate prices - far higher, even, than the London markets. Ship owners complained bitterly to their agents, who were powerless to act, while paupers in the town went hungry.

It was for this express purpose that the famous windmill at Sandown was constructed in 1787 by a syndicate headed by Thomas Oakley, thrice Mayor of Deal. Brewer, banker and prosperous shipping agent for the Dutch East India Company, Oakley endeavoured to break the vicious price ring formed by millers and bakers by selling his own flour at a competitive price. This laudable venture swiftly broke the cartel and rival millers were forced to abandon their nefarious practices.

Despite being a local benefactor, Thomas Oakley was accused of being in collusion with local smugglers by Lieutenant Gabriel Bray, Commander of the revenue cutter *Nimble*. Oakley owned a patch of land furnished with capstans directly opposite his house where he allowed twenty illegal twelve-oared luggers to beach. Further, he provided warehouses protected by carriage guns - loaded and primed - which he rented out to smugglers to store their casks of

Thomas Oakley's mill next to Sandown Castle

brandy, 'the town being full of tea'. The Treasury was reluctant to act on this complaint and required hard evidence before it could contemplate prosecuting the mayor for smuggling. Apparently, smuggling was a family business. Oakley's son was recognised as the organiser of a gang who recovered a consignment of casks seized by Preventive men aboard the revenue cutter *Susanna and Maria*.

Oakley's windmill - painted stark white - was situated prominently at the extreme north end of the town next to Sandown Castle. This was the perfect location for not only did it catch the wind when other mills fell short but it was prominently visible to captains of ships entering the Downs and so compelled them to send ashore for supplies.

Sandown Mill was a tall smock mill with a low brick base, but no staging. It worked two sets of stones and its sweeps ran close to the ground. In an east wind the mill drew motive power direct from the sea and, in consequence, it is said to have established a record when employing four cloth or 'common' sweeps by running forty-eight hours without shortening or in any way altering sail.

It was one of the three mills run by the Chitty family before they moved to Dover. At one time it was damaged by a freak storm that destroyed part of Sandown Castle. The mill survived into the twentieth century but it fell into such a dangerous state that it was demolished around 1910. Dr Gordon Stables, a retired naval surgeon and author, wove a romance about the old mill 'shaking its skeleton arms'. Bathing machines stood on the sea-ward side of the miller's cottage, while the grand meadow west-ward was the venue for the famous Deal Horse Races.

A trio of mills stood inland at the north end of Deal. The first, Town Golf Mill, was a five-storey smock mill erected, it is believed, in 1767. This had two floors under the stage, operated three pairs of stones and latterly worked by means of spring-shuttered sweeps. Also known as North End Mill and Great Mill, this windmill was positioned so close to the miller's cottage that the sweeps, when turning, almost touched the chimney pots. The Mill House still exists at the end of a cul-de-sac opposite College Farm in Golf Road.

Thomas Bushell enjoyed a prosperous trade here for many years, employing three men to work the mill in addition to several carters or loaders. In about 1870 the mill passed into the hands of Richard Chitty, who worked it for the next ten years. Subsequently, the mill was run by Mr GW English who was a respected figure in milling circles of south-east England. An 1895 trade directory carried this advertisement:

> Besides supplying the best qualities of household and fine white pastry flours, Mr English does considerable business as a corn merchant and dealer in offal, horse and poultry mixtures, and feeding stuffs of all kinds, his carts and vans making periodical deliveries for some miles radius from the mill. The mill itself is a well-known feature of the landscape, near the Golf Links, from which it takes its name: and although the motive power is wind, the plant and machinery in the interior have been much improved from time to time, so as to bring the quality of the flour up to the highest standard of excellence. Mr English, who has had a long experience of the milling and kindred trades, superintends personally all departments of the business, which although an old established one, is still of a most progressive character.

Upper Deal Mill and Mill House

195

North End Mill was known to be working in 1894 because at that time a new middling and sweeps were installed by TR Holman. Inevitably, it met the fate of so many of the Kentish windmills, being burned to the ground, according to Mr English's daughter in her reminiscences published in the East Kent Mercury in September 1910.

A second mill in this vicinity was Lower Deal Mill, which stood near the gas works in Cannon Street. This was a smaller smock mill, having two pairs of stones and lacking a stage, worked by Thomas Bushell in conjunction with North End Mill. Also known as Little Mill, it was pulled down around 1870 and the boarding used to build pig styes. Houses on the north side of Cannon Street bore the name Little Mill Cottages.

Mystery surrounds the third mill, which existed to form an impressive triangle. It is clearly marked on Greenwood's map of 1829 as occupying a position half-a-mile south-west of the castle. Pritchard sugests that the construction of this mill, which pumped fresh water through a system of wooden conduits to convey a supply from the North Stream along Northwall Road to a reservoir in Water Street, was prompted by a Parliamentary Act in 1698. An Act was obtained in the reign of William and Mary, for supplying the inhabitants of Deal with water to be brought from the North Stream. A high brick building was erected on land

Town, Great, Golf or North End Mill

once the property of the Cannon family. This was a mill with suitable machinery, attached to which were wooden pipes made by boring through logs of timber, and these were laid all through the streets of the town. A map dated 1796 bears the legend 'Water Wks - Lower Deal Mill'. The mill was demolished in 1854.

Southwards, Walmer Road Mill stood on the foreshore close to Deal Castle. A smock mill, it carried a stage, three pairs of stones, two spring and two cloth sweeps. It was operated in 1839 by John Lawrence and between 1844 and 1849 by John Mummery. It commanded a profitable trade particularly when the black nor'easter blew in from the sea.

Fifteen minutes before midnight on Friday 7 July 1809, during a violent thunderstorm, lightning attracted by the topmost sweep was conveyed to the Old Naval Hospital which stood directly opposite and caused considerable damage. A report by the Governor, detailed the catastrophe. The electricity ripped out the window frames, tore up the floorboards and danced round the iron beds terrifying patients in the wards.

Walmer Mill occupied a prime position and flourished because of the stiff sea breezes. But when the Naval Hospital was rebuilt in 1812 and several large houses constructed for the surgeons in the vicinity, the wind was broken, rendering the mill inefficient. It was demolished in 1858.

Wellington Mill © Deal Library

Clanwilliam House marks its vicinity.

This mill is immortalised in a dramatic painting of the launching of a Deal lugger by Lieutenant Henry Wise Harvey. A member of a great local naval dynasty, Harvey was also Mayor of Deal in 1847. Additionally, a colourful stained-glass window incorporating a windmill was set into the Edwardian villa Oakmead, close to the site in Marine Road.

Two further windmills are remembered in local street names – Mill Road and Mill Hill. Wellington Mill stood in Lower Mill Lane opposite Victoria Park in Mill Road. This was a tall mill having two floors under a stage and, unlike most windmills, was devoted exclusively to the making of flour. It had three pairs of stones for that purpose. Originally, it was owned by Richard Chitty.

Soon after the use of steam became general the sweeps and fantail of Wellington Mill were dismantled, steam power was installed, three further pairs of stones were added and the mill was equipped with the latest machinery for dressing flour. From this modern mill by far the largest business was conducted across East Kent. Eventually the business was transferred to Dover when the miller could no longer compete with cheaper imported flour. Incongruously, the mill ended its days as a laundry before being demolished in 1890.

Walmer Road Mill beside Deal Castle

Remains of the coach house, stables, granary and workmen's cottages are still to be seen at the rear of Wellington House. All traces of the mill, however, have been obliterated. Wellington House, facing the park, was presumably built by the mill owner with his amassed wealth. It is a distinguished dwelling with curved iron railings and an ornate porch originally approached by a flight of steps. Curiously, the basement which contained a warren of domestic quarters, is now concealed at the front elevation by rising ground.

Upper Deal Mill - the last windmill to be constructed - was built about 1855. It stood atop Mill Hill near the waterworks. Surrounded by acres of cornfields, it occupied a position on Deal's highest ground and therefore caught the wind in every direction. Supposedly Quern Road follows the old mill track although, in fact, the road takes its name from the early iron age querns or handmills excavated from the entrenched hill camp and fragments of these are now embedded in a garden wall.

This slim black windmill with its solemnly revolving sweeps was long a familiar landmark. An octagonal smock mill on a stage, it was reputed to be particularly effective in grinding corn by the old stone method. It was the successor of an old post mill that stood nearer to the waterworks on St Richard's Road. The ancient mill appears on Symonson's map of 1596, but an even earlier record, dated 1537, confirms that members of the Foche family possessed lands which included this, the first of Deal's windmills to be built.

In a deed dated 1701 the old post mill is referred to as being bequeathed by John Holloway, mariner, to his four daughters. Later, in 1724, it was sold for £160 to Henry Kenney at which time it was in the tenure of William Carter. In 1840 it was in the possession of Mary Matson, a widow, who built the replacement smock mill for her son.

Constructed soon after the Crimean War by Sweetloves of Wingham, this new mill was regarded as being one of the finest and was once described as 'a worthy example of the art and craft of the millwright'. For a number of years the mill was worked by the Matson family. According to a directory of 1878, Frederick Matson was then the miller and he remained in charge until 1894. A certain Mr Barr held it in 1898 when a new middling was fitted. In 1910, Ernest Fuller, a member of another famous local milling family, hired the mill from a Mr Parker and he was probably the last person to work it.

In 1913 Upper Deal Mill was struck by lightning and it would have been completely destroyed but for the gallant efforts of two men who were working there. Fortunately, the mill was situated near the old Deal Waterworks! All the same, in March 1929 the remains of Matson's Mill were demolished to make way for the erection of the new church dedicated to St Richard. This sought to serve Betteshanger Colliery miners living on the new Mill Hill. And so this too, the last surviving Deal windmill, has gone with the wind . . .

A detailed engraving by Hayward dated 1828 depicts the stunning panorama atop Mill Hill stretching from St.Leonards Church to Walmer Barracks. Probably drawn from the top of Upper Deal Mill, by chance it shows each of the six mills in Lower Deal. William Coles Finch, who compiled the definitive study of watermills and windmills in 1933, noted two long-lost post mills – Walmer Mill south-west of St Mary's church, and Mongeham Mill south-west of St Martin's church. These are both marked on two maps of Kent mills; Symondson's dated 1596 and Bowen's dated 1736.

An eighth windmill which, if counted, would equal the number to the previously named Medway towns, remains on the outskirts of Deal alongside the Dover Road between Walmer and Ringwould. Ripple Mill presents a dramatic spectacle across the skyline - a lonely silhouette against a field of gaudy yellow rape. It has been regarded as an important landmark by shipping in the English Channel and for that reason it was renovated in 1895 by Trinity House.

The mill had a most distinguished visitor. The Duke of Wellington, Lord Warden of the Cinque Ports, often rode over the fields to Ripple from his official residence at Walmer Castle. Without dismounting he used to tap on the door of the mill with his cane: 'That the miller? - Come down and talk.' The unlikely pair would sit on sacks inside the rumbling, dusty interior while the soldier confessed to the miller that war was 'a horrible trade'.

An unique feature of this mill is that it had a mound of earth thrown up against its brick base to take the place of the stage, necessary for unloading sacks of meal on to carts. This improvised construction led to a tragedy in about 1834 when a young girl climbed up the bank to greet her father, the miller, and was struck by the sails. In 1927 two of the sweeps crashed down but they were not replaced because the mill stood in an exposed position with sufficient winds for all the work required.

Ripple Mill was built originally at Drellingore, near Folkestone, at the close of the eighteenth century and transferred to its present site early in the nineteenth century. The method used was to saw the eight corner posts – the 'cants' – down the centre and, when re-erecting, simply bolt them together again. There were three pairs of stones driven from underneath (as in a watermill) instead of from above, known as 'underdrift'.

Ripple Mill appears on a tithe map of 1840 where it states that the 'Mill Fields, house and garden, together with the windmill, stable and yard', were owned by Benjamin Horn and run by John Mummery. Miller Mummery, who hailed from Eastry, had arrived in 1833 to operate the mill and he was succeeded by Henry and William, the latter being described as 'a farmer and miller'. At one time, it was claimed, nearly forty windmills could be pointed out with the aid of a telescope.

Eventually, Ripple Mill was acquired by the Monins family but after the death of Captain John Monins during the Second World War it fell into disuse. In 1955, bereft of cap and sweeps, it was purchased by Rediffusion to support a television mast. Commendably, it has recently been restored to perfection.

Northbourne had the distinction of being the only Kentish village to possess at one time two working windmills - Old Mill and New Mill - each operated with two sweeps only. New Mill, which survives, is located south-west of the village. It was constructed in 1845 by Holman brothers of Canterbury for Richard Fuller in whose family the windmill remained until this last decade.

Originally possessing four sweeps with a phenomenal 70ft span, New Mill was worked in turn by wind, steam and electricity. Until the middle of the last century it continued to function, grinding corn for human and animal consumption. The last owner was Richard Mackney Fuller who took possession of the mill from his father in 1968. He retained the miller's account book from the day the mill was built until it ceased to function in 1951.

Set in a large paddock, this superb example of a late Victorian smock mill preserves its circular stage, original cap and canister which held the sweeps - two of which were carried off by a high wind in the summer of 1915. The remaining pair were rotted by rain. In 1975 the millmill was purchased by designer-silversmith, Paul Harrison, who has imaginatively converted it into a spacious workshop.

DEAL COLLEGE

'Alfred House Academy'

DEAL COLLEGE, from which College Road takes its name, was once an important educational establishment in the town. Situated at the north end of the High Street, the imposing facade faces Alfred Square – the centre of which once boasted an attractive shrubbery. A modest school known as Alfred House Academy was opened there in the eighteenth century. The principal was a Mr Reakes, an example of whose fine penmanship was once proudly displayed in the Town Hall.

Deal College, as it was subsequently termed, achieved a fine reputation as a boarding school under the direction of James Lush. A prominent member of the town council, Lush was five times elected Mayor of Deal, and he was a Cinque Ports and Borough Magistrate. A portrait in oils of Lush hangs in the council chamber at the Town Hall.

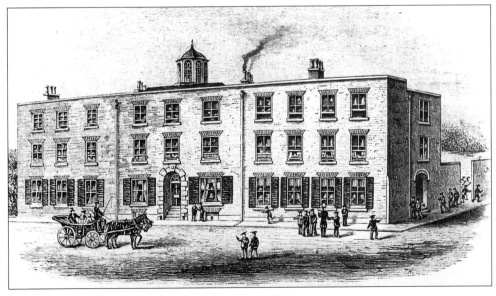

Wood engraving of Deal College

201

College sportsmen and Town Golf Mill

One of the vice-principals was John Sparke, who was the author of a book of verse entitled *The Old Deal Pier - An Autumnal Evening Dream*, concerned largely with his recollections of past inhabitants of the town.

A wood engraving reproduced in Pain's *Reminiscences of Old Deal* (1932) shows Deal College to have been an imposing edifice. The building was composed of three storeys each with a row of ten sash windows, the ground floor having the added distinction of shutters which gave it a Continental air. There was a central doorway fronting Alfred Square with a side entrance in Peter Street. Surmounting the whole was a splendid Deal cupola.

In the sketch a coach and pair with its occupants waits patiently as boys spill on to the street in their formal uniform of mortar boards and Eton jackets. On Sunday mornings these same pupils attended Divine Service at St George's Church, where they occupied reserved seats in the south gallery.

An illustrated guide of 1898 carried a feature on the college which, it claimed, 'ranked amongst the oldest and best known educational establishments in Kent'. Recently modernised, the college had 'commodious and well-ventilated classrooms, a spacious dining hall and an excellent playroom. Additionally, there were numerous comfortably furnished dormitories '. . . a separate bed being provided for each pupil'.

Further features were a laundry, a sanatorium and a dairy farm which supplied fresh produce. The entrance to this farm was in Golf Road where

College Farm exists today and the windmill which stood in this vicinty can be clearly seen in old photographs of the school playing field.

Deal College was divided into two sections. In the Upper Division scholars were prepared for universities, London metriculation and other professional preliminary examinations, while in the Lower Division pupils were tutored in English Grammar, composition, history, geography, arithmetic, French and Latin. Pupils intended for business life received individual tuition in commercial subjects including mental arithmetic, book keeping, mercantile accounts, commercial correspondence and shorthand. Further, there was a preparatory department for boys aged six years and over. There were many facilities for outdoor pursuits as the college had an extensive asphalted area and several acreas of meadows for cricket, football and tennis. And there were ideal opportunities for sea bathing.

A later advertisement appeared in *Dover, Canterbury, Deal and Walmer by Camera and Pen* (1904-1905) announcing that an illustrated prospectus for this 'high class boarding school for boys at the seaside' was available from the then principal, Mr J Stebbings, BA, BSc. The fees - 'strictly moderate and inclusive' - ranged from thirty-six to forty-eight guineas per annum.

Ultimately, the foundation was transferred to Thanet and for some time the premises in North Deal remained unoccupied. The building was acquired as the Lloyd Memorial Home for members of the printing and allied trades. Considerable alterations were undergone; the cupola vanished, the facade was rendered and the interior adapted for its new purpose. The new building was opened on 16 September 1911 by Alderman J Edgar, Mayor of Deal, and the distinguished company included Lord George Hamilton, Captain of Deal Castle.

The name Lloyd Memorial was chosen for the home because of the generous financial assistance given by the family of Edward Lloyd of Sittingbourne, owners of the famous paper mills, who were formerly connected with *Lloyds News* and the *Daily Chronicle*. The home expanded rapidly and, with the aid of prominent men from the newspaper world and the printing industry, extensive alterations were made to the property in Peter Street. Modern flats were also erected for retired printers in Princes Street.

Alternatively known as the Caxton Seaside Home, the sumptuous premises included a billiards room, a smoking room, a comfortable lounge, a spacious dining room, a chapel and a Palm Court. For a time the property also doubled as a convalescent home for the Metropolitan Police. In 1969 the property was vacated, however, and after imaginative modernisation was converted into luxury flats which now bear the name Lloyd Court.

AMBROSE GWINETT

'A remarkable tale of mistaken murder'

A SIXPENNY PAMPHLET in the archives of the British Museum purports to be the autobiography of a certain lame beggar, 'well known to the public', who since 1734 'swept the way between the Mews Gate and Spring Gardens, Charing Cross'. A second, 1770 edition of the pamphlet – entitled *The Life and Strange Unparalleld and Unheard-of Voyages and Adventures of Ambrose Gwinett* – relates a curious case of mistaken murder at a Deal inn.

Ambrose Gwinett - or so the pamphlet claims - was born in Canterbury where his father had a reputable trade in slops (ready made clothes for sailors) at the sign of the Blue Anchor. At sixteen, after a good school education, Ambrose was apprenticed to George Roberts, a city attorney, whom he served for five years. During that time Ambrose's sister married a sea-faring man named Sawyer who, with considerable prizes gained on the high seas, opened a public house three miles from his native town of Deal.

In late autmmn, 1709, Gwinett obtained permission to visit his relatives and he set out on foot one Wednesday morning for Deal. The journey was long and tiring and the road was kept unusually busy with holidaymakers returning from the local fair. Arrived in the town the young traveller felt too weary to go the further short distance to his sister's house so he sought refuge in the immediate vicinity. Several of Her Majesty Queen Anne's ships lay sheltering in the Downs, England being then at war with France and Spain, and so the lodging houses were packed to capacity. Eventually, Ambrose Gwinett took refuge at an inn run by a friend of his sister.

The landlady took Gwinett into the parlour and introduced him to her uncle, Richard Collins, a middle-aged man who sat in his nightgown by a blazing fire, reckoning money. Reluctantly, Collins consented to share his bed with the tired apprentice and shortly afterwards the pair retired by candlelight.

At about three o'clock Gwinett awoke feeling ill with cholic and, desiring fresh air, woke his bedfellow to ask directions for the garden. Sleepily Collins warned: 'You may have difficulty opening the door. The string which pulls the latch is broken.' So saying, Collins lent him a penknife to prise open the door. As Gwinett hurried downstairs a coin, which had evidently stuck between the blade and groove of the handle, fell into his hand. He pocketed it without thinking and found his way to the garden. When he returned to his room half an hour later he was surprised to find his companion had gone. Too ill to worry further, Gwinett fell asleep.

Early next morning he dressed hastily, paid the bill and slipped away quietly into the street. His relatives welcomed him at their inn and made him a late breakfast. Towards midday the family were all standing at the door when three horsemen came galloping towards them. They halted outside the inn, dismounted and seized Gwinett by the shoulder, declaring: 'You are the King's prisoner'. Producing a warrant for his arrest, the leader demanded that Ambrose Gwinett return immediately to Deal to face charges of robbery and murder.

An inquisitive crowd had gathered outside the inn at Deal. The landlady screamed accusations at Gwinett as he was hauled upstairs to the room where he had slept, to be confronted with the scene of a hideous crime. The bedclothes had been turned down revealing sheets, pillows and bolster all stained with blood. Gwinett was searched and his waistcoat pocket was found to contain Collins' penknife and a William and Mary guinea which the landlady recognised as having belonged to her uncle. A canvas bag of money was missing and a trail of blood led from the garden to the seafront. The constable conjectured that Ambrose Gwinett had murdered Richard Collins for his money and, having slit his throat, thrown the body into the sea to be carried away by the spring tide.

A preliminary examination before the Justice of the Peace resulted in Gwinett's imprisonment in Maidstone Gaol. Convinced of his innocence, his relations advertised in the *London Gazette,* offering a reward for news of the missing man. Eventually, the apprentice was brought to trial and was convicted upon strong circumstantial evidence. He was sentenced to be hanged before the door of the inn where the foul deed had been perpetrated, and afterwards to be hung in chains a short distance from his brother's house.

Early one morning Gwinett was placed in a cart and driven to execution at Deal. It was a stormy day. The wind and rain were so violent that the sheriff and his officer were soaked through to the skin. They could scarcely sit on their horses. Gwinett was speedily despatched and cut down to be placed in irons and hung upon a gibbet in a corner of a small common field. (A gallows is prominently marked on the foreshore between Deal town and Sandown Castle on a chart of the Downs dated 1690.)

A lad driving cows home for evening milking stopped to stare at the grisly spectacle and was startled to find the hanging convict return his gaze. The alarm was raised. Gwinett was alive! His relatives rushed to the field and cut him loose with a saw. Freed from his irons, he was blooded and rested in a warm bed. When the authorities discovered that the gibbet had been hacked down, Sawyer was summoned to the Mayor's house for questioning. But he denied all knowledge of the affair and, being a much respected man, he was believed. Thus the daring rescue remained a secret.

Several officers of a privateer had been staying at the Sawyers' public house in preparation for a cruise and were ready to sail. They agreed to enlist Gwinett as an assistant to their steward. Six months at sea, the vessel anchored off the coast of Florida when it fell into the hands of Spaniards, who took the crew as prisoners into the harbour of Havannah. Here Gwinett was confined with forty other English captives for three years. At the end of that time the prisoners were

Scenes from the remarkable life of Ambrose Gwinett © The British Library

put on board transports and shipped to Pennsylvania which was then English territory. Such a release did not exactly suit Gwinett, who was fearful of returning home, so he begged the keeper of the prison to allow him to remain. Finally, the keeper procured him a salary from the governor for Gwinett to become his deputy.

The coast had long been infected with pirates. Scarcely a month passed when one of their ships did not fall into the governor's hands. The captured crews, desperate gangs of ruffians, were always entrusted into the deputy's care, a dangerous and unenviable task. After Gwinett was three months in office, a vessel arrived from Port Royal, a Spanish settlement. As the piratical crew were marched to the governor's house, Gwinett recognised the face of one of the pirates' English prisoners.

'Sir,' asked Gwinett, 'were you ever at Deal?' The man, startled, nodded affirmatively. 'Then your name is Collins, and I was hanged and gibbeted upon your account in England.'

At last Ambrose Gwinett learned the true circumstances of that fateful night at the Deal inn. Unknown to his niece on the day he lodged there, Richard Collins had visited a local barber-surgeon to be bled, and in the middle of the night, he had accidentally discovered his shirt to be soaked in blood where the fresh wound had opened. Without disturbing the household he had left the inn to knock up a neighbouring barber to have the blood stopped and the bandage replaced.

In the street he was accosted by a band of ruffians armed with cutlasses and hangers who seized him and dragged him to the beach. The men were not a press gang but belonged to a privateer, and while the ship's surgeon dealt with his arm, the ship set sail, impressing Collins into service. The considerable amount of money in his nightgown was stolen but upon complaining to the captain he was curtly informed that he should have prize money enough to make amends. He was therefore obliged to submit to the pirates, serving under them as crew member until captured by the Spaniards and taken to Havannah. Nothing, now, prevented Gwinett and Collins from returning to England to confront the magistrates with their bizarre tale . . .

The Voyages and Adventures of Ambrose Gwinett appeared in several London editions – a fourth in 1771, a fifth about 1780. Two Newcastle editions appeared in 1775 and 1800. A second version of the tale, considerably altered and rewritten anonymously, was published in a Liverpool magazine, *The Kaleidoscope*. This revised story appeared in 1825 in Joshua Watt's *Remarkable Events in the History of Man* under the title *Erroneous Conviction Upon Strong Circumstantial Evidence*. In 1864 this account appeared as an episode of local history in Stephen Pritchard's *History of Deal*, while Gwinett's curious narrative was printed in Laker's *History of Deal* in 1917. More recently the story is related in Christopher Lloyd's *The British Seaman* (Collins 1968). In all these instances the story is presented as plain truth.

The second version contradicts the orginal 'autobiography' on several points. It is interesting to compare the two accounts. In Watt's story the unnamed hero is apprenticed to a master sailmaker and he leaves London to visit his mother at Christmas, 1723. Late one evening he arrives at Deal and shares a bed with the boatswain of an Indiaman. After the midnight adventure, the landlady raises the alarm: her uncle is missing and a trail of blood leads directly to the pierhead. At noon young Gwinett is arrested. Blood stains are on his shirt and trousers and in his pocket is discovered a remarkable silver coin. The judge orders his execution for three days' time but at the fatal tree friends support the youth's body so that he is resuscitated and spirited away to Portsmouth.

There, Gwinett joins a man-o'-war and he is soon promoted to master's mate. In the West Indies he transfers ship. Almost the first person who confronts him is the identical boatswain for whose murder he was executed five years before. The two sailors return to England to relate their strange story to judge and jury 'who never after convicted a man on circumstantial evidence'.

In the past this intriguing mystery of how a hanged man met a murdered man has often been cited by writers and historians – who believed the narrative to be factual – to demonstrate the injudiciousness of inflicting capital punishment without sufficient proof that a murder has been committed. Only a few have viewed the story with suspicion. And yet evidence to support the story of a murder at the inn and the existence of a lame beggar who composed the original narrative is absent. Brewery deeds, borough records and county archives are silent. A search for details of the apprentice's naval career, and inspection of the records of the Kent Assizes have revealed no trace of Ambrose Gwinett.

A key to the true authorship may lie in a pencilled note made in the margin by a former owner of the second edition, preserved in the British Museum: 'Dr. Percy told me that he had heard that this pamphlet was a mere fiction written by a Mr. Bickerstaff the Dramatic Poet.' Dr Percy, Dean of Carlisle, author of *Reliques of Ancient Poetry*, was a collector of songs and ballads. Consequently, mention of his name lends authority to the unsigned statement.

Irish dramatist, Isaac Bickerstaff, produced numerous pieces for the stage between the years 1760 and 1761, and he became an intimate friend of Dr Johnson, Oliver Goldsmith and Sir Joshua Reynolds. Bickerstaff died in obscurity having been dismissed from the Royal Marines, in which he had been an officer, under discreditable circumstances. The *Dictionary of National Biography* ascribes the story to him and it therefore seems that the story of Ambrose Gwinett is merely a fictitious romance of bygone Deal.

According to the 1770 autobiography, Gwinett's *Voyages and Adventures* do not end with his confrontation of Richard Collins. Certainly the dramatic incidents continue in a 'strange unparallel'd manner'. As Collins leaves for home, Gwinett prepares to follow, but by mistake boards the wrong ship and falls in with pirates who impress him into further service. Their Irish captain, Brian Walsh, 'a most execrable and bloody villain', befriends him, saves his life and promotes him to purser in charge of immense riches hidden in the pirates' fortification, Swallow Island - twelve leagues west of the Gulf of Mexico. After capturing a Jamaican ship loaded with a cargo of sugar and rum, Walsh is discovered dead, having left Gwinett sole heir to his fortune of £40,000.

At Gwinett's suggestion the rascally crew leave for Jamaica to make a respectable living, but a violent storm wrecks the ship and leaves the pirates destitute. They cast Gwinett overboard but he is picked up by Spaniards who mistake him for a pirate and imprison him for two years. He is condemned to serve in the galleys but during a sea battle against an Algerian rover, in which he loses a leg, Gwinett finally escapes and returns to England. The year is 1730. All Gwinett's relatives are dead and Richard Collins, alas, never arrived home. Penniless, friendless and enfeebled with hardships, the hero of so many daring escapades is now forced to earn his living as a wandering beggar, sweeping the streets of London.

This persistent tale of Ambrose Gwinett was turned into a highly successful play by Douglas Jerrold, who served as a midshipman during the closing years of the Napoleonic Wars. Previously, he had enjoyed a theatrical background since his father was manager of Sheerness Theatre. For many years he worked as a jobbing playwright, drawing inspiration for his creations from Kentish lore. His nautical melodrama, *Black Ey'd Susan*, set entirely in Deal, earned him national fame and fortune.

Ambrose Gwinett, or A Sea Side Story, a melodrama in three acts, was first performed at the Coburg Theatre on 6 October 1828. An acting edition of the script survives, complete with stage directions, notes on the costumes and an introduction by a certain DG. The autobiography is once more rehearsed with the affirmation that Gwinett is 'unquestionably the only person to have written his life after being gibbetted'. And the only deviation from plain truth is, apparently, where Mr Jerrold has 'heightened the interest of his drama by adding the passions of love and jealousy'. A dramatic wood engraving appears based upon a drawing made during a performance in the theatre, entitled: 'Wretch! Heartless ruffian!'

The cast list is entertaining:

> Ambrose Gwinett, a young farmer of Deal in love with Lucy (Mr. Cobham) Lucy Fairlove, in love and beloved by Ambrose Gwinett (Miss Watson) Collins, Host of the 'Blake's Head' (Mr. Mortimer) Label, an itinerant Barber Surgeon and Dentist (Mr E.L. Lewis) Bolt, humane gaoler of Deal Prison (Mr. Porteus) Stephen Reef, leader of the Press Gang (Mr. Elsgood) and George, a Smuggler condemned to Die (Mr. Gale).

Jerrold's popular play was frequently revived including a long run which opened on 4 July 1860 at London's Victoria Theatre.

The Life and Strange Unparallel'd and Unheard-of Voyages and Adventures of Ambrose Gwinett remains one of Deal's most treasured folklores.

SELECT BIBLIOGRAPHY

Anderson, AEO: *A Guide to Deal Parish Church*
Arnold, Tony: *The Coldest Place In England*
Carter, Tom: *The Victorian Garden*
Chapman, Henry: *The Story of Dola*
Chapman, Henry: *A Peep at Olde Deale*
Childs, Virginia; *Lady Hester Stanhope, Queen of the Desert*
Collins, Barbara: *Discovering Deal*
Collins, Barbara: *A Short History of the Civic Church of St. George-the-Martyr*
Douch, John: *The Wicked Trade*
Douch, John: *Flogging Joey's Warriors*
Ellis, Peter Berresford: *Caesar's Invasion of Britain*
Elvin, Charles RS: *Records of Walmer*
Elvin, Charles RS: *Walmer and Walmer Castle*
Finch, William Coles: *Watermills and Windmills*
Harris, Simon: *Sir Cloudesley Shovell, Stuart Admiral*
Haslip, Joan: *Lady Hester Stanhope*
Holmes, T Rice: *Ancient Britain and the Invasions of Julius Caesar*
Holmes, TW: *The Semaphore*
Holyoake, Gregory: *Wellington At Walmer*
Howse, Derek: *Greenwich Time and the Longtitude*
Hutchinson, Lucy: *Memoirs of Col. John Hutchinson*
Jones, ADH: *A Short History of the Royal Marines in Deal*
Kedleston, Marquess Curzon of: *Walmer Castle and Its Lords Warden*
Laker, John: *History of Deal*
Lambarde, William: *A Perambulation of Kent*
Lane, Andrew: *Royal Marines, Deal, A Pictorial History*
Massingham, Betty: *A Century of Gardeners*
Meason, George: *The Official Guide to the South-East Railway and its Branches*
Minter, Alfred: *Deal Railway Station 1847-1995*
Morley, Geoffrey: *The Smuggling War*
Moulton, JL: *The Royal Marines*
Nicoll, Allardyce (ed): *Holinshed's Chronicle*
Oakley, Derek: *Fiddler On The March, A Biography of Lieutenant Colonel Sir Vivian Dunn*
Parfitt, Keith: *Iron Age Burials from Mill Hill, Deal*
Peddie, John: *Conquest: The Roman Invasion of Britain*
Philp, Roy: *The Coast Blockade, The Royal Navy's War on Smuggling in Kent and Sussex 1817 - 31*
Pope, Dudley: *Life In Nelson's Navy*
Pritchard, Stephen: *History of Deal*
Reilly, Robin: *William Pitt the Younger*
Roget, John Lewis: *Sketches of Deal, Walmer and Sandwich*
Saaler, Mary: *Anne of Cleves*
Smith, Graham: *King's Cutters*
Smith, Lucy Toulmin (ed): *John Leland's Itinerary in England and Wales*
Smith, Peter C: *Per Mare Per Terram, A History of the Royal Marines*
Southern, Pat: *Julius Caesar*
Stebbing, WPD: *The Invaders' Shore*
Tomaszewski, Nicholas: *Eight Hundred Years of Worship, St. Leonards Church, Deal*
Vine, Francis: *Caesar In Kent*
Warner, Rex (trans): *War Commentaries of Caesar*
Waugh, Mary: *Smuggling in Kent and Sussex 1700-1840*
West, Jenny: *The Windmills of Kent*
Wilson, Geoffrey: *The Old Telegraphs*
Wiseman, Anne and Peter (trans): *Julius Caesar, The Battle for Gaul*
Also consulted: *Verses, Letters and Remembrances of Sub-Lieut Arthur Walderne St Clair Tisdall, VC*; Major and Mrs Holt's *Battlefield Guide to Gallipoli*; *Early Diary of Fanny Burney Volume II*

NOTES ON SOURCES

Students interested in the history of Deal and Walmer must rely heavily on the published researches of both Stephen Pritchard and John Laker. Fortunately, not only are these books meticulously researched but highly readable, although they are now long out of print. Walmer's fascinating history has been faithfully recorded by the Reverend Charles Elvin.

The Roman Conquest is examined in detail by Peter Berresford Ellis's *Caesar's Invasion of Britain*. The author champions the advanced civilisation of the Celts although he often relies upon their oral tradition (compiled during the medieval period) as hard evidence. Archaeological researches undertaken by Vine, Chapman and Stebbing have been superseded by recent excavations, particularly regarding the discovery of the Iron Age Warrior and Deal Man. Jon Iveson, Curator of Dover Museum, has repeatedly read my chapter on Caesar's invasions of Kent and sent me back several times to the drawing board. Generally, I have followed his considered advice although any mistakes which appear in the text are my own.

Readers interested in finding more about early signalling methods need to consult further two excellent books: *The Old Telegraphs* by Geoffrey Wilson and *The Semaphore* by TW Holmes.

John Douch's acclaimed trilogy of books on smuggling are vastly entertaining to read. *Flogging Joey's Warriors* tells the story of Captain William McCulloch's fight against local smugglers, which is expanded in Roy Philp's masterly volume, *The Coast Blockade*. Both authors have been generous in supplying additional information for my two chapters on Deal's 'Wicked Trade'.

ACKNOWLEDGEMENTS

Tribute must be paid to the host of amateur local historians whose researches often throw light on unusual aspects of Deal and Walmer: David Collyer, Lez Cozens, Julie Deller, Gertrude Nunns, Nicholas Tomaszewski and, paticularly, Terence Williams who has a superb knowledge of the history of the Royal Marines.

Permission to use the reproduction of JMW Turner's watercolour, *Deal In A Storm*, which hangs in the Mayor's Parlour at Deal Town Hall, has been given by John Moir, Chief Executive, Dover District Council, and Deal Town Council.

Special photography by Ian Giles.

Picture credits: British Library; British Museum; Deal Library; Dover Museum; English Heritage; House of Lords Record Office; Kent Messenger Group Newspapers; National Maritime Museum, Greenwich; National Museums and Galleries on Merseyside; Monumenti Musei E Gallerie Pontificie, Vatican City; National Portrait Gallery; Photographic Survey, Courtauld Institute of Art; Reunion des Musees Nationaux, Paris; Rochester Guildhall; Victoria and Albert Museum Picture Library; National Museums and Galleries of Wales; Terence Williams.

Thanks also for special information to: Stephen Alexander; The Antiquarian Horological Society; David Austin Roses; Peter Beales Roses; M Barry; Jonathan Betts, Curator of Horology, Royal Observatory, Greenwich; The British Library; The British Museum; Cllr Marlene Burnham, Mayor of Deal; Clarence House; Denise Coe, Local Studies, Deal Library; Sue Crabtree, Special Collections Librarian, Templeman Library, University of Kent at Canterbury; Ray Dennis, landlord, The Ship Inn, Deal; The Dickens Fellowship; Gerald and Miriam Evans; Mike Feist; Mark Frost; the Rev Gary Gill; Lt Col Ken Grapes, Hon. Sec., The Rose Society; Adam Grummitt, Picture Library, National Portrait Gallery; Rev. David Kendrew; Kent County Council; Dr Andrew Lane; The Law Society; VJ Lewis; David Mallinder; Sally Mewton-Hynds; John Munday; Nigel Knott, Public Relations Officer, HM Customs and Excise, Dover; Alfred Minter; Mr and Mrs Stephen Myatt; Richard Porter; Public Records Office, Kew; Edric and Pauline Radage; Dr Jack Reading; The Royal Horticultural Society; John and Zoe Simpson; David Taylor, Picture Library, National Maritime Museum, Greenwich; The Theatre Museum; Mr and Mrs JAD Thom, Unitarian Chapel, Dover; Tracey Wahdan, General Manager, English Heritage for Dover and Kent; the late Tony Watford.

ABOUT THE AUTHOR

Gregory Holyoake is an actor, writer and school teacher who lives in a restored smugglers' cottage in Deal, the town where he was born fifty years ago. He trained as a school teacher at Culham College of Education, Oxfordshire, where he gained certificates in English and Divinity. As an actor he later trained at Rose Bruford College of Speech and Drama in Sidcup, Kent. He has been acting for twenty-five years in national tours, repertory, repertoire and pantomime. His speciality is comedy and character acting. Gregory has been a freelance writer and photographer for more than thirty years. He is a regular contributor to *Country Life, Country Homes and Interiors, Illustrated London News, Heritage, This England, The Lady* and the *Evening Standard* magazine. He is an authority on Kentish subjects and writes monthly for *Kent Life*. His subjects are diverse: Village Schools, Country Garages, Cricket Pavilions, Country Gardens, Animal Architecture, Rural Post Offices, Ice Cream Parlours, Windmills and Watermills, Church Bells, Beach Fairs and Character Cats. He is the author of *Wellington at Walmer, The Prefab Kid – A Postwar Childhood in Kent* and *Kent,* and *The County in Colour* (with John Vigar) for which he did the photographs. He is currently photographing scarecrows and researching the Goodwin Sands.

Below – The gardens of The Clifton Hotel, a famous temperance hotel, which dates from late Victorian times. The author was born in this building which later changed its name to Redan. The story of his childhood is told in *The Prefab Kid – A Postwar Childhood in Kent* also published by SB Publications.